From Scratch

For Nessie, who insisted on recipes written down, and for Adam, for all the endless washing up, and this life and love.

This book was written at Buena Vista Farm in Gerringong where we acknowledge the traditional custodians of this land, the Wadi Wadi people of the Dharawal nation and their Elders, past and present.

We acknowledge and respect their continuing culture and the contribution they have made and continue to make to life in Gerringong and the Illawarra region.

From Scratch

More than 200 handmade
pantry essentials and other
life-affirming kitchen miracles

Fiona Weir Walmsley

Hardie Grant

BOOKS

About the Author

Fiona Weir Walmsley is a cheesemaker and farmer on a family farm in Gerringong, New South Wales, with a view that does not suck. The family have been on the farm since the mid 1800s, when they arrived from Northern Ireland with nothing except a dream, a small amount of dairy farming knowledge and a cooking kettle that is still on the back verandah today. Fiona's parents are also still on the farm, over the back fence, occasionally enjoying a shiraz and calling in on their mobile when the pigs escape. Fiona and her husband, Adam, raise dairy goats, make cheese and operate a commercial farm kitchen that produces a range of ferments and other deliciousness sold at two big local farmers' markets and to local restaurants. They grow coffee and cut flowers, raise meat chickens, laying hens, bees and pigs (that eat the whey from the cheese room and brewers' grain from a friend's brewery down the hill). In the beginning, before moving home to the farm, Fiona wrote a food blog called *Inner Pickle*.

At the farm, they run a cooking school teaching traditional food skills, such as sourdough baking, cheesemaking and fermentation.

Contents

Introduction

We have taught a class called 'From Scratch' at our on-farm cooking school for almost ten years. In a single day, we lead people through how to make sourdough, yoghurt, butter, labneh, biscuits, crackers, jam, pickles and bone broth. We always talk about how although it seems like such a long list, in fact everything – with the exception of the sourdough and yoghurt fermentation – is pretty quick to make.

That's it, really. We've forgotten that we can make homemade crackers *fast*. Of all the things on the list, crackers are probably the thing people were least likely to make themselves, which is funny, because sourdough – something many more people have attempted – is such a pain in the arse, and homemade crackers take ten minutes.

It's the can-I-be-bothered factor. It's the they-cost-two-dollars-at-the-shop factor. It's the am-I-going-to-waste-my time factor. We're all very busy. Why would you buy the ingredients when you could just buy the product in the next aisle?

There are a few reasons why, but the first is, essentially, freshness. HOMEMADE CRACKERS ARE THE BOMB. Delicious. Crisp. Without weird additives and numbers to keep them that way. And because they are basically only three ingredients. Personal satisfaction. Speed – they take as long to make as an average drive to the supermarket. Variation and originality. Which brings me to the big one: if I can't sell you on flavour and simplicity, then creativity. In a capitalist world, we are consumers first and foremost. All day, every day we are consuming things people make for us: food, media, ideas. How wonderful to take yourself out of that system for a minute and *make* something. Are they ever just homemade crackers? Or are they a beacon of hope in a dark, dark world of boxed two-dollar cheese accompaniments? Without wanting to overstate it, might homemade crackers be the canary in the coalmine in the eventual demise of the twenty-four-hour, fluorescent-lit mega-supermarkets selling you all the things you think you want to eat, made who knows where and when?

We would run a whole morning session of From Scratch in the farm's commercial kitchen, then stop for a lunch in our farmhouse dining room that overlooks the kitchen garden and the sea. More than once, I found class participants in my home kitchen's walk-in pantry. I mean, I get it. I like pantries too. In my mind this is still my grandma's pantry, with super organised neat and tidy rows of tall jars filled with beautifully preserved fruit and tins of homemade fruitcake and scones. I'm sure she had other food in there, but I wasn't interested in it when I was nine. Her peaches, though …

My pantry is not as well organised. There's a lot more in it. And I think what my beautiful class participants were looking for was not whether there were boxes of cake mix or two-minute noodles, or even validation that I was who I said I was, but inspiration. We all need a push. And you want to feel the person pushing you is legit and qualified.

So, do I have cake mix boxes in my pantry? No. That stuff is evil. Two-minute noodles? Yes, occasionally. I have teenagers. Sometimes they sneak them into the house. There was this one time that Matilda, my middle child, convinced her godmother Nessie, one of my best friends, who lives in Sydney, to post her multiple bags of instant noodles that sat in my pantry, potentially compromising my from-scratchness for about a month.

So, let's address this elephant in the room. Do I make everything from scratch all the time, or do I think you should? Nope and nope. Look, if I didn't have to work, maybe I could. If you are lucky enough to have leisure time or just time at home, you'll find sourdough easier. But I don't think it's practical or realistic to make everything from scratch all the time, particularly if you're feeding a family (and particularly if it includes hungry teenagers). I make a lot of the things most of the time, and in between I buy the bread and the butter and the yoghurt and the pasta.

While over the last ten years, my time was predominantly spent running a cooking school and commercial kitchen that produces a range of ferments for sale, now I'm primarily a cheesemaker. We have a beautiful herd of dairy goats – a mix of Toggenburg, Saanen and Alpine – and we milk them every day and turn their milk into cheese (and goat's milk soap) that we sell at local farmers' markets, to local restaurants and caterers, and through our farm shop online and when the farm is open for tours, classes and events.

I started with three goats, who arrived one day, many years ago, on the back of my friend Winnie's red V8 ute. Winnie is a retired local (cow) dairy farmer, we're great friends and we both love goats. When she drove into our driveway with the goats, everything and everyone on the farm stopped to watch. Winnie declared she'd rescued them from an RSPCA-condemned paddock and that she didn't have anywhere to put them at her place and I wanted goats anyway, didn't I? Honestly, without Winnie it might have been years until the first goats made their way here. We didn't have anywhere to put them either. I remember Adam and our market gardener Linda Machon rolling their eyes at each other and putting the goats in the chicken pen – the only fence that was appropriate for them at the time. They dropped whatever else they'd been working on that week and fixed up a paddock and a shelter for them. We named those goats Trudi, Gretel and Franzi and I loved them deeply. Winnie told us there had been a buck in with them, so we hoped they were pregnant. Trudi and Gretel both were. About four months later, Gretel gave birth to the first goat kid born on Buena Vista (as far as we know) and, as suggested by my English brother-in-law Julian, we named him Goaty McGoat Face. Soon after, Trudi gave birth to a doeling who we named Winnie.

I milked the goats every morning on a stand Adam made for me out of an old door. I made cheese in the kitchen. We walked does and kids out to pasture from the hayshed every morning, and brought them back in every evening. We learned that dairy goats hate the wind, and hate the rain even more, that handmade fresh goat's cheese belongs in heaven and that milking goats and making cheese was something we wanted to be doing when we were eighty. It's a dream come true. But it's a lot of work and, as a result, I don't always make my pasta from scratch.

Above all things, this book is not supposed to stress you out. It is not written to tell you that you should make all the things all the time in order to subvert capitalism. (Although that's an excellent idea.) It's supposed to be a friendly guidebook to encourage you to have a go at making some of the things you might regularly eat. And you never know, once you get going on the wonders of homemade crackers (with goat's cheese), maybe you'll never look back.

***

When I first started dreaming about writing a cookbook – about one hundred years ago – I was living in Sydney with two children, not three, and writing a food blog called *Inner Pickle*. Adam and I would periodically foray down to my family farm in Gerringong to visit my parents, and we'd wonder on the way home what was keeping us in Sydney.

We toyed with the idea of moving out of the city and down to the farm for years before actually having the courage to jump and just do it. I mean, what an offer! A family farm, debt free, if we wanted to have a go at it. It was circumstantial that none of my siblings were able, or interested, to take the farm over, and Dad eventually sold off a big portion of the property and paid everyone else out to allow Adam and me to invest in the 18 acres we were left with. Amazing. I thank my lucky stars (and my Dad) every day.

But once we got going and once we started to run on-farm cooking workshops every weekend, that was the end of *Inner Pickle*. With three small children and gardens and chickens and farmers' markets and sauerkraut to make, and admin and bookkeeping and marketing and workshops to teach, I was able to get dinner on the table every night but had absolutely no ability to write a blog post about it.

But, far out, I missed it. Blogging was a tidy combination of creative writing and photography and journaling, but above all, I loved the discipline of it, the scope, the conversations and the record. I worked on the microblogs that are Instagram and Facebook, and it was fantastic for building an online community and for filling last-minute workshop cancellations, but I missed the writing. And so, I started a newsletter called *Slice of Wednesday* (that sometimes comes out on a Wednesday). I'd get feedback and encouragement at the farmers' markets and on farm shop collection days, and this book is a result of that encouragement. Thank you to every single person who has ever suggested I should write it. Some of the stories in this book originated on *Inner Pickle*, some in *Slice of Wednesday*.

It's been an incredible ride. We nearly hit the wall early on after two fairly major chicken losses to fox attacks, and I'd say we came perilously close to the wall pretty regularly for at least five years. Even now, we occasionally consider what our world might look like if one of us took a job off-farm. But then we get back to it because we love working for ourselves, we love living and working here together, and we can't really imagine being this happy doing anything else. I also think a homemade cracker with homemade cheese could turn just about anyone.

Notes

This book uses 250 ml (8½ fl oz) cup measures and 20 ml (¾ fl oz) tablespoons. Oven temperatures are for fan-forced ovens. If using a conventional oven, increase the temperature by 20°C (70°F).

Chapter One

Pantry Lovers

Pantry Lovers

There is often a small relation of mine standing in the doorway of the farmhouse pantry complaining that there is nothing to eat. *There's no food in here, Mum.* That's never true, by the way. They're looking for ready-to-eat, and ingredients alone don't tend to satisfy at afternoon tea time, even if there's yummy nuts and organic dried fruit back there. The popcorn needs to be popped, the dates blitzed into bliss balls or the choc chips baked into bikkies. (*Please put the jar of choc chips down, honey.*) Pantries are places of magic waiting to happen, and while we wait, if you look hard enough, you're sure to find my secret stash of couverture chocolate.

Baking Powder

Oh, baking powder. Sometimes it's all that stands between you and failure. Such a simple little thing: it's the fluffiness in your cake, the rise in your biscuit, the levity in your pancake. We can go for years without even seeing it (hello, self-raising flour), but when it fails us, we feel it deeply.

Shall we talk about the first time I met my publisher? She was driving down to the farm, arriving around morning tea time, and so, perhaps obviously, I whipped up a batch of Visitor Biscuits (page 161), of which I have made one hundred and seventy bazillion batches in my life. Maybe one hundred and eighty. This is the biscuit we have taught for nearly ten years in our From Scratch class and made and sold as part of Buena Vista Farm Bikkies. You've possibly already made them, or eaten these biscuits. Anyway, I pulled them out of the oven, confident, the timing was perfect … and they looked like small warty rocks. Nothing delicious about them. Unable to be covered in icing (confectioners') sugar and resurrected. Chook food. (I served cheese and crackers instead.) It was the self-raising flour. It was dead. By that I mean the raising agent in it was inactive. Honestly, when we had a bikkie business, I would never have dreamed of using self-raising flour; I always declared I wanted to control the rise, and the salt, and also the aluminium (more on that in a sec), but convenience sometimes wins and so I had a bag in the pantry. My bad.

Okay, first let's look at what baking powder is. Your supermarket baking powder is typically bicarbonate of soda (or 'sodium bicarbonate', also commonly called 'baking soda') plus cornflour (cornstarch) and cream of tartar. The cornflour is just there to absorb moisture and stop the powder from clumping. Bicarbonate of soda is an alkali agent, and cream of tartar is an acidic by-product of the winemaking process. Baking powder is stable until it comes in contact with liquid, which is when the magic happens, because with liquid, the bicarb soda and cream of tartar *create* carbon dioxide. Cool, hey? That is, alkali plus acid plus liquid equals carbon dioxide (or, fluffy scones).

So, what's with the aluminium in baking powder? Self-raising flour, if you look at the ingredients, usually contains both 'raising agents' and 'acidity regulators'. Once the first reaction happens, it loses its ability to rise fully again – and delay is fatal to fluff. Aluminium sulphate, however, reacts with the baking soda and cream of tartar when heated, so it's actually called a second acid, or double acting. Almost all self-raising flour contains aluminium sulphate, which I knew, and bought it anyway, so it served me right when it expired and I produced a dreadful tray of inedible biscuits.

The moral? Avoid aluminium in your diet. Research has found aluminium in amyloid plaques in brains with dementia, so let's avoid that shall we?

You don't need double-acting flour. You just need to use fresh baking powder, and not leave whatever it is you're baking sitting around unnecessarily before it goes in the oven. Buy plain (all-purpose) flour and add your own rise!

One last thing: how do you test if your baking powder is still active? Put half a teaspoon in a cup and pour 60 ml (2 fl oz / ¼ cup) boiling water over it. It should froth. If it doesn't, you're going to have a flat cake. Frothing baking powder is the business.

MAKES 20 G (¾ OZ/1 TABLESPOON)

- 1 teaspoon bicarbonate of soda (baking soda)
- 1 teaspoon cornflour (cornstarch)
- 2 teaspoons cream of tartar

Or, depending on how much you are making, use these proportions:
- 1 part bicarbonate of soda (baking soda)
- 1 part cornflour (cornstarch)
- 2 parts cream of tartar

METHOD
Mix together. Store in an airtight container.

Self-raising Flour

Make it up fresh and never accidentally make small-warty-rock biscuits (see intro opposite).

MAKES 150 G (5½ OZ/1 CUP)

> 150 g (5½ oz/1 cup) plain (all-purpose) flour
> 2 teaspoons Baking Powder (see opposite)

METHOD

> Combine the plain flour with the baking powder. Ideally, sift them together, but if you're like me and have a mental block about sifting, combine briskly with a whisk.

Notes

Homemade baking powder will begin to lose potency after about a month, so only make up what you'll use in that time. If you're avoiding corn, substitute arrowroot powder for the cornflour (cornstarch).

If you're making this on the go and not planning to store it, you can leave out the cornflour and then you proportionally only need 1½ teaspoons baking powder to 150 g (5½ oz/1 cup) plain (all-purpose) flour.

Note

If you're making your own Baking Powder (see opposite) and it's freshly made and does not contain cornflour (cornstarch), reduce the amount of baking powder to 1½ teaspoons per 150 g (5½ oz/1 cup) plain (all-purpose) flour.

Breadcrumbs

Really? Is it worth it? Well, yes! Recipes often call for just a handful, and the ones you make are seriously going to be exponentially better than a shelf-stable packet from the supermarket. My only gripe is that recipes for homemade breadcrumbs almost inevitably instruct you to use bread without crust, so it's the crust that's always left behind. This is because the crust is usually harder to blend, and for uniform white breadcrumbs you need uniform white bread. FORGET THAT! Who needs uniform?! Ensure the bread you're using is a few days old (easy, right?), use a high-powered blender and embrace non-uniformity. You can use seeded bread – those breadcrumbs are even prettier – just either use it fresh or freeze immediately; you don't want rancid seeds in your crumbs. If you look at your breadcrumbs and need them to be finer, just make sure they are dry

(and cooled if just out of the oven) and pulse them again until they are as fine as you like. If you don't have a food processor, you can tear the bread up into crouton-sized pieces (don't use the crusts if you're doing this by hand), dry it out thoroughly either on the bench or in a low oven, then pop inside a zip-lock bag that's not totally sealed (so it can't pop) and bash with a rolling pin.

You can use frozen bread that's been defrosted. Sit the defrosting bread on some paper towel to absorb the water.

Gratin Topping

150 G ROUGHLY TORN FRESH BREAD
MAKES 150 G (5½ OZ/2 CUPS)
FRESH BREADCRUMBS

TO MAKE FRESH BREADCRUMBS

Using stale bread, tear into small pieces and whiz in a food processor to fine breadcrumbs.

TO MAKE DRIED BREADCRUMBS

Take your fresh breadcrumbs and put them on a lined tray in an oven preheated to 120°C (250°F).

Bake for approximately 15 minutes, stirring every few minutes.

Cool completely on the tray before storing in a jar in your pantry for 2–3 weeks. (Minimise their exposure to air as much as possible – use an airtight container and fill it right up.)

Look, I know you can use breadcrumbs to coat chicken, in meatballs, in homemade stuffing and in Christmas pudding, but really, the very best use of breadcrumbs – in my opinion – is mixed with cheese, herbs, garlic and lemon zest and sprinkled over everything. Let your bread go stale to make this stuff – you won't regret it.

I've called it 'gratin topping' because I don't know what else to call it. I first heard Annabel Crabb talk about breadcrumbs and cheese and herbs on her podcast *Chat Ten, Looks Three* years ago, and it stuck with me. Sprinkle this over potatoes or pasta bake, or scrambled eggs, or breakfast cereal (just kidding) – it improves everything it adorns.

MAKES APPROX. 120 G (4½ OZ/1½ CUPS)

80 g (2¾ oz/1 cup) fresh Breadcrumbs (see opposite)
35 g (1¼ oz/⅓ cup) parmesan, finely grated
2 teaspoons finely grated lemon zest
1 garlic clove, very finely minced, or ¼ teaspoon garlic powder
1 teaspoon dried oregano
1 teaspoon dried parsley
½ teaspoon salt

METHOD

Mix everything together. You can substitute fresh herbs if you have them – use twice the amount. Store in a sealed bag in your freezer to improve countless weeknight pasta bakes.

Notes

You can keep fresh breadcrumbs in a sealed jar in the fridge for about a week, and they freeze well for about 3 months.

Dried breadcrumbs also freeze beautifully, so if the weather is muggy at your place, don't risk them going mouldy, freeze them!

Fresh breadcrumbs take up approximately twice the volume of dried, so if you're following a recipe you may need to adjust if using fresh.

When defrosting breadcrumbs, put them on a sheet of paper towel to absorb moisture.

Condensed Milk

You can totally make your own condensed milk. This is useful to know if you are, you know, in a cabin in the middle of nowhere with a stove and sugar and milk and a desire to make no-churn ice cream. Because that scenario sounds likely. Or maybe you have a hankering for caramel. Or so you can eat it with a spoon. Or just make it for the joy of demonstrating that something you always bought in a can *can* be made from scratch. For fun. If that's your kind of thing. (Totally my kind of thing.)

I make my own condensed milk because I'm a mad keen from-scratch cook who really likes making slices, and many of my slice recipes, as you'll see, have condensed milk in them.

MAKES 250 ML (8½ FL OZ/1 CUP), APPROX. EQUIVALENT TO 1 × 400 G (14 OZ) TIN

500 ml (17 fl oz/2 cups) full-cream (whole) milk
220 g (8 oz/1 cup) white sugar

METHOD

Mix the ingredients together in a heavy-based saucepan and stir over a low heat until the sugar dissolves.

Once the sugar is fully dissolved, simmer over a very low heat for approximately 40 minutes, stirring occasionally. It's done when it has halved in volume from the start.

Store in the fridge for up to 1 month.

Brown Sugar

The first time I learned I could make my own brown sugar my mind was a bit blown. What? It's white sugar with molasses added back in? So why don't we just use white sugar and molasses in the recipe then? Feel free to try that if you're into experimentation (I am), but turns out, it's really not the same. Particularly in baked goods, the way the butter interacts with different sugars is elemental. Butter creamed with brown sugar and butter creamed with white sugar with molasses added after equals very different results. It's dead easy to make your own brown sugar if you've run out, and if you happen to conveniently have white sugar and molasses on hand.

MAKES 230 G (8 OZ/1 CUP)

220 g (8 oz/1 cup) white sugar
1 tablespoon molasses

For a darker brown sugar
220 g (8 oz/1 cup) white sugar
2 tablespoons molasses

METHOD

Put the sugar in a bowl and drizzle the molasses over the top. With your fingers (it won't work with a fork) rub the molasses into the sugar. I know it's messy but bear with me – it's a little bit of magic. Keep rubbing, it'll look like white sugar and clumps of molasses until it magically turns into brown sugar! There you have it. You're a wizard. I'll be honest, sugar technically lasts forever, but homemade brown sugar doesn't store beautifully for that long; it tends to go hard and lumpy. Apparently, you can mitigate this by sticking a slice of white bread into your sugar jar, which absorbs the moisture and stops it from clumping. Or you can just make as much as you need for 2–3 weeks.

Curry Powder

When you're making your own curry powder from scratch, you want to use whole spices, toasted and then ground. This will give you the very best flavour and fragrance. Technically, once you do this, the shelf life of your homemade curry powder is shortened. The longest-lasting homemade curry powder is made with ground versions of the spices below, but you compromise the flavour. Use whole spices, toast, grind, then don't assume it still has pungency two years later, okay? (Alternatively, use ground versions of the whole spices below, really, no hard feelings.)

MAKES 50 G (1¾ OZ)

2 tablespoons whole coriander seeds
½ tablespoon whole cumin seeds
1 teaspoon whole cardamom pods
1 teaspoon whole black peppercorns
½ tablespoon ground turmeric
½ tablespoon ground ginger
1 cinnamon stick
1 teaspoon chilli flakes
1 teaspoon garlic powder

METHOD

Toast the coriander, cumin, cardamon pods and peppercorns in a dry frying pan over a medium heat for 1–2 minutes until fragrant.

Remove from the pan and cool the spices to room temperature before placing in a high-speed food processor with the remaining ingredients and pulse together until finely ground, or pound by hand with a mortar and pestle.

Mix all the ingredients together and store in an airtight jar in your pantry for up to 2 months.

Taco Seasoning

This is a simple and handy spice mix to have in your pantry to pimp just about anything from roast potatoes to bolognese mince. This is something you should make, not buy; the flavours will jump out at you with none of the nasty chemicals or preservatives frequently found in commercial versions.

MAKES 60 G (2 OZ)

2 tablespoons ground coriander
2 tablespoons ground cumin
2 tablespoons dried oregano
2 tablespoons smoked paprika

METHOD

Mix all the ingredients together and store in an airtight jar. It will last about 6 months, depending on the freshness of the spices used.

Garam Masala

I'm giving this to you in largish proportions because you want to make a reasonable-sized jar, and use it! It will last in a sealed jar in your pantry for six months. If you're not already putting this into butter chicken or cheese sauce or homemade chai, you need to. It's delicious. Alternatively, you can easily halve this recipe.

MAKES 60 G (2 OZ)

1½ tablespoons whole cumin seeds
1 tablespoon whole coriander seeds
1 tablespoon whole cardamom pods
1 tablespoon whole black peppercorns
1 cinnamon stick
1½ teaspoons whole cloves
1½ teaspoons ground or freshly grated nutmeg
½ teaspoon fennel seeds
1 star anise
1 bay leaf

METHOD

In a frying pan, dry-roast the cumin, coriander, cardamom and peppercorns for 1 minute over a medium heat until fragrant.

Remove from the pan and cool the spices to room temperature before placing in a high-speed blender with all the other ingredients. Pulse together until finely ground, or pound by hand in a mortar and pestle.

Store in an airtight jar in your pantry for up to 6 months.

Za'atar

I first discovered this spice blend travelling in Israel in my twenties, sprinkled over labneh that had been drizzled with olive oil, and eaten with really good flatbread. Israeli za'atar tends to be dried thyme, salt, sesame seeds and sumac. Egyptian za'atar usually includes cumin and coriander.

Za'atar is also the name of a rare plant that is a protected species in Israel, with restrictions on harvesting to protect it from extinction. It has a long history, including being part of the biblical leper-cleansing ritual. Apparently, it was the plant the Israelites used to sprinkle lamb's blood over their doors at Passover when God sent the angel of death to kill all the first-born sons of Egypt.

In more cheerful news, it's absolutely great used to roll a log of goat's cheese in, or sprinkled over avocados and tomatoes, or used as a dry rub for roasting meat or veggies.

I still hold fast that the very best way to eat za'atar is sprinkled over homemade Labneh (page 261), drizzled with olive oil and eaten with homemade Yoghurt flatbread (page 56). Ideally with wine. (Unless it's 10 am.)

MAKES 30 G (1 OZ)

1 tablespoon toasted sesame seeds
2 tablespoons dried thyme
1 tablespoon sumac
2 teaspoons sea salt flakes, or other granulated salt

METHOD

Toast the sesame seeds in a dry frying pan over a medium heat, stirring often, then allow to cool thoroughly. Mix all the ingredients together.

Store in an airtight container in your pantry for up to 1 month (you don't want those toasted sesame seeds going rancid).

Flavoured Salt

First, why would you bother with flavoured salt?

Here's why: almost without exception, flavoured salt improves everything it touches. Do not underestimate it. Use it on meat or fish as a rub, or sprinkled on top before cooking, or over the finished dish before serving. Sprinkle it on popcorn to revolutionise movie night. Hop up your bolognese. Shake it over hot potatoes (with butter), use it as a 'finishing salt' over eggs. THERE ARE SO MANY THINGS. It also makes a great gift. (Maybe include a swing tag telling the recipient how to use it!)

Rosemary Salt

MAKES 40 G (1½ OZ)

2 fresh rosemary sprigs
3 tablespoons sea salt flakes

METHOD

Strip the leaves off the sprigs onto a tray and leave to air-dry for approximately 24 hours.

Once dry, blitz the rosemary in a high-speed blender until fine, remove and stir into the salt by hand. Sprinkle over hot potato wedges. AMAZING.

OTHER FLAVOURED SALTS TO TRY:

Chilli and lime (great with fish)

Smoked paprika (excellent with barbecued steak and tacos)

Sage salt (lovely with pasta – upgrades macaroni and cheese significantly)

Notes

1. Air-dry any fresh ingredients you're going to use. For example, dry zested citrus on a tray for a day or two before using. Alternatively, dry it in your oven on the lowest setting for about 1 hour.
2. Once dry, blitz the dry herbs or zests in a high-speed blender until very fine.
3. Use coarse salt – for example, sea salt flakes.
4. Remove dry ingredients from the blender and mix your herbs or spices into the salt with a fork, or use your fingers directly, at a ratio of 3:1 salt to flavour.

Egg Pasta

Homemade pasta with homemade pesto is fast food.

Really? Is she smoking tea tree with a side of overt earnestness? Perhaps she has too much time to poke around in gardens and lacto-ferment pickles and hand-make every last piece of family clothing including hand-stitched underwear?

Actually, no. I've never made underwear. But I frequently poke around in gardens and I'm a huge fan of lacto-fermentation and, for a fast dinner, YOU CAN MAKE PASTA FROM SCRATCH. I promise.

Start with the sauce. What have you got that's green? My mum grows wild rocket (arugula), and it really is wild. Grows like mad. I've usually got a few nuts on hand (edible as opposed to immediate family members, also handy), and if you happen to have a scraping of parmesan, a bit of lemon left over from that cup of tea you made, garlic and some olive oil, you're all set. You may not even have to shop for this meal.

The recipe for my Basil Pesto is on page 304, but if you're feeling creative, you don't really need a recipe. Try freestyling with a couple of big handfuls of greens of some kind (leftover carrot tops, beetroot [beet] greens, kale) plus some kind of toasted nut, some lemon juice, minced garlic and salt and a good stream of olive oil. Whiz it up. Taste it. Lovely. You're done.

Right. We're here for the pasta. Basic egg pasta is always simply 100 g (3½ oz/⅔ cup) plain (all-purpose) flour and one egg per person. I have a family of five, so typically times this by five, but make as little or as much as you like. Fresh pasta freezes well.

Engage child labour only if you have an extra twenty minutes plus clean-up time. Do not be deceived by willingness and enthusiasm. Small hands will slow you down and frustrate the bejaysus out of you if you're in a hurry. Ah, yes. Good for their maths. Teach them to cook, they said. Oh, for sure. Not when the wheels are falling off and you're looking for fast food though, right?

Pasta-making machines: excellent if you have one but not necessary. You can roll out your pasta dough nice and thin with a rolling pin, then roll it in a loose cylinder and slice into ribbons with a knife. Extremely satisfying.

Fresh homemade pasta cooks in boiling water for 2–3 minutes, and that's not some mad make-it-from-scratch lunatic exaggeration. It's literally 2–3 minutes. If you can mix up flour and eggs and get it rolled out quick smart (and then go do something else while you rest it), you've got fresh pasta in the same time it took to open a bag and boil it for 12 minutes. It's not only tastier – and you wear that earnest glow of someone who *just cooked pasta from scratch dammit* – it's much more nutritious. The fresher the flour the better, ideally unbleached, and that's some good carbohydrate.

Fast food. And you didn't have to drive to get it, no animal lived in misery to supply it and no kid worked for some compromised multinational to serve it. It'll fill you up and hopefully someone else will clean up the kitchen.

SERVES 5

500 g (1 lb 2 oz/3⅓ cups) plain (all-purpose) flour (ideally strong or bakers flour)
5 free-range eggs

METHOD

Place the flour in a large bowl, make a well in the centre and add the eggs while whisking with a fork. Incorporate the flour with the fork, and then with your hands, take the dough out, put it on the bench and knead it until it's really smooth. Wrap in plastic or wax wrap and rest in the fridge for half an hour.

Next, divide the pasta dough into large pieces and just work with one at a time, keeping the others covered (with one dry tea towel [dish towel] on the pasta and another damp tea towel over the top) so as not to dry the dough out. Using a pasta machine, roll and re-roll from the largest to the smallest number on the machine, until the dough is 1–2 mm (1⁄16–⅛ in) thin. Or roll as thin as you can with a rolling pin, keeping the dough well floured.

You can cut the pasta however you like – into long, thin noodles, or into chunky strips – just keep them well scattered with flour to stop it all sticking together.

Bring a large pot of lightly salted water to the boil, then reduce to a simmer. Cook the pasta (in batches if there's too much) until it is just cooked and floats to the surface, about 2–3 minutes, then remove with a slotted spoon.

Notes

If you have a food processor, the simplest way to make this recipe is to put the flour and eggs together in the bowl of the processor and whiz until they are a lovely amalgamated pasta dough. Take out the dough, put it on the bench and knead it until it's really smooth. Wrap in plastic wrap/wax wrap and rest in the fridge for half an hour.

Pasta freezes really well. Twirl little well-floured 'nests' of pasta with a fork or tongs, pop into a sealed bag and freeze. Then you can cook them from frozen, straight in the boiling water.

Vanilla Extract

Homemade vanilla extract is a simple thing, a trick up your sleeve and a gorgeous gift. It's a straightforward alcoholic extraction. You can use cheap or luxurious vodka, and you get two goes at it. Make it once, pour off the extraction and top up with vodka again. Fresh vanilla beans should give you two good batches of vanilla extract, and then when the beans are a bit worn out, you can use them to make Vanilla Sugar (see on right).

MAKES 250 ML (8½ FL OZ/1 CUP)

> 5 vanilla beans
> 250 ml (8½ fl oz/1 cup) vodka

METHOD

> Place the vanilla beans in a narrow bottle that holds about 250 ml (8½ fl oz/1 cup) and top up with the vodka.
>
> Leave to extract for 8–12 weeks for maximum flavour.
>
> Either use (or gift) with beans in, or pour off the extraction and bottle it.
>
> It does not need refrigeration and has an indefinite shelf life, as long as you don't accidentally leave the lid off, in which case it will evaporate.

Vanilla Sugar

Use this in place of white sugar in any recipe calling for white sugar, for an additional vanilla-y hit.

Version 1

MAKES 440 G (15½ OZ/2 CUPS)

> 1 or 2 whole vanilla beans, roughly broken or cut into pieces
> 440 g (15½ oz/2 cups) white sugar

METHOD

> Blitz the vanilla and sugar together in a food processor, then store in an airtight container.

Version 2

MAKES 1 KG (2 LB 3 OZ)

> 5 used dried vanilla beans
> 1 kg (2 lb 3 oz) caster (superfine) sugar

METHOD

> Pour the sugar into a jar that will hold all of it with some space left.
>
> Stick the beans into the sugar, seal the jar and leave for at least 1 week.
>
> The sugar will take on the flavour of the vanilla, and you can just leave the beans in there.

Version 3

MAKES 125 G (4½ OZ/1 CUP)

> 125 g (4½ oz/1 cup) icing (confectioners') sugar
> 3 teaspoons Vanilla Extract (see on left)

METHOD

> Mix the sugar and extract into a paste. Spread on a lined baking tray and let dry out completely. Break into pieces and powder with the back of a spoon. Store in an airtight container.

Red-wine Vinegar

Red-wine vinegar seems like such an excellent thing to do with leftover red wine. What you really need is a vinegar mother, which you'll have made after you successfully make your first batch of this. For your first batch, you need patience. Without a mother (even using your raw apple-cider vinegar), this first batch can take 8–12 weeks, in my experience, sometimes even longer.

MAKES 875 ML (29½ FL OZ/3½ CUPS)

500 ml (17 fl oz/2 cups) red wine
125 ml (4 fl oz/½ cup) apple-cider vinegar, with the mother
250 ml (8½ fl oz/1 cup) filtered water

METHOD

Wash a 1-litre (34 fl oz/4 cup) jar with a lid in very hot soapy water, rinse well with very hot water and air-dry.

Put all the ingredients into the jar and shake really well.

Take the lid off and replace it with a piece of muslin (cheesecloth) or a hanky fastened on with a rubber band.

Label the jar with the date. Put it in a cupboard or on a shelf away from direct light.

Check it after about 8 weeks, but it's possible nothing will happen for 3 months. You're looking for a 'mother' culture to form, usually floating on top. It will look a bit like a jelly. Once you've grown this mother you can use it in all future wine vinegar endeavours and the fermentation will take approximately half the time.

Taste the wine vinegar. When it's tart and finished, bottle it in a bottle with a tight-fitting lid, otherwise it will evaporate.

Pizza Sauce

We make pizzas every Saturday night. It's one of the ways we mark out the week. You can rely on it, our friends all know Saturday is pizza night, and we're pretty good at making large amounts of pizzas in one go, at short notice. Our pizza dough recipe is on page 56, and I make up this pizza sauce in large batches every summer when the tomatoes are on, and store it in the pantry. I never, ever manage to make enough to get us through to the next summer, and every year in spring as I'm pulling the last jar of sauce out of the pantry I promise myself I'll make more this year.

MAKES 3 × 300 ML (10 FL OZ) JARS (PLUS A BIT EXTRA)

- 2 tablespoons olive oil
- 1 onion, finely diced
- 2 garlic cloves, minced
- 1.5 kg (3 lb 5 oz) fresh tomatoes, chopped into eighths
- 15 g (½ oz/½ cup) fresh thyme, basil and oregano leaves, finely chopped, or 1 tablespoon mixed dried herbs
- 500 ml (17 fl oz/2 cups) water
- 1 teaspoon salt
- ½ teaspoon freshly ground black pepper
- 1 tablespoon Brown Sugar (page 28)
- 1 tablespoon apple-cider vinegar

METHOD

Heat the olive oil in a large heavy-based saucepan over a medium heat.

Pop the onion and garlic into the oil and cook until translucent and your kitchen smells delicious.

Now add the chopped tomatoes and the herbs and mix well, cooking for a few minutes, stirring so it doesn't brown or stick to the bottom.

Pour the water over the tomatoes, stir well and leave the heat on medium until it starts to bubble, then reduce the heat to low, add the salt, pepper, sugar and vinegar and leave to cook for 45 minutes, stirring occasionally.

Once cooked, allow to cool fractionally so you're not blending boiling hot liquid, then carefully transfer to a food processor and blend until smooth, or use a hand-held blender.

You can either put the sauce into clean jars and keep in the fridge for up to 3 months, or you can hot-water process them for longer storage (see below).

HOT-WATER BATH PROCESSING

Sterilise your jars (see Note on page 86). Fill the sterilised jars with the sauce and leave a 2 cm (¾ in) space at the top between the sauce and the lid. Close the lids.

Put the jars in a large clean saucepan of water that covers them by at least 5 cm (2 in). Put the pan over a medium heat and allow the water to boil. Turn down to a simmer (otherwise your jars are going to roll around and crack) and leave, making sure the jars are constantly submerged, for 15 minutes.

Carefully remove the jars from the water with tongs and/or rubber gloves (or you can leave them to cool down in the water if that feels safer) and leave on the bench until the lid sucks in or becomes slightly concave, which means a seal has formed.

If for some reason a seal hasn't formed, just put that jar in the fridge and use it first.

If a good seal has formed, it's safe to leave this sauce in your pantry for 1 year, then refrigerate after opening.

A Tale of Chickens...

We've been growing pastured chickens for years now. This means we're highly attuned to stray dogs, strong winds (mobile field shelters at risk), and big overhead birds. Adam and I can be seen running at high speed out of the farmhouse if we spy goshawks anywhere near the chickens in the paddock. The goshawks are beautiful and enormous but can be seriously problematic for free-ranging chickens. Having said that, we haven't lost any birds to overhead predators recently – whenever one appears we put one of the farm dogs in with the chooks to babysit (they don't love that job; they complain that it's a bit boring). An unfortunate chicken died recently when a crow flying over dropped a golf ball on it. That was not a risk we had planned for.

Who'd be a farmer, eh? It's something Adam says when stuff goes wrong, or, you know, escapes or dies or doesn't grow or gets eaten or breaks or we hit the wall financially.

He always says it wryly, as if he's the farm kid and I'm the townie and this farming idea is a permanent foregone conclusion. Like he's in it past his boots, and we might have had a disastrous day but he'd still rather be here than anywhere.

He said it one day after we'd gotten over the initial shock of losing a batch of meat chickens to a fox. Not quite the whole batch this time. Two weeks previously it was the whole batch. The whole mature batch that were due for processing the following week. That we'd paid for up-front (of course), paid for all the feed, all the infrastructure, and then received zero income for. Which is not what it's about for us anyway, but it does drive us closer to that wall. We had to call Feather and Bone, the lovely sustainably-raised meat providore that we supplied in Sydney, and explain that we'd be letting them down. We had to remember to call the abattoir and tell them we wouldn't be coming. We had to compost all the carcasses, because a fox doesn't actually eat a hundred chickens, it just eats a few and kills the rest to collect later.

It's brutal, sometimes, the dark side of small-scale farming.

And because there's no straightforward roadmap, it was easy to make mistakes in the early days of chicken tending. We checked and double checked the fences. We invested in fox lights. But the fox somehow got over the electric netting fence.

We won't bait on this farm although that's what the Department of Primary Industries strongly recommends we do. It only takes one person to have a living memory of losing a dog to 1080 poison to make it impossible to bring that poison onto your land. My dad, in this case. Aside from the fact Adam ethically objects to baiting.

We see foxes out in the paddocks almost every night. But now we have strong, purpose-built steel shelters with really well-fitted doors that are closed at night. There's a humane trap down in the gully. There's a dog in a mobile kennel tied up at night next to the shelter.

We choose to raise our birds in open-range paddocks, because this environment is significantly healthier for the birds. But because they are not safely locked in an enormous stinky shed, inhaling toxic poop air and needing antibiotics in their feed to survive, they're potentially vulnerable to predators, however diligent we are.

Raising poultry on pasture is risky, and the farmer carries that risk. Customers share the risk by supporting the pastured-poultry farmer and buying product at a premium price, priced that way to reflect the costs in doing things on a smaller scale: the hand raising, the bucket feeding, the water checking, the fox lights, scarecrows, fake owls, and late night head-torch-wearing circuits of the meat chickens, checking the fences in the winds, checking when it gets too hot, checking when the temperature drops, and picking up a hundred small birds and putting them under the hoop house shelters on the first few nights they're in the paddock until they figure out where to sleep. If you think pasture-raised poultry is expensive, you're damn right it is.

Who'd be a farmer, eh? He would. I would. (And the dogs are lying about it being boring.)

Chapter Two

A Bakery Item, *Please*

A Bakery Item, Please

There are ups and there are downs. For every story there's another one.

For every earnest heart wishing for a small farm in a friendly town with an orchard and room for chickens and a big veggie garden, there's an orchardist lying in bed tonight wondering how she's going to pay her water bill and how she'll keep those damn chickens out of the veggie patch.

For every exhausted working mother facing down the long fortnight of a school holiday juggle, complete with guilt and deadlines, there's a stay-at-home mother itching to do something else, dreaming of a quiet coffee in a clean house, feeling frustrated and undervalued.

For every bad apple there's a crate of good ones.

In every workshop that we poured our hearts into, every farmers' market we dragged ourselves to, every moment we hung on by the skin of our teeth hoping the whole idea would fly, we looked up and discovered a magical transfer of energy. The amazing people coming through the farm are energising the hair off our heads. The staff who arrived then stayed for years and became family. The volunteers who became staff. The international backpackers who taught us all their things and became lifelong friends. The customers who showed up week after week and bought whatever we made. The people around us, reminding us that for every down, there's an up. Those people: MAKE THEM SOME HOMEMADE BAKERY ITEMS. That is all.

Breadsticks

These are the champion of your cheese plate or grazing platter. The perfect thing to poke into a dip, and a crunchy snack in a jar in the pantry. While they are Italian in origin (called grissini there), I was surprised and thrilled to find them in jars on tables in restaurants in the States, offered as an appetiser. You can serve them with soup or beers, or they double very efficiently as a Harry Potter wand. Kids love them.

MAKES 24

200 ml (7 fl oz) warm water
1 teaspoon instant dried yeast
1 teaspoon white sugar
350 g (12½ oz) bread flour (strong or high-protein flour), or plain (all-purpose) flour
1½ teaspoons salt
60 ml (2 fl oz/¼ cup) olive oil
salt, cheese, seeds or herbs, to sprinkle (optional)

METHOD

Put the warm water into a jug and stir in the yeast and sugar. Set aside for a few minutes to froth. (If it doesn't froth at all your yeast isn't active and you'll need a new packet.)

Add your flour, salt and olive oil to a large bowl and pour in the yeast mixture.

Mix together until well combined, then knead for 2–3 minutes. You can do this whole process in the bowl of a stand mixer fitted with the dough hook attachment, or in a Thermomix or by hand.

Cover the bowl with plastic wrap or wax wrap and leave to sit for an hour at room temperature.

Preheat your oven to 180°C (360°F) and line two baking trays.

Divide the dough into 24 pieces and roll each piece into a log about 25 cm (10 in) long. (Don't roll on an overly floured board; they won't roll properly. Stainless steel is ideal, or a well-anchored chopping board. With two hands, roll from the middle of the breadstick outwards, to get it to the right length.)

Place on the trays, leaving space in between as they're going to expand, and use a pastry brush to brush with water and sprinkle with extra flaky salt or parmesan cheese, sesame seeds, fresh finely chopped rosemary, poppy seeds, whatever you like.

Bake for about 18 minutes, or until golden and crisp. Allow to cool completely either on the trays or on a wire rack before storing. They'll store in an airtight container for about 1 week.

Muffins

Muffinos. Doesn't everyone call them that? These are a favourite afternoon tea treat, eaten warm out of the oven. I really don't like a cakey muffin. Muffins are not cake. If it was a cake, it would be a cupcake and not a muffin, amirite? Technically, cake is usually made with butter and muffins are made with oil. They should be lighter, entirely more scoffable, and best eaten within a day or two. Anyway, this is my muffino recipe, for your enjoyment. Pictured on page 48.

MAKES 12

Base Muffin
155 g (5½ oz/⅔ cup, firmly packed) Brown Sugar (page 28)
300 g (10½ oz/2 cups) Self-raising Flour (page 25)
250 ml (8½ fl oz/1 cup) grapeseed oil, or canola, vegetable or light olive oil
2 free-range eggs, beaten
170 ml (5½ fl oz/⅔ cup) full-cream (whole) milk
1 teaspoon Vanilla Extract (page 36)

Scoffable Raspberry Muffins
125 g (4½ oz/1 cup) fresh or frozen raspberries

METHOD

Preheat your oven to 180°C (360°F).

To make the base muffin mixture, combine the sugar and flour in a large bowl.

In a jug, ideally a heatproof 500 ml (17 fl oz/2 cup) one if you have it, combine the oil and eggs (which you can beat into the oil), then add the milk, which will take your liquid up to a satisfying 500 ml (17 fl oz/2 cups) total. You are welcome. Mix together, then pour into your dry ingredients.

Add the vanilla and beat until smooth.

Spoon into 12 muffin cases and bake in the oven for 20 minutes, or until golden and the top of the muffino bounces back when pressed.

For Scoffable Raspberry Muffins, just add the raspberries to the mix when you add the vanilla and fold through.

VARIATIONS
Use 155 g (5½ oz/1 cup) blueberries or 175 g (6 oz/1 cup) chocolate chips, or both. Or 60 g (2 oz/½ cup) oats and 120 g (4½ oz/½ cup) mashed banana. Or 2 tablespoons poppy seeds and the zest of an orange, replacing the milk with orange juice. Add the fruit or other ingredients with the vanilla.

Lemonade Scones

What's a break in routine for if not to make scones and, more importantly, to sit and eat them with jam and cream with the people you love?

My scone recipe came from my friend Angela Thompson, who I knew when she was Angela Hyslop, in fact who I knew when she was two (and I was three) and she was like my fourth sibling.

Anyway, Ange can cook. And she gave me this recipe written on a napkin after I ate one of her scones hot, about twenty years ago, when she shared an apartment with my sister Naomi in Sydney. I still have that recipe on the napkin. How's *that* for hoarding?! Kind of shocking, frankly.

And then, surprising to me, when I worked as the cook in a kindergarten for a hundred children the following year in Brisbane, this was their scone recipe too. It's the best. Sorry, Nan.

MAKES 14 USING A 7 CM (2¾ IN) ROUND SCONE CUTTER

600 g (1 lb 5 oz/4 cups) Self-raising Flour (page 25; see Note)
300 ml (10 fl oz) lemonade (lemon soda; see Note)
300 ml (10 fl oz) pouring (single/light) cream

METHOD

Preheat the oven to 200°C (390°F) and line a large baking tray with baking paper.

Mix all the ingredients together, as lightly as you can, until the mixture is evenly combined.

Flour your work surface, press or lightly roll out the dough into a roughly A4-sized rectangle and cut out your scones with a 7 cm (2¾ in) round biscuit cutter. Lightly re-work all the remaining dough until you've used it up. You can then (1) flour the tops of the scones, or (2) brush with milk for a professional finish. (I rarely do either because, honestly, they're coming out of the oven and going onto a plate to be covered in butter or jam or cream, or golden syrup or lemon curd.)

Scones need to be cooked hot and fast. Pop them into your oven and bake for 13–15 minutes, or until well-risen, cooked through and light brown on top.

I hope you get to eat scones with someone you love, sometime soon.

Note

Ange has a note written on the napkin: Tip – use a new packet of flour and good lemonade.

Nan's Scones

If the controversial use of lemonade in a scone recipe is deeply shocking to you, please accept my apologies and this traditional scone recipe as a peace offering.

This recipe is my nan's. Hazel Le Quesne, my mum's mum, gave great hugs, told funny whimsical stories, drew gorgeous floral illustrations, and we all miss her, she was marvellous. Nan also made excellent scones.

MAKES 7 USING A 7 CM (2¾ IN) ROUND SCONE CUTTER (DOUBLE THIS RECIPE FOR A CROWD)

300 g (10½ oz/2 cups) Self-raising Flour (page 25)
1 good tablespoon white sugar
1 good tablespoon butter
250 ml (8½ fl oz/1 cup) full-cream (whole) milk

METHOD

Preheat your oven to 200°C (390°F) and line a large baking tray with baking paper.

Mix the flour and sugar together, then rub in the butter. Stir through the milk.

Knead, and cut into scone-like shapes (scone cutters are good for this, my favourite is a 7 cm/2¾ in round one).

Bake for about 15 minutes, or until golden on top.

That's it. Enjoy.

Shortcrust Pastry

Pastry is one of those things that's easy to buy. It's in your freezer, it's convenient, and a surprising number of very competent cooks have a mental blank about their capacity to make good pastry. (Also, the blind-baking puts people off.)

I'm here to encourage you. Give this a go. It's straightforward and *so much better* than a store-bought version. This recipe makes enough for a 28 cm/11 in pie crust, top and bottom. If you only need a tart base, halve the recipe.

MAKES 650 G (1 LB 7 OZ)

350 g (12½ oz/2⅓ cups) plain (all-purpose) flour, plus extra for dusting
250 g (9 oz/1 cup) butter, chilled and cubed
1 free-range egg yolk
2 tablespoons cold water

METHOD

In a food processor, process the flour and butter with a pinch of salt until combined and crumby.

Add the egg yolk and water and process until it comes together as a dough.

Wrap and refrigerate for about 30 minutes before using. (Why do we do this? Because it gives time for the flour to fully absorb the liquids, and for the gluten in the flour to relax. The result is a crisper crust and less shrinkage when it's baked.)

Preheat your oven to 175°C (345°F).

Once rested, roll the dough out on a floured board to approximately 5 mm (¼ in) thick, line your pie dish with it, and always blind-bake. Don't skip this step, unless you are making a pie with a lid.

Place a piece of baking paper over the pie crust and fill with either ceramic baking beads or rice or dry chickpeas/beans. (If you use rice or pulses, consider these sacrificial and keep in a labelled jar for future use for the same purpose.)

Bake for 15 minutes, then take out of the oven, remove the beads/beans and the paper and return to the oven for another 5 minutes.

Then it's ready for filling. Don't be put off by the fuss. This is a memorable pie you're making, whereas bought pastry is completely forgettable.

Note

To make a sweet shortcrust pastry, add 2 tablespoons icing (confectioners') sugar with the flour.

Shortcrust Pastry (with shortening)

Adam draws the line at lard in our house, but I can get away with vegetable shortening, and it really does make delicious flaky pastry.

MAKES 750 G (1 LB 11 OZ)

375 g (13 oz/2½ cups) plain (all-purpose) flour, plus extra for dusting
½ teaspoon salt
90 g (3 oz/⅓ cup) cold unsalted butter, cubed
150 g (5½ oz) vegetable shortening, chopped
120 ml (4 fl oz) iced water

METHOD

Put the flour, salt and butter in a food processor and whiz until the mix is sandy.

Add the shortening and process until well combined. Add the water and pulse until it forms a ball of dough.

Remove the dough to a floured board and roll it into a rough rectangle with a floured rolling pin. Fold one-third into the centre and the other third over the top, turn and fold in thirds in the other direction until you have a neat parcel.

Roll out again into a rough rectangle, then fold again into thirds, turn and fold into thirds again.

Roll out again – it may still be a bit speckled with shortening, that's okay!

Fold up tightly one last time and wrap in a large wax wrap or piece of plastic wrap and pop in the fridge for half an hour.

Once rested, roll out on a floured board to approximately 5 mm (¼ in) thick, line your pie dish with it, and blind-bake according to the Shortcrust Pastry recipe (see on left).

THEN it's ready for filling.

Sour Cream Pastry

I worked for a talented woman called Kirsten McHugh in Gerringong for a short while right before we got the farm business going. Kirsten was a cheesemaker and tea grower; she ran a beautiful cafe and cheese shop locally and this was her go-to pastry recipe. She'd make it in a flash and line rectangle tart cases with it and fill them with egg and cream and handmade cheese and herbs, and those tarts were heavenly. I never saw her blind-bake these cases; the pastry would be chilled and rolled out in a flash, filled and baked as one.

MAKES 650 G (1 LB 7 OZ)

300 g (10½ oz/2 cups) plain (all-purpose) flour,
  plus extra for dusting
200 g (7 oz) cold butter, cubed
125 g (4½ oz/½ cup) sour cream

METHOD

In a food processor, process the flour and butter together until it looks like fine breadcrumbs.

Next, add the sour cream and process until it comes together as a dough.

Wrap in plastic wrap and put in the fridge to rest for half an hour.

Roll out on a floured board to 5 mm (¼ in) thick and use as required.

Blind-bake as per the Shortcrust Pastry recipe (see opposite page).

Rough Puff Pastry

Of all the pastries, this is the one I make the most. Rough puff pastry is particularly perfect for encasing samosas or hand pies, or pasties or sausage rolls. You can make it and keep it wrapped in the fridge for about five days, pull it out and use it and it's still perfect. This is useful if you have it on hand to wrap lunchtime leftovers into a pie – because everything tastes better wrapped in rough puff. YUM.

MAKES 550 G (1 LB 3 OZ)

250 g (9 oz/1⅔ cups) plain (all-purpose) flour,
  plus extra for dusting
200 g (7 oz) cold butter, chopped
½ teaspoon sea salt
100 ml (3½ fl oz) cold water

METHOD

In a food processor, blitz the flour, butter and salt together well.

For images of the following steps, see page 52.

Pour this dry mix into a large bowl. Make a well in the centre and add the water. Mix with your hands until it comes together as a dough. There will be small chunks of butter visible – this is fine!

Remove to a floured board and form into a rough rectangle. With a floured rolling pin, roll out thinly and fold one-third into the centre and the other third over the top, then turn and fold in thirds in the other direction until you have a neat parcel.

Roll out again into a thin rectangle and fold into thirds, then turn and fold into thirds again.

Roll out again – it should no longer be speckled with butter. If it is, fold again and roll until you can't see flecks.

Fold up tightly one last time, cover and put into the fridge to rest for half an hour before using.

When using, roll to approximately 5 mm (¼ in) thick and bake for about 20 minutes, or until golden.

FROM SCRATCH

Cinnamon Scrolls

I've been making cinnamon scrolls for many years, primarily as a birthday morning treat for my middle child, Matilda Daisy, who LOVES them, and also on Christmas morning as a family tradition.

Another of our family food traditions is Sunday morning bakery pastries. I'm not sure how that happened, but I'm not arguing. It's a tradition tightly held by my children (and husband, let's be honest) and occasionally, instead of buying pastries on a Sunday, I'll break with the birthday-and-Christmas-only tradition and make cinnamon scrolls.

This recipe works best of all with white bread flour. They are a roll, after all, and the high gluten content in bakers flour yields the fluffiest and softest roll of all. I sometimes use 100 per cent organic unbleached spelt, which works beautifully too, but if you're after show-stopping softness, sweetness and lightness, use bakers flour, bread flour ('strong' flour) or high-protein flour.

Right. Let's do this. These are simple and DELICIOUS. You won't regret it.

MAKES APPROX. 14

Rolls
- 250 ml (8½ fl oz/1 cup) full-cream (whole) milk
- 7 g (¼ oz) instant dried yeast, or 2 teaspoons
- 110 g (4 oz/½ cup) white sugar
- 2 free-range eggs
- 125 g (4½ oz/½ cup) butter, melted
- 1 teaspoon salt
- 750 g (1 lb 11 oz/5 cups) bread (strong) flour, plus extra for dusting

Filling
- 125 g (4½ oz/½ cup) butter, softened
- 165 g (6 oz/¾ cup) Brown Sugar (page 28)
- 2 tablespoons ground cinnamon

Glaze
- 125 g (4½ oz/½ cup) butter, melted
- 125 g (4½ oz/1 cup) icing (confectioners') sugar
- 2 tablespoons full-cream (whole) milk

METHOD

To make the rolls, warm the milk in the microwave (or on the stove) for approximately 50 seconds, or until it is warm to the touch. Put it into the bowl of a stand mixer, if you have one, and sprinkle the yeast on top. Add the sugar, eggs and butter and mix well. Now add the salt and flour and stir until combined. If you're using a stand mixer (best!) use the dough hook and mix for a good 5 minutes. If there is dough sticking to the bottom of your bowl add an extra tablespoon of flour. It should form a nice elastic dough ball. If it's not stretching (which means it's too dry) add another tablespoon of milk. If you don't have a stand mixer, you can just mix and then knead by hand for 5 minutes on a floured surface.

Transfer the dough to an oiled bowl, cover and leave to stand for approximately 1 hour, or until the dough doubles in size. After it has doubled, roll it out onto a large floured cutting board into a 30 × 50 cm (12 × 19¾ in) rectangle.

To fill the rolls, spread the softened butter over the whole dough rectangle. Sprinkle the brown sugar and cinnamon over the top. Tightly roll up the dough from the long edge until you have a long sausage. Cut into 2–3 cm (¾–1¼ in) pieces. You should get about 14.

Place the rolls onto a lined baking tray (I use one that's about 30 × 40 cm/12 × 15¾ in), cover with a clean tea towel (dish towel) and leave to rise for another 30 minutes.

To bake the rolls, preheat the oven to 180°C (360°F) and bake for about 20 minutes, or until lightly golden.

Make your glaze by mixing your melted butter, sugar and milk. Beat with an electric mixer if possible, or by hand, enthusiastically, until perfectly combined. Drizzle over the rolls or paint on with a pastry brush. It's fine to do this while they're hot, and also fine to eat one while they are still the temperature of the sun.

You can actually make the rolls the night before. After you've rolled them out and cut them up, but before the second rise, cover and refrigerate overnight. The next day, get them out and do that 30-minute second rise before baking.

I hope you love them as much as we do!

Pizza Dough

Homemade pizza dough changes everything. More than anything, it's a vast, vast improvement on frozen, shrink-wrapped bases from the supermarket in terms of freshness, flavour and the satisfyingly delicious way it bakes. We make this every Saturday.

MAKES 5 MEDIUM (25 CM/10 IN) BASES OR 4 LARGE (35 CM/13¾ IN) BASES

- 300 ml (10 fl oz) warm water
- 2 teaspoons instant dried yeast
- 1 teaspoon white sugar
- 500 g (1 lb 2 oz/3⅓ cups) bread (strong) flour, plus extra for dusting
- 1 teaspoon salt
- 2 tablespoons olive oil

METHOD

Put the water in a jug and stir in your yeast and sugar. Leave to froth – this will take about 5 minutes. If it doesn't froth, it means your yeast is no longer active and you'll need to buy some more.

Either by hand or in a stand mixer fitted with the dough hook attachment, mix together your flour, yeasty water, salt and olive oil until well combined, then knead for about 3 minutes. The dough should feel smooth and elastic.

Roll into a ball and leave in a bowl in a warm spot for about an hour, or until doubled in size.

Knock the air out of it, cut the dough into four or five pieces and roll each piece into a tight ball.

On a floured board, roll each ball out into a circle of between 25–35 cm (10–13¾ in).

Top with Pizza Sauce (page 39), mozzarella and basil leaves (or whatever you like) and bake in a hot oven (210°C/410°F) for about 25 minutes, or until the edges are puffy and the underside is lightly browned.

Yoghurt Flatbread

We make this flatbread A LOT. It's cheap and quick and fills a gap when a snack is needed, or when you need something to dip into your Pumpkin Soup (page 102), or to mop up your chicken curry, or to eat with Labneh and Za'atar (pages 263 and 31).

Here's how it goes …

MAKES 6

- 300 g (10½ oz/2 cups) Self-raising Flour (page 25), plus extra for dusting
- 250 g (9 oz/1 cup) natural yoghurt (see page 259–60)
- 2 teaspoons salt

METHOD

Mix the self-raising flour and yoghurt in a bowl. Add the salt and mix until it comes together into a loose dough. Form into six balls. Ideally allow to rest, covered, at room temperature for between 15 minutes and 2 hours, but they'll still work if you skip this step.

Heat a dry heavy-based frying pan over a high heat. Take one ball at a time and roll it out on a floured board with a floured rolling pin until it's about 5 mm (¼ in) thick.

Place the flat dough into the hot, dry pan and cook for 2 minutes, then flip and cook on the other side for 2 minutes. Keep the flatbreads warm and soft by wrapping in a tea towel (dish towel) until serving.

Notes

You can brush the hot, just-cooked flatbreads with butter or ghee or garlicky butter, but it's not really necessary. You can store these for a couple of days in an airtight container and bring them back to life by lightly brushing with water and popping in a moderate oven for 10 minutes.

Flatbread

What is the logic behind making your own flatbread or wraps when you can buy them so cheaply from the supermarket? Is it sensible when you're going to have to go to the shops anyway to buy the ingredients and one aisle over you can buy the finished product? The logic is that sometimes flatbread isn't just flatbread. (Sometimes it is. Ask me on a school day when lunchboxes need filling and everyone is trying to get out the door and someone ate the last lunchbox bikkie late last night. At that moment I am grateful for an emergency bag of bought frozen wraps.) But on the days when you can find the energy, when you're feeling creative, when you've handily got the ingredients and you are energetically pursuing zero waste and anti packaged foods, there is no denying that homemade flatbreads taste supremely better. There's no weird numbers or un-food-like ingredients listed. There's no plastic. There's no mould-inhibiting sachets. There's just flatbread to wrap around leftover veggies or to mop up curry or top with hummus for a snack.

This flatbread is worth the rising wait time just for the puffiness it acquires when it hits a hot, dry frying pan – so satisfying.

MAKES 8

2 teaspoons instant dried yeast
1 teaspoon white sugar
375 ml (12½ fl oz/1½ cups) warm water
450 g (1 lb/3 cups) plain (all-purpose) flour,
    plus extra for dusting
1 teaspoon salt

METHOD

Mix the yeast and sugar into 125 ml (4 fl oz/½ cup) of the warm water and let it begin to froth. This can take 5 minutes. If there is zero froth, you need to ask yourself how long that yeast has been in your pantry. Is there any chance that it's older than the hills? If your yeast has lost its oomph, you might need new yeast. Mix the activated yeast into a large bowl with the flour, salt and remaining 250 ml (8½ fl oz/1 cup) warm water.

Knead for a few minutes (use a stand mixer fitted with the dough hook attachment if you have one) then roll into a ball, put it back in a bowl, cover with a cloth and let it sit somewhere warm until doubled in size, usually around 1½ hours.

Cut into eight equal pieces and roll each piece into a ball.

Ideally allow to rest, covered, at room temperature for another half an hour, but they'll totally work if you skip this step.

On a floured board with a floured rolling pin, roll out each ball into a thin disc about 5 mm (¼ in) thick. I roll out one, get one cooking, roll out the next. If you want to roll them all at once, don't stack uncooked flatbreads on top of each other – they'll stick together.

Heat a dry heavy-based frying pan over a medium heat and cook the rounds, one at a time, for approximately 2 minutes per side. They should puff up, particularly when cooking on the second side. If they're cooking too fast, turn the heat down to low. Keep them warm and soft by wrapping in a tea towel (dish towel), or store them in an airtight tin for later use. They keep well for about 3 days. You can refresh them by sprinkling them with a little water and popping them into a warm oven for a few minutes.

Flour Tortillas

These are a yeast-free flatbread, with no rising/resting time, which makes them perfect for a quick turnaround. No bread for lunch? These are a really cool solution. They make great fish taco casings, or a great lunch with leftover shredded chicken, Sixty-second Mayo (page 85) and lettuce.

MAKES 12 SMALL (10 CM/4 IN) OR 8 LARGE (15 CM/6 IN)

450 g (1 lb/3 cups) plain (all-purpose) flour, plus extra for dusting
1 teaspoon salt
1 teaspoon Baking Powder (page 24)
80 ml (2½ fl oz/⅓ cup) olive oil
250 ml (8½ fl oz/1 cup) warm water

METHOD

Combine the flour, salt and baking powder in a bowl and mix until well combined.

Make a well in the centre and add the oil and the water, stirring until well combined and it comes together into a ball.

Turn out onto a floured surface and knead for 1 minute until the dough is smooth. (You can use a stand mixer fitted with the dough hook attachment for this step.)

Divide into twelve (or eight) pieces and form into balls.

Roll your dough balls on a floured board with a floured rolling pin into flat circles about 5 mm (¼ in) thick. (I roll one, get it cooking while I roll the next. Don't answer your phone while you're doing this. Also don't stack uncooked flatbreads on top of each other – they'll stick together.)

Heat a large, dry heavy-based frying pan or cast-iron skillet over a medium heat.

Once the pan is hot, place a tortilla in the saucepan and cook for about 1 minute (the underside will have brown spots and the top should bubble a bit). Flip the tortilla and cook for another minute on the other side.

Remove with tongs and keep warm and soft wrapped in a tea towel (dish towel) while you cook the rest.

Homemade tortillas don't store fresh particularly well – I'd say 2 days in an airtight container or sealed bag. You can refresh them by microwaving with a damp paper towel in the bottom of a microwave-safe container for about 30 seconds. They also freeze well – just put some baking paper in between them and freeze in a sealed bag.

A Love of Loaves

I love a loaf. Really love it. In fact, please 'scuse me for one minute while I go and make some toast to accompany the writing of these recipes.

I love toast. I love it with peanut butter. Even at 10.15 pm at night. (Maybe most of all then.)

I'm unclear how many bread recipes are appropriate for one cookbook, but I get all giddy at the sight of a hunk of bread on a board so there's going to be a few.

I have three types of bread I make. Two do not involve much work and the other is sourdough. Nonetheless, without getting too preachy, there is an awful lot to love about sourdough. It's pre-fermented so it's easy to digest. It's got great chew due to the fermentation process. It's got great flavour and structure. It's basically better bread. But it's a bit of a pain in the arse to make. You have to maintain the starter. The starter has to be at a fever pitch of activity for the bread to be great, and it only reaches fever pitch if you use it all the time. The whole thing takes ages. After you've made your own sourdough, paying $9 for a loaf no longer feels like daylight robbery.

Anyway, in addition to sourdough, I also love a good no-knead loaf and a breadmaker or stand mixer loaf. Oh yes. I love the idea of hand-kneading bread, really I do, but I much prefer letting the stand mixer or the mysterious genius of long-ferment no-knead do the work for me.

Sourdough

Sourdough Starter

First, a note about flour.

Not all flour is created equal. There are multiple types of wheat grown that produce different flours for different purposes, aside from the myriad ways flour is processed. But from a baking perspective, there is soft wheat and there is hard wheat. Soft wheat is great for biscuit and cake baking. It's general, or all-purpose. Hard wheat is your bread-baking wheat. Australia grows some of the best hard wheat in the world, and we export an enormous amount of it to Italy. Hard wheat is higher in protein, yields better gluten development and is processed to produce what is sometimes called 'strong flour'. It's the flour you want to use to make bread, or pizza: bread flour, or strong flour, or bakers flour.

(The '00' and '000' flour refers to the sift, not the type of wheat. It's very fine flour, so is really nice for making smooth and silky pasta.)

Also, a note about water.

When making and maintaining sourdough starter and bread, you always need to use filtered water rather than town or tap water. Tap water in Australia has chlorine added to it, which is an antibacterial agent that ensures the water is safe to drink. It feels stupid to be complaining about safe and clean drinking water, but from a sourdough point of view it's problematic because that antibacterial chlorine will compete with the wild yeasts and bacteria in your sourdough, it'll ultimately kill them off and you'll be left with a flat, lifeless starter. If you feed your starter chlorinated water once, don't throw it out or assume it's dead. But if you feed it chlorine on an ongoing basis, you'll eventually kill it. The best way forward is to invest in a water filter if you can – because if you're drinking chlorinated water it's also killing all the bacteria in your gut – or leave a jug of water out overnight on the bench and the chlorine will evaporate.

How to Make a Sourdough Starter From Scratch

Mix 100 g (3½ oz/⅔ cup) bakers or bread (strong) flour and 100 g (3½ oz) filtered water in a glass or plastic jar/container. Cover with a tea towel (dish towel). It shouldn't be airtight because it needs to be able to consume oxygen and release carbon dioxide.

Leave your starter on your kitchen bench for one to two days. Keep an eye out for any signs of activity – the process of feeding it over the next few days is really dependent on what sort of activity you're getting out of it. What you're looking for is elevation or growth, and usually bubbles.

After two days, whether you've seen activity or not, tip out approximately three-quarters of the starter and give it the same feed again: 100 g (3½ oz/⅔ cup) flour and 100 g (3½ oz) filtered water. Leave it for another two to three days, looking for signs of activity again. You may get some, you may not (weather will affect this, with colder months slowing the process). Just persist with it. It'll be starting to develop, and those strains of yeast, which are there and are present, need to become more active – and time is the only thing that's going to permit that.

If you're not getting activity, keep giving the same feed every couple of days – tip three quarters out and mix in 100 g (3½ oz/⅔ cup) flour and 100 g (3½ oz) water, continuing to observe, until you do. Once you start getting activity it's critical to maintain a steady feed and to observe how quickly it's multiplying. You want it to get to the point where it will visibly increase in size and you'll get to know how long this takes – some starters are at peak activity in four hours, some at ten hours.

In the next feed that follows some activity, give it the same feed again – tip three-quarters out and add 100 g (3½ oz/⅔ cup) flour and 100 g (3½ oz) water. Observe it at intervals – four, five, six, seven, eight hours later, and see where it peaks/doubles in size and then starts to decline. You can mark your starter jar with a rubber band to make the observation simpler.

Getting the starter ready for baking

When you begin using your starter to bake you will ideally want it to be a little bit before it peaks, because that's when it's at its highest activity. When you feed it at that point it's going to have the greatest ability to multiply again, which is the process you want when you start making the bread.

So now you'll feed it again to get it ready for baking with. Note how long it took to peak last time and give it this feed that length of time before you want to bake your bread. So, say it took six hours to peak, feed it six hours before you want to bake.

For this pre-bake feed, tip out a portion so that just 100 g (3½ oz) of the sourdough starter remains. Give it 100 g (3½ oz/⅔ cup) bakers flour (I use an organic unbleached stoneground) and 100 g (3½ oz/⅔ cup) rye flour (again, I use a whole organic rye) and 200 g (7 oz) filtered water. Once it has grown to its peak, remove 250 g (9 oz) to use. That's the leaven for your bread recipe. *Note: A good trick to determine if the starter is ready to bake with is if a teaspoon of it floats in a cup of water.*

Maintaining your starter

If you want to make a daily practice of baking bread, you'll want to give your sourdough a consistent feed each time prior to baking.

Discard a portion of your starter leaving about 100 g (3½ oz) behind, then feed it 200 g (7 oz/1⅓ cups) flour and 200 g (7 oz) water – I always use half organic bakers flour and half organic whole rye. And then use it when it's at its peak.

If you don't want to use it the next day, continue to feed in smaller amounts (100 g/ 3½ oz/⅔ cup flour and 100 g/3½ oz water) every couple of days, discarding a decent portion first.

Feed refrigerated sourdough starter on a weekly basis

If you do not bake often, maybe only weekly or monthly, it may be more practical to keep your sourdough starter in the refrigerator, in a tightly closed container, and feed it once a week.

1. Remove at least 50 g (1¾ oz/¼ cup) starter from the refrigerator. Discard the remaining starter.
2. Feed the starter with flour and water. Use a scale to measure the ingredients and combine equal amounts by weight of starter, water and flour: 50 g (1¾ oz) starter, 50 g (1¾ oz) water, 50 g (1¾ oz/⅓ cup) flour. (Again, I always use half organic wheat flour and half organic rye flour.)
3. Cover and let the starter sit for 1–2 hours at room temperature, until light and bubbly.
4. Put a tight lid on the jar and return to the refrigerator.
5. Repeat weekly even when not baking with your sourdough culture.

Sourdough Bread

This is our 'teaching' recipe, which we've used for many years in the cooking school. It's technically a low-hydration sourdough recipe, meaning it has less water to flour in ratio than other recipes, such as Chad Robertson's well-known Country Loaf from his book *Tartine*. Why we worked with this low-hydration recipe, and why I give this one to you now, is because it was by far the most reliable in different environments. High-hydration sourdough requires you to have a very active and bubbly starter (i.e. frequently used) and, because of the higher water content, high-hydration bread is more susceptible to temperature changes in your kitchen. This recipe just seems to work in most homes.

If your bread is not rising beautifully with good aeration, the fault is less likely to be the recipe or process or oven and almost certainly your starter. The best bread is made with a starter that's used often, and not sleepy from being in the fridge.

MAKES 2

250 g (9 oz) active starter (see page 62)
650 g (1 lb 7 oz) warm water
1 kg (2 lb 3 oz/6⅔ cups) white bread (strong) flour, or bakers flour or high-protein flour (see Notes), plus extra for dusting
2 teaspoons salt
olive oil, for oiling
polenta, for sprinkling

METHOD

See images on page 63. Weigh your active starter into a bowl and stir the water into it. Then weigh in the flour, add the salt and mix well. Bring it together and shape into a rough ball. Cover and leave for 30 minutes.

With a wet hand, pull the sides of the dough over the top of itself, forming as tight a ball as possible. Turn the bowl as you go, pulling the bottom of the dough up and over itself. Cover and leave for 1 hour.

After an hour, either in the bowl or on a floured surface, pull or fold the dough into a new, tighter ball from the outside into the centre (like an envelope). Return to the bowl for another hour, covered.

After another hour, take it out again. On a floured surface, pull or fold the dough again into a ball shape from the outside inwards. It should be starting to feel puffier and more aerated. Place back into the bowl. (It's at this stage that you would add in olives/raisins/nuts/seeds/sprouted grains, etc. Stretch out your dough, sprinkle them on, work them in, shape and fold.) Cover and leave for 1 hour.

After the hour, take out the dough, divide it into two and shape into loaves, placing the shaped dough into two bannetons or bowls lined with a floured cloth. Leave, covered, to rise for 2–3 hours.

Preheat your oven to 235°C (455°F), oil a baking tray with a little olive oil and sprinkle with some polenta. Tip the dough out of the banneton or bowl directly onto the baking tray. Score the top of the loaves with a sharp serrated knife or a razor blade, and bake (see Notes) for 30 minutes or until darkly golden with a crispy crust.

Alternatively, tip out the dough onto a piece of baking paper, score the top of the loaf, then use the paper as a sling and place the dough carefully into a pre-heated cast-iron Dutch oven casserole dish (heat in your oven for at least half an hour) with a lid.

Bake your loaves, one at a time, with the lid on for 30 minutes, then remove the lid and bake for another 15 minutes, until the loaf is crusty and golden and sounds hollow when tapped on the bottom.

Notes

If you use wholegrain (whole-wheat) flour, increase the water to 800 g (1 lb 12 oz).

Getting steam into your oven: If you don't have a Dutch oven casserole dish to bake in, it's a good idea to create steam in your oven by preheating it with a baking tray in the bottom. When you are ready to bake, pour boiling water into this hot tray and also spritz the walls and ceiling of the oven with a water spray bottle to increase steam. Steam softens the outside of the loaf and allows it to rise well, otherwise it may form a hard crust too early on and not rise as it should.

Daily Bread

I went off the no-knead recipe for a while as I went down the rabbit hole of what a breadmaker can do … then I burnt my breadmaker cord (Adam had suggested I move the breadmaker *away* from the stove where I tended to drape the cord across the back of hot elements … oops). I shelved my breadmaker recipe and got back on the sourdough wagon and learnt that the more you make it, the better and more active the starter is, and suddenly you're turning out really good sourdough.

My incredibly wonderful dad showed up at my place in Sydney one day (this is before we moved to the farm) with some tools and in a wink had replaced the breadmaker's cord for me, and I can vouch that sandwich loaf, fruit loaf and grainy bread (pages 68–9) all work beautifully in a breadmaker. Obviously, you don't need a breadmaker; you can make all of the following recipes by hand. But if you have one languishing in a cupboard, get it out. This'll be fun.

No-knead Bread
(long ferment using yeast)

Jim Lahey from Sullivan Street Bakery New York was the father of the no-knead bread (without stacks of yeast) many years ago now, and this recipe is based on his.

If maintaining a sourdough starter starts to rob you of the will to live, I want you to try this, because the final result looks very like sourdough, and it is incredibly straightforward.

MAKES 1

450 g (1 lb/3 cups) bread (strong) flour,
    plus extra for dusting
¼ teaspoon instant yeast
½ teaspoon salt
300 ml (10 fl oz) water

METHOD

In a large bowl, combine the flour, yeast and salt. Add the water and stir well – the dough will be wet and sticky. Cover the bowl with a cloth (or a shower cap!) and let it rest for at least 12 hours (you can leave it up to 18) at room temperature.

The dough is ready when the surface is dotted with bubbles. After the long fermentation, and leaving the dough in the bowl, pull the dough from the bottom over the top of itself, turning the bowl as you go. Keep working until you form a ball. It'll still be pretty wet. Leave it to rest. Come back half an hour later and pull the dough up and over itself, turning the bowl as you go. The dough should feel more elastic and be able to hold its shape. Leave for another half an hour. Do this one more time – so you've folded and flipped the dough into a ball three times over about 1½ hours.

Then, using just enough flour to keep the dough from sticking to the work surface or your fingers, flip the dough out of the bowl and gently shape it into a ball. Sprinkle a cotton or linen tea towel (dish towel) with flour and place the dough, seam side up (that is, top-down), on the towel and dust with more flour. Fold the tea towel over the dough and let it rise for about 2 hours. When it is ready, the dough will be more than double in size and will not readily spring back when poked.

At least half an hour before the dough is ready, preheat your oven to 230°C (450°F). Put a heavy covered pot (cast iron, enamel or ceramic) in the oven as it heats. When the dough is ready, carefully remove the pot from the oven. Slide your hand under the tea towel and turn the dough over into the pot, seam side down. It may look like a mess, but it's okay, it will straighten out as it bakes. Cover with the lid and bake for 30 minutes, then remove the lid and bake another 15 minutes until the loaf is beautifully browned and sounds hollow when tapped on the bottom. Cool on a rack, and don't cut into it when it's hot.

Sandwich Loaf

MAKES 1

300 ml (10 fl oz) warm water
2 teaspoons instant dried yeast
1 teaspoon white sugar
450 g (1 lb/3 cups) bakers flour, or protein-enriched or bread (strong) flour, plus extra for dusting
1½ tablespoons olive oil
1 teaspoon salt
sesame or poppy seeds, for topping

METHOD

To make this bread in a breadmaker, add the water to the breadmaker with all the ingredients, in order, except the seeds. Set to 'dough'. Once it's ready, take it out and transfer to a 22 × 11 × 10 cm (8¾ × 4¼ × 4 in) loaf (bar) tin. Sprinkle with sesame or poppy seeds, or both – or none, whatever you fancy.

Allow to rise for about 40 minutes. Once it has risen by at least half its size, bake in a 200°C (390°F) oven for about half an hour, or until toasty on top and hard if you poke it (and it's making your house smell like heaven).

To make this bread by hand, combine the water, yeast and sugar in a large cup or small bowl and leave until it froths, usually 5 minutes. (If it doesn't froth up the yeast might be inactive – try a new packet.)

In a large bowl, mix the flour, olive oil and salt together. Add the yeast mix and mix together until combined. Turn out onto a floured board and knead for 5–10 minutes until the dough is springy and stretchy.

Put the dough back into the bowl and leave it, covered, in a warm spot until the dough has doubled in size (approximately 1½ hours). This is called the 'first rise'. Punch it down and turn it out of the bowl to form a loaf or put it into a loaf (bar) tin. Sprinkle the top with sesame or poppy seeds, or both – or none.

Leave the loaf somewhere warm to rise again by at least half, covered, for another 40 minutes or so (this is the 'second rise') and then bake in a 200°C (390°F) oven for 30 minutes. The loaf is cooked when it sounds hollow on the bottom when tapped.

Fruit Loaf

As a student, I was obsessed with fruit toast. Having arrived in Sydney and discovered proper bread (hello, early nineties), to also discover lovely dense fruit loaf made with spices and sometimes nuts was heaven. You can substitute whatever dried fruit you fancy here. My favourites have always been sultanas and apricots.

MAKES 1

300 ml (10 fl oz) warm water
2 teaspoons instant dried yeast
1 tablespoon Brown Sugar (page 28)
450 g (1 lb/3 cups) bakers flour, or protein-enriched or bread (strong) flour, plus extra for dusting
1½ tablespoons olive oil
1 teaspoon salt
1 tablespoon ground cinnamon
60 g (2 oz/½ cup) sultanas (golden raisins)
90 g (3 oz/½ cup) dried apricots

METHOD

To make this bread in a breadmaker, add the water to your breadmaker with all the ingredients, in order. Set to 'dough'. Once it's ready, take it out and transfer to a loaf (bar) tin. Allow to rise for about 40 minutes, lightly covered with a cloth or, ideally, with a reusable shower cap!

Once risen by about half its size, bake in a 200°C (390°F) oven for about half an hour, or until toasty on top and hard if you poke it (and it's making your house smell amazing).

To make this bread by hand, start with the lukewarm water. Mix in the yeast and brown sugar and leave until it froths, usually 5 minutes. (If it doesn't, the yeast might be inactive – try a new packet.)

In a large bowl, mix the flour, oil, salt, cinnamon and dried fruit together. Add the yeast mix and mix together until combined. Turn the dough out onto a floured board and knead for 5–10 minutes until the dough is springy and stretchy.

Put the dough back into the bowl and leave it, covered, in a warm spot until the dough has doubled in size (approximately 1½ hours). This is called the 'first rise'. Punch it down and turn it out of the bowl to form a loaf or put it into a 22 × 11 × 10 cm (8¾ × 4¼ × 4 in) loaf (bar) tin. Leave the loaf somewhere warm to rise, covered, for another 40 minutes or so (this is the 'second rise').

Bake in a 200°C (390°F) oven for 30 minutes. The loaf is cooked when it sounds hollow on the bottom when tapped.

Grainy Bread

MAKES 1

300 ml (10 fl oz) water
450 g (1 lb/3 cups) wholemeal (whole-wheat) flour
2 tablespoons wheat bran
2 tablespoons wheatgerm
1 tablespoon cracked wheat
1 tablespoon linseeds (flax seeds)
1 tablespoon sunflower kernels
1½ tablespoons milk powder
1½ tablespoons oil (I use macadamia nut)
1 teaspoon salt
2½ teaspoons instant dried yeast
sesame or poppy seeds, for topping

Handmade version
1 teaspoon white sugar

METHOD

To make this bread in a breadmaker, add the water to your breadmaker with all the ingredients, in order, except the seeds. Set to 'dough'. Once it's ready, take it out and transfer to a 22 × 11 × 10 cm (8¾ × 4¼ × 4 in) loaf (bar) tin. Sprinkle with sesame or poppy seeds, or both – or whatever you fancy. Allow to rise for about 40 minutes, lightly covered with a cloth or, ideally, with a reusable shower cap!

Once risen by about half its size, bake in a 200°C (390°F) oven for about half an hour, or until toasty on top and hard if you poke it (and it's making your house smell like heaven).

To make this bread by hand, start with 300 ml (10 fl oz) lukewarm water. Mix in the yeast and the sugar. Combine the remaining ingredients in a bowl, add the yeast mix and knead for about 10 minutes. Give it two rises (let it double, punch it down and let it double again), then bake as above.

Apologies to any gluten-free readers that have stumbled in here.

A Simple Life

I totally signed up for the simple life – the living on the farm, living more sustainably, with a smaller ecological footprint, and feeding our family home-raised, home-grown, dynamically nutritious food. Turns out, there's nothing bloody simple about it at all.

I read *Possum Living* by Dolly Freed and, while it was all very interesting, I personally don't think you can live without money. Well, not with children that you want to do stuff with, and (before you can afford to invest in the tanks and the solar power) if you need to pay bills, right?

Don't know about you, but I'm no good without internet. (And that was before we had to homeschool through a pandemic while working full-time. You too?) I need to pay the internet service provider bill, and I suspect they're not so interested in bartering home-grown broiler chickens.

And you know what? I *bought Possum Living*. Ridiculous? I could have walked the mile into town to the public library that's only open for four hours once a week and put my name on the list to borrow it in six weeks, but I'm in the commercial kitchen prepping for the markets the day the library opens. Oh, the irony. I can't escape the need to work for a living. Who can?!

I adored the book *Radical Homemakers* by Shannon Hayes, but I cannot see how you can completely disentangle yourself from the commercial reality of needing some kind of income. You're lucky in the extreme if you have no debt to repay, or don't need to pay for school excursions or the jars to put your preserves in.

Still, how did we get so busy? And can we dial it back? When did I last lie in the paddock with a kid, looking at the clouds? That was pretty much the principal reason I moved back down here. (That, and the desire to have dairy goats and a flock of ducks.)

So, in a vague effort to find some kind of rhythm, some degree of calm, I make bread. I make the time to make bread. Because when I'm flat out like a lizard drinking, it's the breadmaking that falls by the wayside. I find myself making sandwiches with a bought loaf of sliced bread. And even though the scaffolding is all there, I feel like the simple life has fallen away from me, or me from it.

Is there *one* thing that makes you feel like you're on track? Making time for breadmaking? Finding calm in a downward dog? Looking at clouds? Holding knitting/a hammer/an instrument? I hope there is. I'm off to knead mine …

Because simple takes time. The homemade laundry powder, all those hankies on the line, all the from-scratch food in lunchboxes and on the dinner table, the chemical-free cleaning, the vegetable garden, the chickens and, for heaven's sake, the twenty-four-hour sourdough process. But, for some reason, I really, really, really believe in it. I believe it's a better way to live, if you can, if you're inclined. Not at all simple, but fresh out of the oven it's a little bit of awesome.

Baguette

Ooh la la, so perfect for a picnic, for garlic bread, for bruschetta. Perfect split and served for lunch with soup or thinly sliced minute steak and Horseradish Cream (page 85), or goat's cheese, sliced tomato and fresh Basil Pesto (page 304), or buttered and filled with crispy bacon, avocado and lettuce.

You will need to start this recipe in the evening for baguettes the next day.

MAKES 3

500 g (1 lb 2 oz/3⅓ cups) bread (strong) flour,
    plus extra for dusting
350 g (12½ oz) water
2 teaspoons salt
2 teaspoons white sugar
1 teaspoon instant dried yeast

METHOD

Mix all the ingredients in a bowl and cover with plastic or wax wrap and allow to rest for 15 minutes.

Pull the bottom of the dough over itself, turn the bowl, pull the dough over itself, turn the bowl, pull the dough over itself. The aim here is to stretch and fold the dough into a nice tight ball. Cover the bowl and let the dough rest for 30 minutes.

Repeat the above steps, and again another half an hour later.

Cover the bowl with plastic wrap and refrigerate overnight, at least 12–14 hours.

The next morning, turn the dough out onto a lightly floured surface and divide into three. Shape into rough rectangles, cover and allow to rest for 45 minutes to an hour.

Form each dough rectangle into a tight cylinder, sealing the seams well. Roll each sausage from the centre and stretch to the right length, tapering the ends until each is about 40 cm (15¾ in) long.

Create a couche (a bed/resting place of canvas or linen used to support the bread while it proves) with floured linen, if you have it, or a large tea towel (dish towel).

Put the baguettes in the couche, seam side up. Cover and prove for 30–60 minutes, or until proved and puffy.

Preheat your oven to 230°C (445°F). Place a baking stone, if you have one, on the upper rack, and a tray of water on the bottom rack.

Transfer the baguettes to a piece of baking paper (if you're using a stone), or a lined baking tray, seam side down, and score the top of the baguettes with a razor blade or sharp knife in a swift, firm motion.

Carefully slide the baguettes onto the baking stone, or place the baking tray with baguettes into the oven and bake for 10 minutes.

Remove the tray of water, rotate the baguettes, and turn the oven down to 215°C (420°F) and bake for another 10 minutes, or until deep golden brown.

Garlic Bread

Garlic bread is one of my kids' favourite things. It's on the menu for most birthday dinners, or when we have lasagne, or when there's soup.

MAKES 1 BAGUETTE (APPROX. 10 SLICES)

1 × Baguette (see opposite)
2 garlic cloves, finely minced
2 tablespoons salted butter, softened to room
    temperature

METHOD

Preheat your oven to 180°C (360°F).

Slice the baguette diagonally in 5 cm (2 in) pieces, but don't cut the whole way through.

Mix the garlic into the butter, then spread onto the cut sides of the baguette.

Wrap the baguette tightly in aluminium foil and place on a tray in the oven for 15 minutes.

Serve warm!

If you have leftover garlic butter, just pop it in a jar and leave it in the fridge to add to the frying pan when you start your next bolognese mince/soup/sauce – anything! I quite like having a jar of garlic butter in the fridge – it's super handy.

Hot Cross Buns

Oh, Easter.

You can keep your chocolate eggs, your bunnies and your bilbies, all I need is a hot cross bun. Ideally warmed (not toasted), with a lick of proper butter.

Hot cross buns are dead simple and quick. It's a satisfying bake that, without the extremely distinctive cross, doesn't need to be relegated to merely a once-a-year affair.

MAKES 12

600 g (1 lb 5 oz/4 cups) plain (all-purpose) flour, plus extra for dusting
14 g (½ oz) instant dried yeast
115 g (4 oz/½ cup) caster (superfine) sugar
3 teaspoons mixed (pumpkin pie) spice
1 teaspoon ground cinnamon
½ teaspoon salt
225 g (8 oz/1½ cups) currants
50 g (1¾ oz) butter
300 ml (10 fl oz) full-cream (whole) milk
2 free-range eggs, lightly beaten

Flour paste for the cross
75 g (2¾ oz/½ cup) plain (all-purpose) flour
100 ml (3½ fl oz) water

Sticky glaze
2 tablespoons caster (superfine) sugar
80 ml (2½ fl oz/⅓ cup) water

METHOD

Combine the flour, yeast, sugar, mixed spice, cinnamon, salt and currants in a large bowl. Melt the butter in a small saucepan over a medium heat and add the milk. Heat for 1 minute, or until just lukewarm. Add the warm milk mix and the eggs to the flour mix. Stir gently until the dough comes together, then use your hands to finish mixing to form a soft dough.

Turn the dough out onto a floured surface. Knead for 5–8 minutes, or until the dough is smooth (you can use a stand mixer fitted with the dough hook attachment for this). Place the dough in a lightly oiled bowl. Cover with plastic wrap and set aside in a warm place for 1–1½ hours, or until the dough doubles in size.

Line a large baking tray with baking paper or a silicone baking mat. Punch the dough down to its original size. Knead for 30 seconds on a lightly floured surface until smooth. Divide into 12 even portions. Shape each portion into a ball. Place the balls onto the lined tray, spread apart. Cover with plastic wrap and set aside in a warm place for 30 minutes, or until the buns double in size. Preheat the oven to 190°C (375°F).

Make your flour paste by mixing the flour and water in a small bowl until smooth, adding a little more water if the paste is too thick. Spoon into a small sealed bag. Snip off a small corner of the bag and pipe the flour paste over the tops of the buns to form crosses. Bake for 20–25 minutes, or until the buns are cooked through.

Make the glaze by putting the sugar and water into a small saucepan over a low heat. Stir until the sugar dissolves, then bring to the boil and boil for 3–4 minutes. Brush the warm glaze over the warm hot cross buns. Serve warm or at room temperature, cut in half and spread with butter.

Soda Bread

I've always imagined this was probably the bread cooked by my great-great-grandmother Mary when she arrived at this farm pretty much straight off the boat from Ireland at eighteen years old, with a newborn baby and her determined and headstrong young Irish husband. Traditionally cooked in the coals, or at the bottom of the cooking pot (I recommend you use an oven), this bread is satisfyingly quick and easy to make. The addition of the egg means the loaf has better lasting power and will stay fresh for a few days, unlike its Australian counterpart, damper, which needs to be eaten on the day it is made.

MAKES 1

600 g (1 lb 5 oz/4 cups) plain (all-purpose) flour, plus extra for dusting
1 teaspoon bicarbonate of soda (baking soda)
1 teaspoon salt
80 g (2¾ oz) unsalted butter, cubed
400 ml (13½ fl oz) buttermilk
1 free-range egg

METHOD

Preheat the oven to 200°C (390°F). Line a baking tray with baking paper or a silicone baking mat.

In a large bowl whisk together the flour, baking soda and salt.

Cut the butter into the flour mix and rub together with the tips of your fingers until the butter pieces are pea-sized and as incorporated as you can get them.

In a separate jug or bowl, whisk the buttermilk and egg together.

Pour the buttermilk mix into the flour mix and bring together with a spoon until it's too heavy to handle, then turn out onto a floured board and, with floured hands, knead together into a ball. If it's way too sticky add a bit more flour, 1 tablespoon at a time.

Transfer the dough ball to your baking tray, cut an X into the top and bake for about 40 minutes, or until it sounds hollow when tapped on the bottom. If it's browning too rapidly on top, you can cover it with aluminium foil halfway through the bake.

Remove from the oven and serve hot or cold or toasted.

Soda bread stores well for a couple of days in an airtight container or tightly wrapped. It's best eaten toasted after this time.

Chapter Three

A Deep Love of Condiments

A Deep Love of Condiments

Once upon a time when I was a food blogger, a lovely reader called Susan asked a good question in the comments that got me thinking. And thinking. And thinking. She asked, why do I cook from scratch? Is it because it's cheaper? It tastes better? Or is it for environmental reasons to cut down on food miles?

It's so weird, Susan, I thought. No one had ever asked me that question.

They'd asked me if I'm bonkers (well, my sisters had), because really, who makes their own butter? People have asked about the time commitment because, again, who really has time to make all their own bread and crackers and pasta if they have a job? Even if, or especially if, that job is at home raising small people!

Let me answer the fundamental question first.

Although I've cooked forever, and for a living, I first started diligently cooking from scratch when I figured out that my son Henry, then about three, reacted to artificial colours, flavours and preservatives.

Everyone knows kids react to sugar. That's obvious. But it was when he would get completely hyper after eating 'healthy' rice crackers and dried fruit that I started paying attention. After discovering the amazing Sue Dengate, who wrote *Fed Up*, I started by taking him off dairy. This wasn't easy, as his diet at the time was pretty much made up of milk, cheese and yoghurt. But after about three days, he was an exponentially calmer boy and I wondered if I was onto something.

I started really reading the back of packets (particularly of rice crackers and dried fruit). I was surprised to find nasty flavour enhancers in plain rice crackers (not to mention the sodium) and discovered an insidious preservative called 160b in lots of things, which really seemed to affect his behaviour. Anyway, the first step was avoiding all artificial preservatives. The natural next step was to make everything myself.

I should say one thing: although I'm a huge advocate for kicking all artificial stuff out of kids' diets, and I have first-hand experience of how much this affects concentration and calmness, I don't think it's wise or even correct to attribute all behavioural issues to food. What I mean is that I think sometimes kids get ratty, and it's not necessarily because of something they've eaten. If you're constantly telling a kid that their behaviour is being moderated by the MSG-laden chips they just ate, I wonder if they might stop taking responsibility for the way they're feeling and behaving? Just a thought.

So, that was my first motivation.

Then I discovered how much deep joy I got from making stuff from scratch. I am so intensely proud of my homemade yoghurt, and pulling a jar of homemade butter out of the fridge makes me freakishly happy. Maybe you start because it's a good idea. It is definitely cheaper: bread, 50 cents a loaf! But you keep on, until you discover yourself making not just breakfast cereal and peanut butter and ice cream and hummus and stock and baked beans and pies and quiches, but all your own cleaning products and washing powder too. Because it's FUN. Really fun. Freaks that we are. (You're here, aren't you? I'm betting you've at least made a loaf of bread once.)

And yes, food you make yourself from scratch tastes better.

Well, food made by someone else can sometimes taste better! Adam made a lasagne the other night that brought a tear to my eye.

But food from a box or a bag or a packet? It never does. Those frozen watery vegetables? Anaemic boxed microwave meals? They never do.

Time, though. That is an issue.

To make everything from scratch takes time. But for me, so does going to the supermarket with three children. I figured out a while ago it was much quicker making my own pastry from my bulk bag of flour, an egg and some butter than going to the supermarket, buying frozen pastry, then waiting for it to defrost. (If you don't make your own pastry, this should be the one thing you try. It's so fast that if you have a food processor, you will never go back.)

And food miles?

I remember when I was quite little and Victorian milk started being brought into New South Wales, undercutting the local milk price. I was a dairy farmer's daughter. It was a big deal. You supported the local dairy co-op or the local farmers went out of business.

I'll admit though, since then, I didn't give a whole lot of thought to food miles until I found myself lucky enough to live in an area with an excellent farmers' market focused on reducing food miles and supporting local farmers.

I also saw *Food, Inc.* and started listening to impressive local market advocates like Joel Salatin.

So, Susan, in answer to your question, I cook from scratch for lots of reasons. Because it's healthier, because I love it, and because I want to know where the ingredients have come from.

There's one more major reason – it takes me outside of the ridiculous and evil market manipulation that is large grocery chains. It unlinks me from the chain of commoditisation that consumers are pushed into, ending with people putting crazy 'fruit strings' in their kids' lunchboxes. (They're lollies, people. Don't let anyone tell you they are a healthy snack choice.) It's my little up-yours to giant food companies who have successfully convinced people that it's cheaper to buy frozen pies and chips for dinner than a bag full of vegetables. Cheaper how?

Anyway, that's enough of that.

I'm off to make relish.

Beetroot Relish

We've been making this relish commercially at the farm since the first COVID-19 lockdown, when we needed to ask our wonderful kitchen crew, Sarah Worboys and Stephanie Debeck, formerly working on our on-farm workshops and events (all cancelled), to focus on commercial kitchen production, making things we could sell online and at our farmers' markets. We started producing things that go well with goat's cheese, and this was and still is a crew favourite.

MAKES 3 × 300 G (10½ OZ) JARS

- 1 large bunch (approx. 650 g/1 lb 7 oz) beetroot (beets)
- 1 brown onion, finely chopped
- 1 tart cooking apple, peeled, cored and finely chopped
- 185 g (6½ oz/1 cup, lightly packed) Brown Sugar (page 28)
- 250 ml (8½ fl oz/1 cup) white-wine vinegar
- 1 tablespoon fennel seeds
- ¼ teaspoon ground cloves

METHOD

Trim the beetroot stems, wash the beetroots thoroughly and place in a large saucepan. Cover with cold water. Place over a medium–high heat and cook for 20 minutes, or until the beetroots are just tender. Drain and rinse under cold water. Wearing rubber gloves, peel the beetroots and coarsely grate.

Meanwhile, combine the remaining ingredients in a saucepan. Bring to the boil over a high heat, stirring to dissolve the sugar. Reduce the heat to medium–low and simmer for 10 minutes, or until the apple is tender.

Add the grated beetroot to the apple mixture. Simmer for 45 minutes, or until the mixture is syrupy. Carefully spoon into clean jars and put the lid on tightly. This relish keeps well refrigerated for 3 months, or hot-water-bath-processed for 1 year (see page 39).

Harissa

I had a job in a kitchen in Glebe when I was eighteen years old. I started as a waiter, worked my way up to barista, then across into desserts and finally into the kitchen proper, where I worked with two wonderful, imaginative and hilarious chefs, John Svinos and Virginia Seymour. Some of the things I made regularly in that kitchen have never left me. One of them was harissa. This isn't the Rose Blues Café recipe, but it's an echo. In Glebe, in the mid-nineties, we spread that harissa on trendy new focaccia, topped with sour cream and chicken with garlic cooked in white wine. I've loved harissa ever since and try to always have a jar handy, in case I ever come across focaccia. It's great smeared on a salad sandwich, added to a stew or casserole for a hearty chilli kick, or add a teaspoon to mayonnaise to make a fab chilli mayo.

MAKES 220 G (8 OZ/1 CUP)

- 1 tablespoon ground cumin
- 1 tablespoon whole cumin seeds
- 1 tablespoon ground coriander
- 150 g (5½ oz/approx. 5) fresh long red chillies, deseeded and chopped
- 5 garlic cloves, peeled
- 2 teaspoons salt
- 2 tablespoons olive oil, plus extra if needed

METHOD

Put all ingredients except the oil in a food processor and blend to a paste.

With the processor running, slowly drizzle in the oil until it's as smooth as you can get it. Add extra oil if needed but don't let it get too runny.

Store in the fridge with a layer of oil on top for up to 2 months.

Mustard

Mustard is super simple to make yourself, and super customisable, which I think is what I love most about it. You can make it grainy or smooth, flavour it or smoke it up with paprika (or not). Basically, it's just mustard seeds soaked and blended. Please note: LET IT SIT! Don't try your mustard on day one and chuck it. It takes a few days for the flavour to mellow. Repeat after me: slow food, slow food, slow food. And also: sourdough with pickles, cheese and homemade mustard is one of life's utter joys.

MAKES 1 × 300 G (10½ OZ/1 CUP) JAR

- 100 g (3½ oz) yellow mustard seeds
- 80 ml (2½ fl oz/⅓ cup) apple-cider vinegar
- 2 garlic cloves, minced
- 2 teaspoons salt
- 3 tablespoons honey
- 60 ml (2 fl oz/¼ cup) water

METHOD

Put the mustard seeds in a bowl and cover with cold water to about 10 cm (4 in) above the seeds. Cover and sit at room temperature overnight or for at least 12 hours.

Drain any remaining water from the seeds. Combine the soaked seeds, vinegar, garlic, salt, honey and water in a blender and blend until smooth.

Transfer to a jar and cover, then refrigerate.

Don't eat it for the first two days; it'll be super spicy and you'll wonder why on earth you bothered, but it will mellow after a few days.

It will keep in the fridge, covered, for months.

Mango Mustard

My dear friend of more than twenty years, Leah Horstmann, is a mad foodie and now lives in Cairns. When I see her, she often gives me a bag of dried mango. I like dried mango, but not as much as I like mango mustard. I've never actually told Leah that her gorgeous very-well-travelled mango always ends up in mustard. I'm sure she would understand.

MAKES 1 × 300 G (10½ OZ/1 CUP) JAR

- 50 g (1¾ oz) yellow mustard seeds
- 50 g (1¾ oz) brown mustard seeds
- 85 g (3 oz/1 cup) roughly chopped dried mango
- 80 ml (2½ fl oz/⅓ cup) Red-wine Vinegar (page 38)
- 1 tablespoon smoked paprika
- 2 garlic cloves, minced
- 2 teaspoons salt
- 2 tablespoons caster (superfine) sugar
- 60 ml (2 fl oz/¼ cup) water

METHOD

Put the mustard seeds into a bowl and cover with cold water to about 10 cm (4 in) above the seeds. Cover and sit at room temperature overnight or for at least 12 hours.

Drain any remaining water from the seeds.

Put the mango in a bowl, cover with boiling water and leave to stand for about 15 minutes to reconstitute, then drain.

Combine the soaked seeds and softened mango in a blender with the remaining ingredients and blend until smooth.

Transfer to a jar, cover and refrigerate.

Don't eat it for the first two days, it'll be super spicy, but it will mellow after a few days.

It will keep in the fridge, covered, for months.

Whole Egg Mayonnaise

This recipe is for everyone other than my beloved sister-in-law, Rachel, who truly believes mayonnaise is the work of the devil and would rather die than be in the same room as it.

This is a staple in our house. In the last week, I've dressed salads with this mayo, dipped zucchini (courgette) sticks in it and spooned it over eggs. It's a great thing to have in the fridge to make a quick and yummy coleslaw with, to serve with homemade hot chips, or to improve a lunch wrap no end. And it's easy to make.

MAKES 1 × 300 G (10½ OZ/1 CUP) JAR

1 free-range egg, separated
1 tablespoon apple-cider vinegar
1 teaspoon mustard (see page 82)
250 ml (8½ fl oz/1 cup) light-flavoured oil,
    such as grapeseed or rice bran oil
½ teaspoon sea salt

METHOD

To make the mayo in a food processor, place the egg yolk, vinegar and mustard in the bowl of the food processor and process until the mixture is pale. With the motor running, add the oil in a VERY SLOW but steady stream until the mayonnaise is thick and emulsified. Add the egg white and mix until well combined. Add the sea salt.

Refrigerate until needed. It will keep for 1 week in the fridge.

To make your mayo by hand, place the egg yolk, vinegar and mustard in a large bowl and whisk with a balloon whisk until the mixture is pale and fluffy. Then, while still whisking vigorously, begin to add the oil in very small amounts, very slowly, until the mayonnaise becomes thick and emulsified. Add the egg white and sea salt and mix until well combined.

Aioli

At our farm workshop lunches, we almost always serve our pasture-raised chicken tossed in this garlicky mayo. Aioli is also absolutely excellent served with fish and chips, or piped over pizza made with broccoli. One of my favourites.

MAKES 1 × 300 G (10½ OZ/1 CUP) JAR

3 garlic cloves, very finely diced
1 free-range egg yolk
1 tablespoon lemon juice or white-wine vinegar
1 teaspoon dijon mustard
250 ml (8½ fl oz/1 cup) grapeseed oil

METHOD

To make the aioli with a food processor, place the garlic, egg yolk, lemon juice and mustard in the bowl of the food processor and process until the mixture is pale and well mixed. With the motor running, add the oil in a VERY SLOW but steady stream until the mayonnaise is thick and emulsified, then season with salt and pepper.

Refrigerate until needed; it will last for 1 week in the fridge.

To make the aioli by hand, place the garlic, egg yolk, lemon juice and mustard in a large bowl and whisk with a balloon whisk until the mixture is pale and well mixed. Then, while still whisking vigorously, begin to add the oil in very small amounts, very slowly, until the mayonnaise becomes thick and emulsified, then season with salt and pepper.

Sixty-second Mayo

Our ordinary mayo (see opposite) is really pretty quick to make, but there's an even quicker method. To get a lovely thick mayo you need to do a slow emulsification, but you can get a perfectly decent mayo by mixing it all at once, no slow drizzle. Sometimes, when you feel like mayo with your hot chips and they're actually already out of the oven and on the table, remembering that you can make mayo in literally a minute might motivate you to do it.

Rules: Don't make this in a bowl. It has to be made in a jar or jug that your hand-held blender fits in, so it can whip everything together simultaneously.

MAKES 1 × 300 G (10½ OZ/1 CUP) JAR

1 free-range egg yolk
1 tablespoon apple-cider vinegar
1 teaspoon mustard (see page 82)
250 ml (8½ fl oz/1 cup) light olive oil
½ teaspoon sea salt

METHOD

Put all the ingredients in a jug or a jar and blitz together with a hand-held blender until emulsified and thick.

Store in the fridge for up to 1 week.

Horseradish Cream

Horseradish cream has many uses, but I think its very best use is served on a fresh baguette with hot, just-cooked minute steak. I think it might be one of the very best lunches in life.

MAKES 1 × 300 G (10½ OZ/1 CUP) JAR

250 g (9 oz/1 cup) sour cream
20 g (¾ oz/¼ cup) grated fresh horseradish, or you can use store-bought, in a jar
1 tablespoon mustard (see page 82)

METHOD

Whisk all the ingredients together in a bowl, cover and refrigerate for at least 2 hours before using, if possible, to allow the flavours to meld together.

Keeps in the fridge for up to 1 week.
Pictured opposite.

Tomato Chilli Jam

I adore tomato chilli jam. I serve it with lots of things: cheese on toast, quesadillas, under smashed avo, with cheese platters, spooned into bolognese or stew. Once, our hero, the US regenerative farmer Joel Salatin, came to stay here while filming with our friends Kirsten and Nick for their amazing permaculture education business, Milkwood. Kirsten emailed me after they'd all left and said that Joel had asked for my tomato chilli jam recipe. I did a little happy dance. And sent it immediately. I like to think Joel Salatin is eating chilli jam under his pasture-raised eggs, and it's like a grateful bow from me to him, because without his inspiration (and Kirsten's endless encouragement), we might not be here farming at all.

MAKES 4 × 300 ML (10 FL OZ) JARS (SEE NOTES)

- 2 kg (4 lb 6 oz) tomatoes, finely chopped
- 660 g (1 lb 7 oz/3 cups) white sugar
- 120 ml (4 fl oz) lemon juice
- 2 teaspoons freshly grated ginger
- 1 teaspoon ground cinnamon
- ½ teaspoon ground cloves
- 1 tablespoon salt
- 1 tablespoon red chilli flakes, or chopped fresh chilli

METHOD

Combine all the ingredients in a large, non-reactive pot. Bring to the boil, then reduce the heat and simmer, stirring regularly, until the mixture reduces to a sticky, jammy mess. This will take between 1–1½ hours, depending on the temperature.

When the jam has cooked down, remove from the heat and fill into jars, leaving 2 cm (¾ in) head space at the top of the jars. Wipe the rims and put on the lids. Process the jars in a boiling water bath (see page 39) to make them shelf-stable for 12 months, or just keep the jars in the fridge for 6 months.

Notes

The yield on this recipe varies depending on the tomato you use, your pan and the thickness to which you cook it.
  In my kitchen, the word 'simmer' means to cook just below a boil. There should still be a few bubbles, but it shouldn't be splashing all over your cooktop. If you cook at lower temperatures, the cooking time will increase.

Sweet and Sour Pickles

These pickles are delicious – REALLY good on a cheese sandwich. They're great made with cucumbers, and just as good made with zucchini (courgette).

MAKES 1 × 1 LITRE (34 FL OZ/4 CUP) JAR OR 3 × 300 ML (10 FL OZ) JARS

- 5 Lebanese (short) cucumbers, cut into thin slices
- 1 brown or white onion, halved and thinly sliced
- 1 tablespoon salt
- 185 ml (6 fl oz/¾ cup) white-wine vinegar
- 115 g (4 oz) white sugar
- 2 teaspoons mustard seeds
- 2 teaspoons coriander seeds
- 1 teaspoon dried juniper (optional)
- 1 teaspoon celery seeds (optional)

METHOD

Place the cucumber, onion and salt in a bowl. Mix well with your hands to combine.

Place the vinegar, sugar, mustard, coriander, juniper and celery seeds, if using, in a saucepan over a medium heat. Cook, stirring, until the sugar has dissolved.

Pack the cucumbers and onion into sterilised jars (see Notes) and pour over the hot pickling liquid. Leave just under a 1 cm (½ in) gap at the top.

Screw down tightly with sterilised lids and store in a cool place.

These pickles last well for 6 months.

Notes

You can use white vinegar, apple-cider vinegar, Red-wine Vinegar (page 38) or white-wine vinegar, or a combination – see what you like!
  To sterilise jars, wash the jars and lids in hot soapy water, then put the jars on a tray in a moderate oven (150°C/300°F) for 15 minutes. Put the lids into a bowl and pour boiling water over them.

Gravy

There are a hundred ways to make gravy. You can buy a packet mix and add water, you can use pan juices, you can use stock cubes. But before all that, shall we talk about the importance of gravy for a sec?

Oh, gravy.

It's the sauce that improves everything. Its glistening loveliness takes roast chicken from average to memorable. With beef of any kind, including sausage, it's like a unifying force, adding flavour and moisture and deliciousness to every mouthful.

We even use it as a metaphor, *well everything else is just gravy*. The extra. The bonus.

Can you make a vegetarian gravy? Of course you can! Douse your falafel with it. Spoon it over your chickpea steaks. It 100 per cent brings a solo dish of mashed potato to life.

But gravy comes into its own with meat. Made with proper meat-based flavours, without any 1970s starch, it'll always improve dinner. MAKE IT. IT'S EASY. Here's how.

(A quick note about 'broth' and 'stock': I'm a big fan of bone broth, the difference between broth and stock essentially being time. You can make an excellent stock in about half an hour, but bone broth takes longer – see page 94–7 for details. You can use either stock or broth to make gravy.)

Gravy using pan juices

If you've roasted meat and there's lots of lovely juice in the bottom of your roasting tin, this is an invitation to make the best and most flavourful gravy.

MAKES APPROX. 500 ML (17 FL OZ/2 CUPS)

about 250 ml (8½ fl oz/1 cup) pan drippings
2 tablespoons butter, chopped
2 tablespoons plain (all-purpose) flour
250 ml (8½ fl oz/1 cup) beef or chicken stock
  or broth

METHOD

If you've just taken your meat out of the oven and there's heaps of fat in the pan, you might want to let it sit for 15–20 minutes for the fat to separate and spoon it off the top of the pan juices. If you're about to serve dinner and don't have time to do this, you can just use the juices and fat but, depending on the meat, it may need to be adjusted for liquid-ness.

Pour the pan juices into a small saucepan over a medium heat. Whisk the butter in until it's emulsified. (If you have heaps of fat in the juice, halve the butter.) Whisk in the flour. Slowly pour in the broth and keep stirring until it thickens. If it becomes too thick, you can thin it with either extra broth or whole milk, adding a splash at a time so you don't overdo it. If it doesn't thicken before it comes to the boil, you need more flour. Add an extra tablespoon. Season with salt (this will depend on how much seasoning was on the meat originally – taste it to see).

Gravy without pan juices

Maybe you made steak. Or sausages. Or there just wasn't enough juice under your roast chook. Here's a recipe for gravy without pan drippings that is delicious and works every time.

MAKES APPROX. 500 ML (17 FL OZ/2 CUPS)

2 tablespoons butter
2 tablespoons plain (all purpose) flour
1 teaspoon onion powder (see Note)
½ teaspoon ground black pepper
500 ml (17 fl oz/2 cups) chicken or beef stock
        or broth

METHOD

Melt the butter in a saucepan over a medium heat.

Add the flour, onion powder and black pepper and whisk together.

While whisking, slowly pour in the broth or stock. (I've made this with hot and cold stock – it works both ways – but cold stock obviously takes longer.)

Once fully incorporated, stir until it thickens to a good gravy consistency. Taste it and season with salt if it needs it.

Note

I don't use onion powder in anything else in my life except this recipe. I buy a small amount and it kind of lasts forever. I recommend it, but if you can't come to terms with the processed-ness of it, finely dice and cook ½ onion in a little oil, then blitz as fine as possible with a hand-held blender or in a food processor.

Chapter Four

Broths (and Soups) of Life

Broths (and Soups) of Life

I have a deep respect for broth. It feels like an old food to me. As if somehow all the research on its capacity for anti-inflammation and mineral-richness and fabulous amino acids is unnecessary if we *just listened to our bodies on broth*. Humans have been reaching for bone broths for millennia, since we figured out how to boil bones in vessels. Broth is cheap and nutritious, and if made with properly-raised bones, it's gelatine-rich and filling and great for people with digestive issues and nourishing enough to build up bodies recovering from disease or injury. It doesn't take much making, and these recipes should be guides only. Make it your way. Add veggies if you want to, or seaweed, or herbs. Please just make it! Don't throw away those bones! If you've had a whole roast chicken dinner with wine and it's late, don't compost the bones. Chuck them in a bag in your freezer until you have enough bones for a huge potful. Broth shouldn't be underestimated; it's a fundamental food for life and I'm here to help encourage you to make (and drink) lots of it. Our farm crew have always known there is a two-litre jar of broth in the door of the farmhouse fridge, almost permanently, and are encouraged to see HOW GOOD IT IS at 3 pm when you're feeling pulled towards needing something uplifting. It's satisfying and full of minerals that will give you vigour and energy in a surprising dose.

So, make the broth. Warm it up and drink it by the cupful. Use it as the base for soups, stews, casseroles, gravy and even porridge. Freeze it in ice-cube trays and drop one into your green smoothie for a collagen kick. Pass a mug to anyone who is sniffling. Take a jar to someone who is sad or grieving or so unwell that they just can't face food. Have it in your fridge and your freezer and see what happens if you replace one caffeinated beverage a day with a mug of bone broth. You might find yourself all evangelical about it too.

A note about bones: the reason you want to use pasture-raised or grass-fed is because the difference in the animal's life makes a big difference to its bones. Pasture-raised animals that live with more robust nutrition throughout their lives tend to have mightily more calcium in their bones. A good example of this is if you pick up a cooked bone of a conventionally grown chicken from the supermarket. You can usually snap it. This is not the case with a pasture-raised meat chicken. You actually cannot usually even break the bones with two hands.

This nutrition, of course, is extended to the broth made from these bones. It's more expensive to grow chickens in small batches on pasture than it is to grow them by the thousands in large, temperature-controlled sheds. It's less economic to give cows heaps of space and manage them in rotated paddocks than to grow them in yards feeding them grain for quicker growth.

Please pay the extra money and buy pasture-raised and grass-fed, for sustainable farming, for a better quality of life for the animals being farmed, and for your own very good health.

Chicken Bone Broth

MAKES APPROX. 2.5 LITRES (85 FL OZ/ 10 CUPS)

1 chicken carcass (ideally pasture-raised)
1 onion, skin on and roughly chopped
3 garlic cloves, unpeeled
2 bay leaves
2 teaspoons sea salt
1 tablespoon whole black peppercorns
2 tablespoons apple-cider vinegar

METHOD

Take one free-range chicken carcass and put it in a stockpot. You can use the bones raw or cooked, though roasted bones tend to lend the broth some extra colour and flavour. Use all the pan scrapings, including the chicken skin, in your broth.

Add the onion (use the skin too for added colour), garlic and bay leaves. Add the salt and the black peppercorns.

Cover the bones with water and add approximately 1 tablespoon of apple-cider vinegar per litre (34 fl oz/4 cups) of water (this helps draw the gelatine and other goodness out of the bones) and bring slowly just up to the boil, then reduce the heat to a simmer. Put the lid on, slightly ajar (we usually prop the lid open with a wooden spoon on its side). Simmer slowly for 6–8 hours for a lovely, mineral-rich broth. You need to simmer it on a low enough heat that it does not evaporate. For a lovely jelly-like finish you don't want to be adding too much extra water as it cooks.

Strain out the vegetables and bones and store the finished broth in the fridge for up to 2 weeks. It also freezes really well for 6 months.

Beef Bone Broth

MAKES APPROX. 2.5 LITRES (85 FL OZ/ 10 CUPS)

1 kg (2 lb 3 oz) grass-fed beef bones
2 whole onions, skin on
3 garlic cloves, unpeeled
2 bay leaves
1 tablespoon whole black peppercorns
2 teaspoons sea salt
2 tablespoons apple-cider vinegar

METHOD

To make beef bone broth, start with good grass-fed bones, ideally knuckle, marrow and neck bones if you can get them. Roast them off at 180°C (360°F) for 20 minutes.

Put the bones in a big pot – ideally stainless steel – with the rest of the ingredients and cover with water.

Heat until the water starts to boil, then reduce the heat to a simmer and put the lid on, slightly ajar. (We usually prop the lid open with a wooden spoon on its side.)

Beef bone broth should be simmered for 12–24 hours. You need to simmer it on a low enough heat that it does not evaporate. For a lovely jelly-like finish you don't want to be adding too much extra water as it cooks.

Strain out the bones and vegetables and cool the broth in the fridge.

Once the broth is cool, the fat should solidify on top and you can remove it easily – you can keep this in a jar (it's called tallow) and use it as a cooking fat if you like.

Bone broth lasts for 2 weeks in the fridge or freezes well for 6 months.

Note

You can freeze this broth in ice-cube trays and throw frozen cubes into your green smoothie for an extra mineral hit. If you're planning to do this I would not salt the broth.

Fish Bone Broth

MAKES APPROX. 2.5 LITRES (85 FL OZ/ 10 CUPS)

1 kg (2 lb 3 oz) fresh fish carcasses
2 whole onions, skin on
3 garlic cloves, unpeeled
2 bay leaves
1 tablespoon whole black peppercorns
2 teaspoons sea salt
1 tablespoon apple-cider vinegar

METHOD

Put all the ingredients in a large pot – ideally stainless steel – and cover with water.

Heat until the water starts to boil, then reduce the heat to a simmer and put the lid on, slightly ajar. Fish broth should be simmered for about an hour.

Strain out the bones and vegetables and cool the broth in the fridge.

Fish broth lasts for about 1 week in the fridge or freezes well for 6 months.

Veggie Broth

MAKES APPROX. 2 LITRES (68 FL OZ/ 8 CUPS)

2 onions, skin on and roughly chopped
5 celery stalks, roughly chopped
3 carrots, skin on and roughly chopped
3 garlic cloves, roughly chopped
2 litres (68 fl oz/8 cups) water
2 tablespoons olive oil
2 bay leaves
½ tablespoon ground black peppercorns
½ tablespoon sea salt
80 g (2¾ oz/4 tablespoons) tomato paste
(concentrated purée)
2 tablespoons nutritional yeast (optional)
handfuls of fresh parsley, rosemary and thyme, torn or very roughly chopped

METHOD

In a large heavy-based pot – ideally stainless steel – sauté the onion, celery, carrot and garlic in the olive oil.

Pour the water over the veggies and add all the other ingredients. Simmer over a medium heat for about an hour.

Strain out the veggies and jar the broth. It keeps in the fridge for approximately 2 weeks and freezes well for at least 6 months.

Soup Weather

It's the last day but one of winter here. My favourite season, gone for another year. For the love of winter; for me it was the hardest thing about living in Brisbane (Winter? You call that winter?) and the best thing about living in London.

I chased winter one year with Adam many years ago, right up to Swedish Lapland. It was early March and still a frozen wonderland. We each got on the back of a sled filled with dog food (and little else) pulled by a team of six or seven sled dogs, and led by an insane Norwegian dog musher (who actually had a belt made out of baby seal fur, I'm not even kidding) and we mushed north for five days.

I tell you, I've never met happier dogs. They obviously thought Kenneth (the musher) was one of them, but they were uber happy. They slept outside in the snow, which I couldn't believe, but they were fine. Better than fine.

Other things I love about winter? Soup, soup, soup, soup.

GOSH we eat a lot of soup in this house. It's the best way of cleaning out the bottom of the fridge and getting a bunch of veggies into non-veggie-eating small-fry.

Do you have once-taut broccoli languishing in your crisper? Go right now to your kitchen, cook a chopped onion in some oil in a heavy-based saucepan, chop your broccoli in and cover with broth or stock of whatever kind you have, and cook. Season it. Stir through a little fresh or sour cream if you're feeling fancy. Add chilli or a heaped teaspoon of smoked paprika if you're inclined. But you've just salvaged your lovely broccoli and made something delicious and nutritious. It can be dinner tomorrow night, it will just need reheating. Maybe consider making some Yoghurt Flatbread (page 56) to dunk in it. There are SO many reasons to love winter.

Here are some more ...

Simple Cauliflower Soup

This is a warming and satisfying soup, fragrant with a touch of nutmeg, quick to make and an excellent use of slightly past-it's-prime cauliflower.

SERVES 4–6

1 onion, finely sliced
3 garlic cloves, finely chopped
splodge of olive oil
1 cauliflower, broken up
4 large potatoes, peeled and diced
1.5 litres (51 fl oz/6 cups) Veggie Broth (page 97)
freshly grated nutmeg, to taste

METHOD

In a large pot, sauté the onion and garlic in the oil. Stir the cauliflower and potato into the onion and garlic then pour over the broth.

The broth should only just cover the vegetables – if you've used a bigger or smaller cauliflower, adjust the volume of broth accordingly.

Cook on a low boil for approximately half an hour, or until the vegetables are soft. Mash or blend with a hand-held blender if you have one. Season with sea salt, freshly ground black pepper and nutmeg to taste.

Green Split Pea and Bacon Soup

Do you have a random bag of green split peas in your pantry?

Did you know that if you haven't quite got around to soaking them overnight as most recipes instruct, you can simmer them for five minutes then soak them for an hour to the same effect? Try it! I promise it works.

SERVES 4

2 brown onions, sliced
1 tablespoon olive oil
3 bacon rashers (slices), chopped
2 carrots, sliced
3 potatoes, peeled and sliced
440 g (15½ oz/2 cups) green split peas (ideally soaked overnight, or as above)
1.5 litres (51 fl oz/6 cups) Chicken Bone Broth (page 94)

METHOD

In a large pot, cook the onion in the olive oil. Add a pinch of salt to help it sweat. Throw in the bacon and cook. Add the other vegetables and the soaked peas and cover with the chicken broth. Cook for about 30 minutes, or until the peas collapse and are soft and the veggies are cooked well. Blend with a hand-held blender or in a food processor. Season to taste with sea salt and freshly ground black pepper.

Serve with some bread or not. Wouldn't it be awesome if that was the hardest decision you made today?

Chilled Avocado Soup Sip with Prawns

This is, perhaps obviously, a summer soup. In fact, it dates back to when Adam and I were young and child-free and one of our favourite things to do was make elaborate degustations for our friends and family. This little soup sip has featured on our Christmas and dinner party menus and I give it to you now because it's elegant and you can make it on the spot (if you can find your food processor in among the chaos of a fourteen-course degustation).

SERVES 4 AS SMALL BOWLS, OR UP TO 20 IN SHOT GLASSES

2.5 avocados, peeled and stones removed
1 garlic clove, finely minced
2 tablespoons lime juice
1 litre (34 fl oz/4 cups) cold Chicken Bone Broth
    (page 94)
peeled cooked prawns, for garnish

METHOD

Process the avocado, garlic and lime juice in a food processor until smooth. Add the cold broth slowly and process until combined. Season to taste with salt and freshly ground black pepper.

Divide between shot glasses or bowls and serve topped with prawns.

This soup keeps well in the fridge (separately to the prawns) for about a day, if you want to take the edge out of thrash catering and make it the day before.

Pumpkin Soup

I've never met a kid who won't eat pumpkin soup. Big call, I know, but I have met some seriously dedicated non-veggie-eating children who will wolf down a bowl of this.

I worked for a while, what feels like one hundred years ago, as a cook for a big preschool in Brisbane. I was a solo cook, and I fed a hundred children each day. (Actually, not each day, I had Wednesdays off.)

It was a hoot. It was a hot little kitchen (they all are) and the equipment wasn't fantastic, but the director gave me free rein to recreate the entire menu (morning tea, lunch, afternoon tea) and encouraged a really healthy menu.

I loved that job.

On my first day, the day after my interview, I arrived in the kitchen only to find there were no recipes, no procedures, no 'cook this much pasta for this many children'. Nothin'.

There were sporadic ingredients (the last cook had been fired on the spot the week before) and the director had been doing the cooking herself, as far as possible. They'd had a few days of sandwiches I think. But there were lots of pumpkins in the veggie bin. And potatoes. And I found some stock cubes (they'd do). And onions.

So, for lunch on my first day, the kids had pumpkin soup. Proportions wildly guessed at and luckily sufficient. I peeped into the rooms to see the kids mopping it up from their bowls with bread and butter.

You can bake the pumpkin first, and some people swear by this. But you really don't need to. I now add coconut milk and garam masala, which I think improves it no end, but you can omit both of these if you don't have them. (Or you can make them both – see pages 294 and 31.)

Anyway, here's the recipe. It's quick, and failsafe.

SERVES 4

1 onion, chopped
2 garlic cloves, finely chopped
1 tablespoon olive oil
3 small- to medium-sized potatoes, peeled and chopped
1 butternut pumpkin (squash), or whatever kind you have, enough to fill a 1.5 litre (51 fl oz/6 cup) jug or container when chopped
1 litre (34 fl oz/4 cups) broth or stock (chicken works well, vegetable too; see pages 94 and 97)
250 ml (8½ fl oz/1 cup) Coconut Milk (page 294)
1 teaspoon Garam Masala (page 31)
sea salt and freshly ground black pepper, to taste

METHOD

Cook the onion and garlic in the oil in a heavy-based saucepan until translucent. Add the potatoes and the pumpkin. Of course, you can use different kinds of pumpkin here, but one type of pumpkin is fine. Just keep the proportions to about 3:1 pumpkin to potato.

Cover the veggies with the stock by about 2 cm (¾ in). Stir in the coconut milk and garam masala. Bring to the boil, then reduce to a simmer and cook for about 30 minutes. It's ready when you poke the veggies with a knife and they're soft enough to collapse. Blend with a hand-held blender.

Cool before serving to smallies! (Add salt and pepper for the adults, or the room group leaders at the preschool who I still miss; they were terrific gals, and they were relieved to see the end of sandwiches!)

For the record, for people feeding smallies, from my time at the preschool, the kids' favourite hot lunches (other than pumpkin soup) were:

- Fried rice

- Chicken and vegetable risotto

- Pumpkin, spinach and ricotta bake

- Oodles of noodles with ham and cheese

- Pasta Roma (a simple tomato/egg/cheese pasta bake)

- Tuna mornay with brown rice

- Zucchini (courgette) slice

- Meatballs with mashed potato

- Vegetable pizza slices

In my humble experience, these are also terrific meals to teach kids to make, particularly those who may be leaving home at some stage!

Chapter Five

Breakfasts of Champions

Breakfasts of Champions

On the side of my big bag of flour it says 'for manufacturing purposes only'. Manufacturing. Why can't it say, 'for cooking' or 'for feeding people with' or, seriously, what's wrong with 'for making food'?

There are so many shortcuts at this point in commercial cooking, there are all these moments where 'real food' vanishes and, suddenly, you could be manufacturing snack food. Empty junk food. Packaged and processed.

Fake food worries me deeply. I get a dreadful unsociable twitch about it.

Is there much manufactured food in your pantry? In your fridge or freezer? How many raw ingredients are there compared to sealed bags or boxes of something made a long way from your kitchen? You're here, reading this, you're probably about to (if you haven't already) make your own bread, you might even make your own yoghurt. If you don't, can I highly recommend it? And can I encourage you to find one thing that you might usually buy – peanut butter or butter or sour cream or tomato sauce or pasta or crackers or whatever, and make it yourself *this week*? I bet you'll find it forehead-slappingly easy and cheaper. There's over two hundred recipes kicking around in this book for making stuff from scratch. Knock yourself out. (Don't actually.)

Hey, join in with the crazy people making their own crumpets! It takes an insane make-it-from-scratch kinda person to know one! I SEE YOU THERE!

Here's to real food.

Fried Scones

Oh, my goodness, fried scones. If you didn't grow up with them, they are probably like Vegemite to Americans: unappetising to the point of being completely unapproachable.

I grew up with them. They were our Sunday morning breakfast treat, the way you might have pancakes or bacon and eggs or French toast. We had them smothered in golden syrup and we adored them. We'd gobble them up with their crisp brown outsides and fluffy soft insides. My mum would deep-fry batch after batch, and even though we knew she hadn't eaten even one herself, my brother and sisters and I would wait for the next plateful to come from the kitchen and fall on them like small desperate people. No one stood between the Weirs and their fried scones.

If you dunked them in cinnamon sugar they would be very close to a doughnut. (We never did.) With nothing resembling a thermometer in my mum's kitchen, sometimes they were very, very dark on the outside and sometimes they were perfect and golden. Mostly, they were fluffy all the way through, and sometimes they weren't quite cooked. We children were good at spooning out any uncooked middles and just filling them up with golden syrup. Sticky smiling happy Sundays.

And then, one day, after many, many years of fried scone goodness, Mum made one bad scone. No one is quite sure what happened. I wasn't there; I think it was just after I'd left home. She thinks the outside cooked too rapidly, or maybe there was some water in the oil. One minute she was cooking fried scones, the next minute a scone exploded in the boiling oil, splashing it all over the underside of her arm, causing a pretty awful burn. (She's fine, everyone.) This was many years ago, but it left a scar. And that was the end of fried scones; she never ever made them again. I'd occasionally ask, or suggest I might make them, but no one had the appetite and my own family developed a Sunday morning bakery pastries tradition, which gave me a morning off brekky prep so I didn't argue.

I recently decided to get back on the horse, but after however many hundreds of batches of fried scones the woman must have made, Mum for the life of her could not remember her recipe and had not written it down anywhere. I rang my Auntie Margie, and thankfully she remembered it off the top of her head. It's basically damper. Flour and milk. It is, as it turns out, an old colonial Australian recipe that was originally called 'Puftaloons'. After a bit of hunting, we found a version of it in the original *The Commonsense Cookery Book* with measurements in pounds and gills!

Anyway, I made the recipe according to Margie and there they were: fried scones. With fluffy insides and crispy golden outsides, smothered in golden syrup. The original Puftaloon recipe tells you to shallow-fry these. I tried it, but you don't get the hilariously satisfying moment of the bottom of spherical fried scones cooking and then turning themselves over in the oil to cook the other side. I HAD FORGOTTEN THEY DID THAT!

Look, shallow-frying (please beware of any water near your oil) mitigates the risk of an exploding scone, but honestly, isn't life meant to be lived? I have no fear of it. I spoon balls of scone dough into boiling oil with complete confidence, I really do, and you should too.

Do not walk away from oil on the stove. If it ever starts to smoke, it's way too hot, so turn it off. Let it cool. You can test the oil's readiness by dropping a tiny bit of scone mix in and if it sizzles it's good to go. Getting the heat right is a bit of a trick – if it's not hot enough your scone will absorb too much oil; too hot and the outside will cook faster than the inside (and you'll be making scooped-out golden syrup bombs a la small Weir children).

It's no harder than getting the pan temperature right for pancakes though. Make one scone and you'll know if it browns too fast and the middle is uncooked. You want it to turn golden on the underside in about 2 minutes, then if it flips itself over to cook the other side in about 2 minutes, you've nailed it.

Nothing will shift my family's great attachment to bought pastries on Sunday mornings, but fried scones appear here on rare and special occasions to remind me of my own golden childhood and sticky plates and happy days.

MAKES ABOUT 12

1 litre (34 fl oz/4 cups) rice bran or canola oil
300 g (10½ oz/2 cups) plain (all-purpose) flour
1 tablespoon Baking Powder (page 24)
250 ml (8½ fl oz/1 cup) full-cream (whole) milk
golden syrup (light treacle), to serve

METHOD

Preheat a large heavy-based saucepan with approximately 1 litre (34 fl oz/4 cups) light oil, such as rice bran or canola.

In a bowl, mix together the flour and baking powder until well combined. Stir in the milk and keep stirring until it's mixed very well.

You should be able to tear off a piece the size of a golf ball – if it's too wet, add more flour by the tablespoon until you can.

Roll a golf ball–sized piece together with wet hands and quickly and carefully put it into the hot oil. Use a spoon if you're more comfortable with that. Put in as many as will fit with a bit of space for them to move. Once the bottoms are cooked, if they're spherical they should roll over. If not, don't stress, just carefully turn them over with a fork until the underside is also golden – another 2 minutes or so.

Carefully lift out with a slotted metal spoon (do not accidentally use a plastic slotted spoon in boiling oil! It will melt. I have done this, and I'm here to save your plastic slotted spoons)

Drain on a piece of paper towel or a clean tea towel (dish towel) and serve immediately with golden syrup.

Hash Browns

I've put these in the breakfast section, but we will eat them at any time of the day. Under an egg, in a sandwich or hamburger, as a dinner side. Hash browns are all the good things: crunchy, carby, salty. And easy.

MAKES 4

1 large starchy white-skinned potato (see Note)
1 tablespoon olive oil
1 teaspoon salt

METHOD

Peel your potato. Grate it on a box grater. Don't leave the grated potato sitting around or it'll oxidise and go pink. If you have a potato ricer, chuck the grated potato into the ricer and squeeze out as much liquid as you can (do this in batches; it's a great way to get rid of potato juice). Alternatively, pop the grated potato in a clean tea towel (dish towel) and squeeze out as much liquid as you can.

Put a heavy-based frying pan over a medium heat with a good tablespoon of olive oil.

Salt the potato and divide into four. Pick up one-quarter of the mix with wet hands and form into a ball.

Put into your hot frying pan and press down with a spatula until it's flat.

Cook until the underside is brown, then flip and cook the other side. Serve immediately, and enjoy!

Note

A note on spuds: waxy potatoes will hold their shape better in your hash brown, but starchy will give up their moisture more efficiently and you'll get a crispier hash brown.

Pancakes

For a long time, we've had a Wednesday morning pancake tradition at our breakfast table. I couldn't tell you why it was Wednesdays except that it wasn't Saturdays because Adam and I were running the cooking school and no one was getting a cooked breakfast that day. Wednesday was a school day and worth celebrating with pancakes.

My beautiful friend of many years, Jodi Mullen, an extremely good cook and very serious about pancakes, brought her own frying pan on a holiday we went on once to Byron Bay, on the plane, so she could make pancakes in the holiday house we'd rented. I love a woman who travels with a skillet. She knew exactly how long it took to heat up, and the temperature the pan needed to be to make a perfect fluffy pancake. That was about twenty years ago now (before restricted luggage allowance) and I'm *still* impressed. The moral of the story is: use a good heavy-based frying pan. I favour cast iron. Jodi's was stainless steel, but her current favourite is cast iron – probably less likely to be packed on holiday.

This recipe is for fluffy pancakes, not thin and rollable. Perfect with a smear of butter and a good drizzle of pure maple syrup.

MAKES 6

1 tablespoon butter
300 g (10½ oz/2 cups) Self-raising Flour (page 25)
500 ml (17 fl oz/2 cups) full cream (whole) milk
1 free-range egg

METHOD

Melt the butter in a heavy-based frying pan over a moderate heat.

Mix the flour, milk and egg together well and stir in the melted butter.

Put a half-cup measure of the mix into the frying pan and cook until you can see bubbles forming all over the surface. Carefully flip the pancake over and cook the other side.

Either serve immediately or keep warm in the oven or covered with foil or a tea towel (dish towel) on the bench.

You can make the mix the night before and store it in the fridge, but it's so simple and quick you can make these before the coffee even kicks in.

Crumpets

Ever made your own crumpets?

It kinda does seem like one of those things that might just not be worth the time, right? They come conveniently packaged at the supermarket ... but so do bread and crackers, and the homemade versions of those are exponentially more delicious.

Fresh homemade crumpets are too.

MAKES 7

150 g (5½ oz/1 cup) plain (all-purpose) flour
1 teaspoon Baking Powder (page 24)
½ teaspoon salt
½ teaspoon white sugar
1 teaspoon instant dried yeast
250 ml (8½ fl oz/1 cup) warm water
butter, for greasing

METHOD

Put the flour, baking powder, salt, sugar and yeast in a large bowl and mix together using a whisk. Pour the water into the dry ingredients and beat together with a whisk until you have a smooth batter.

Cover the bowl with plastic wrap or a clean tea towel (dish towel) and leave the mixture in a warm spot for about 15 minutes until it's bubbly. (If you leave this too long, you'll lose your bubbles.)

Lightly grease a heavy frying pan with about 1 tablespoon butter and put over a high heat. Grease egg rings with butter – I use 8 cm (3¼ in) round cookie cutters – and put them in the pan. Fill the rings with 60 ml (2 fl oz/¼ cup) per ring.

Cook over a high heat for the first 2 minutes to get the bubbles going, then turn down to a low heat to cook for about a total of eight minutes. Feel free to pop any surface bubbles that haven't popped themselves, it's immensely satisfying. Slip the rings off using tongs and flip the crumpets over to cook the top for about 30 seconds.

They're perfect with butter and golden syrup. Or honey. Or whatever. Delicious. You can serve them straight away, fresh, but actually I think they're even better the next day, toasted.

Do my kids eat them? The girls do.

Henry is really not much of a morning person and I have to work hard to make him a breakfast person at all. He has all his life hated eggs.

Since he was very young, he has always very reluctantly peeled himself out of bed, then flopped on a nearby couch or chair until I could coax him to the breakfast table with a banana smoothie. Now he's grown, it's a flat white coffee instead of the smoothie, as hard as I've tried (crumpet, nah, thanks Mum).

Our two girls, though, have their whole lives bounced out of bed and straight to the breakfast table.

I remember when Tilly was really little, before Ivy was born, she would happily 'Good morning!' everyone (including Henry's imaginary friend, who lived in his foot) and cook herself an egg (with some help). She still does everything fairly enthusiastically, including making eggs for her sister (but not her brother).

Total crumpets, all three.

Toasted Muesli

Ah, muesli. Or granola, depending on where you're from. I love, love, love it with a love not usually reserved for muesli. I love it mostly for breakfast and sometimes for lunch. Most recently with a glossy glob of yoghurt, but traditionally just with milk.

You don't really need a recipe for muesli. Every muesli-eater I know has their own, and it's the very best. My mum makes hers raw, with just grains. I know people who add cocoa or cacao nibs to theirs. Adam likes his with dried fruit, mostly apricots, and I like it with a handful of almonds and dried cranberries. I've watched Dutch farm volunteers toast theirs daily on my stove, in a big pan, just turning it until it goes golden.

So, for the recipe you neither need nor want because you'll make this however you damn well please …

MAKES APPROX. 1 KG (2 LB 3 OZ)

175 g (6 oz/½ cup) golden syrup (light treacle)
   or honey
3 tablespoons vegetable oil
3 tablespoons butter
625 g (1 lb 6 oz/5 cups) rolled oats
60 g (2 oz/½ cup) sunflower kernels
65 g (2¼ oz/½ cup) pepitas (pumpkin seeds)
80 g (2¾ oz/½ cup) linseeds (flax seeds)
2 teaspoons ground ginger
2 teaspoons ground cinnamon
nuts and dried fruits of your choice (optional)

METHOD

Preheat your oven to 170°C (340°F) and line two baking trays.

In a small saucepan over a medium heat, stir the golden syrup, oil and butter together until the butter melts.

In a large bowl, stir together all the other ingredients, except the fruit, if using. Pour the melted butter mix into the bowl and mix until the oats are well coated.

Spread out on the trays and bake for approximately 15 minutes, stirring occasionally, until evenly golden.

Add dried fruit(s) of your choice. Once cool, store in an airtight jar or container for up to 2 months.

Tilly's Baked Oatmeal

This recipe is inspired by my teenage daughter Matilda, who found something similar on TikTok and made it every morning for a week until she was happy with it, which made me heart-burstingly proud. Tilly tends to add fresh or frozen berries on top too – just a handful, right before popping it in the oven.

SERVES 1, OR MULTIPLY AS REQUIRED

butter, for greasing
60 g (2 oz/½ cup) rolled oats
60 ml (2 fl oz/¼ cup) milk of your choice
   (Tilly uses soy)
½ banana, mashed
¼ teaspoon Baking Powder (page 24)
2 teaspoons pure maple syrup
pinch of salt
¼ teaspoon ground cinnamon
handful of berries of choice (optional)

METHOD

Preheat your oven to 180°C (360°F).

Grease a 500 ml (17 fl oz/2 cup) capacity ramekin or ovenproof bowl.

Crush your rolled oats fine, like flour; we do this in big batches in the food processor and store a week's worth in a jar.

Mix all your ingredients together and put in the ramekin. Add the berries, if using. Bake for 15 minutes.

Photograph or video that wonderment. Slay queen! #healthy #breakfastgoals #foodgram #loveyoubabes

Lentil Dahl

Dahl for breakfast?! Hear me out.

Dahl, I find, is quite divisive. People either get it or they don't. A bit like IKEA.

I love, love, love dahl – probably due to protracted bouts of vegetarianism before we started growing animals ourselves – and I'd wheel this one out regularly. (Truly, what's not to love about red lentils I ask you?!)

I make big batches of it at a time. And it's more delicious the day after. And the day after. And it's GREAT for breakfast. Nourishing, filling, interesting, warm. Once you get past the western cultural insanity of breakfast cereal, everything makes sense. Dahl for breakfast makes perfect sense.

The provenance of my dahl recipe is hazy. I think I first learnt to cook dahl thanks to my darling friend Leah, now in Cairns, who Nessie and I once worked with and started a lunch club with (in which one of us brought in lunch for three and then the next two days you had lunch cooked for you). It was totally fab. We'd do awesome salads and bring in cold quiche, and swapped recipes like women possessed. And Leah cooked a fabulously simple dahl. I have cooked this off the top of my head for years, but I think this is where it came from.

I cook dahl because I love it. It's tasty and I can imagine one day eating it while hiking the Annapurna Circuit in Nepal with Adam and our eventually grown-up kids.

But another reason I love it is because it costs about 10 cents to make. Well, maybe not 10 cents, but damn it's cheap. About $10 for an entire family dinner. And it's super nutritious. Gotta love that.

SERVES 4–6

1 tablespoon cumin seeds
1 tablespoon coriander seeds
2 tablespoons ghee, or olive oil
1 tablespoon ground turmeric
1 large onion, finely diced
2 garlic cloves, crushed
3 cm (1¼ in) piece fresh ginger, chopped
1½ teaspoons salt
1 teaspoon freshly ground black pepper
375 g (13 oz/1½ cups) red lentils
1–1.25 litres (34–42 fl oz/4–5 cups) chicken broth (see page 94), or vegetable stock or water
steamed rice, yoghurt and fresh coriander (cilantro), to serve

METHOD

Smash the cumin and coriander seeds in a mortar and pestle if you have one. Warm the ghee in a large heavy-based saucepan or a cast-iron pot over a medium heat and add the cumin, coriander and turmeric. Cook for a minute until fragrant, then add the onion, garlic and ginger. Cook until the onion is translucent, stirring fairly constantly, and add the salt and pepper.

Add the lentils and stir until coated, then cover with the broth – sometimes I just use water, which is fine – and simmer until cooked, usually about 30 minutes. I keep checking and stirring and adding broth or water if it looks dry.

You can add chilli, which spices the whole dish up (add with the spices), but leave it out if cooking for kids.

I remember that this was one of the dishes I had on high repeat when I was a young mum, for the lovely reason that you can cook it one-handed! And dinner seems to run into breakfast anyway. Chuck it all in. Stir. Serve. All with a baby with a head cold on your hip!

Or enjoy it for breakfast while dreaming about Annapurna.

Chapter Six

Life *is* Sweet

Life is Sweet

There is a woman I used to know, you may know her.

I can tell you what she used to look like.

She used to match. Have a $250 haircut. Often manicured. Always smooth, combed, clean.

You wouldn't see her without mascara at the very least. Some nice cheek gloss. Lip gloss. All on expensively moisturised skin, recently facial-ed.

Seriously, WHAT is she wearing now?

Are they Blundstone boots? With jeans and a sundress?

Has she got anything in that wardrobe with any shape?

Did she actually look at herself before she got in the car? (No, she didn't.)

And I mean, really. Where IS the novel? Where's the PhD? Where's the big job, the world changer, the mover and shaker, the girl most likely? And I'm sure that the whole outfit is hand-me-down or second hand. (It is.)

Where's the girl who drank soy lattes and furiously scribbled verse? That's not really her, sitting by the swimming pool for another swimming lesson? Is that her in daggy pants at the school pick up? Pushing a trolley in the supermarket, putting on another load of laundry, dosing out junior Panadol and breaking up an argument over who sits in what chair at the dinner table?

And, really, you should see her house. Piles of washing. Toys all over the floor. The children skating across the floor on board books. (I saw a guest actually pause once before sitting down on a chair that had obviously been occupied by someone eating breakfast cereal earlier.)

You know once, she would have been able to tell you exactly how much she weighed. Now she knows how much all her children weigh and just that she intends to lose 10 kilograms.

Which illustrates my point: she really has let herself go.

She can't remember when she last had an undisturbed night's sleep, but she is laughing out loud and loudly at the baby blowing raspberries.

She hasn't worn a nice pair of heels in months, but her heart is bursting because she caught her children being randomly kind to each other.

She has nothing to show for herself at the end of the day but she's whisking eggs in pure joy.

She's blinking in amazement that her children can independently take themselves off to the toilet.

She let herself go, let the self-imposed rules and restrictions, all the insecurities, the vacuous meaningless nonsensical self-centeredness go, and she found she was genuinely happier than she'd ever been in her whole life.

Sweet life, it's often never what you thought it would be.

Cake of Sunday

I don't know about you, but in my house, Sunday is a good day to make cake. Unless it's your birthday – then any day of the week is cake day. It never occurs to me to make a cake mid-week. It doesn't travel well in lunchboxes. It's not something I would hurl into a container to give my gymnast for afternoon tea on the trip between school and the gym three afternoons a week. But if we make a cake on Sunday, with any luck there'll be leftovers for fika through the week.

Fika is a tradition held tight by everyone working on the farm, led by Adam. No, he's not Swedish. He just worked for IKEA for many years and one of his favourite and enduring memories of it was stopping for fika with his team.

Fika is not technically morning tea; it's actually a ritual, taking time out with friends and colleagues for coffee or tea and maybe a little slice of cake or something else delicious. Our fika is always mid-morning. Here, a long way from IKEA, it is a little doorstop between an early breakfast and a late lunch, when everyone is in opposite corners of the farm and, at 10.30 am, whoever is nearest the farmhouse makes sure the coffee machine is on and has a hunt in the pantry for leftover cake. Sometimes it's the little things that make life really sweet. In particular, the beautiful people who work with us, and sharing a slice of cake with them.

Simple Butter Cake to Save the Day

This was the very first thing I learnt to cook. Ever. I think I was eight.

But I also have a memory of a moment in time when this was more than a cake: it was how we held out-of-control days together with small children and a new farm business and building a commercial kitchen, and sometimes Sundays were a struggle.

Here's a journal entry from October 2013:

Today we made a butter cake. You could call it Butter Cake. Or perhaps it could be Grumpy Cake. Three Year Old Tears Cake. Cracking-It-Big-Time Cake.

Grumpy children, sleep-deprived grown-ups, terribly hot and sticky for October, no Sunday picnic today, what was there left to do but save the day with cake?

The salvage was led by Tilly and her friend Katie. They hovered for the cake-making, actually participated in the clean-up and controlled the food colouring for the icing: bright pink.

By late afternoon, and as soon as the cake was sprinkled, the girls led the charge to evacuate to a friend's pool, and so we did, even extracting Adam to join us. It was lovely.

So, no one got cake, except me, when I was making early dinner for everyone in their pyjamas. (Aka throwing leftovers onto the table, eggs into boiling water and grilled cheese into the griller. 'If-its': if it's in the fridge or on the table you can eat it.) I took one look at that cake on the bench and decided I couldn't go another moment without a mouthful.

And then, even though it wasn't Tuesday Night Dessert Night, after boiled eggs and if-its, we all had cake. We licked bright pink butter frosting off our fingers. Day saved.

SERVES 8–10

125 g (4½ oz/½ cup) butter, softened, plus extra for greasing
220 g (8 oz/1 cup) white sugar
2 free-range eggs
300 g (10½ oz/2 cups) Self-raising Flour (page 25)
250 ml (8½ fl oz/1 cup) full-cream (whole) milk
Buttercream Icing (page 124; optional)

METHOD

Preheat the oven to 180°C (360°F).

Prepare a 20 cm (8 in) round or square cake tin by greasing well with butter then lining with baking paper. You can split the cake between two smaller tins and sandwich together with jam and cream. You can make it in a loaf (bar) or a ring (bundt) tin – whatever you like.

Cream the butter and sugar together until light. Add the eggs, one at a time, and mix well. Beat in the first cup of flour, followed by half of the milk. Beat in the second cup of flour, then the rest of the milk.

Scrape the cake batter into your prepared tin and bake immediately for approximately 30 minutes, or until golden and a skewer inserted in the centre of the cake comes out clean.

Cool in the tin for 15 minutes, then carefully remove and cool on a cake rack before icing (if you like).

Buttercream Icing

I resisted buttercream icing for years, based mainly on cupcakes that were doubled in size by it: did we really need to add so much extra butter and sugar to a cake? You know though, sometimes we do. Sometimes life just calls for *the icing on the cake*. In these instances, it's better not to skimp. For this we go all in, and it is altogether perfect for topping things off.

MAKES APPROX. 300 G (10½ OZ)

> 125 g (4½ oz/½ cup) butter, softened
> 180 g (6½ oz/1½ cups) pure icing (confectioners')
>   sugar (see Note)
> 1 tablespoon full-cream (whole) milk

METHOD
Mix together the butter and icing sugar, ideally with an electric mixer if you have one. Add in the milk while mixing until you get a soft and creamy consistency. Add a few drops of natural food colouring if you like, or a whole capful if you're six and very determined that happiness is bright-pink icing on fresh cake. You're right, it is.

Note
If your icing (confectioners') sugar is hard and lumpy, break the lumps up first. Either whiz in a food processor or thump the bag with a rolling pin.

My Friend, the Chocolate Cake

Ten things before cake:

1. When I first met Adam, I *may* have pretended to be more outdoorsy than I actually am. (Although I don't believe he was fooled by my shiny mountain bike for a second. Might have been the black beret/9-hole Doc Martens that gave me away.)
2. I keep talking about learning French but never get around to it.
3. I have a partially researched PhD topic that I would love to go back to one day. It was on the food supply of the armies of the Crusades. I may have been the only person on earth who thought it was terribly interesting.
4. A small piece of my heart currently lives in Hong Kong (one of my beloved sisters moves around a lot).
5. There's an Australian band called My Friend the Chocolate Cake that I used to love, I even went to see them in concert. They are currently (according to Wikipedia) on hiatus. I feel like I lived through my twenties with them playing in the background.
6. In high school, I wanted to be a composer. I started writing a musical with a friend of mine when I was fifteen. (He's gone on to become a very accomplished composer. I now compose silly songs to amuse small children and embarrass teenagers.)
7. My favourite novel is *Middlemarch* by George Eliot. I think. Or maybe it's a slightly trashy Sharon Penman historical fiction. Or *The Little Bookroom* by Eleanor Farjeon.
8. My favourite food has been, variously, baklava, cheesecake, grilled cheddar on toast, marinated goat's cheese and a really good apple, or blackberry pie. I am a fickle, fickle lady.

9. The job I've held down longest was in corporate marketing and communications in financial services. My shortest job was as a private investigator reporting on a medical professional under investigation for fraud. My favourite (and lowest-paid) job before my current rest-of-my-life beloved cheesemaking job was for six months only, as a cook for a big preschool in Brisbane.

10. I've lived in Gerringong (country New South Wales), Sydney, London, Brisbane, and Edinburgh, for the duration of the Fringe Festival for two seasons. Of the places I've visited, I'd most like to go back to Jerusalem and Istanbul. Of the places I've never been, the one I'd love to go to most is India. Or Nepal. Or Tibet.

And so, we've made it this far, and albeit a bit one-sided, I'm hoping we're friends?

For you, here's a friendly chocolate cake recipe.

It's light, not dense, and delicious iced with chocolate ganache or just sprinkled with icing (confectioners') sugar. I hope you love it.

SERVES 8–10

125 g (4½ oz/½ cup) softened butter
345 g (12 oz/1½ cups) caster (superfine) sugar
1 teaspoon Vanilla Extract (page 36)
3 free-range eggs
½ teaspoon bicarbonate of soda (baking soda)
60 g (2 oz/½ cup) unsweetened cocoa powder
300 g (10½ oz/2 cups) Self-raising Flour (page 25)
250 ml (8½ fl oz/1 cup) full-cream (whole) milk

Chocolate ganache icing (optional)
200 g (7 oz) chocolate, finely chopped
125 ml (4 fl oz/½ cup) fresh pouring (single/light) cream

METHOD

Preheat the oven to 180°C (360°F). Grease and line a 20 cm (8 in) round cake tin.

Start by creaming the butter and sugar together. Add the vanilla and eggs to the mix and beat well.

Sift the bicarbonate of soda, cocoa powder and flour into the wet mix and stir together well, then mix in the milk.

Beat for 3 minutes on medium speed, either in a mixer, if you have one, or using hand beaters. Alternatively, use a wooden spoon and stir enthusiastically.

Pour the cake batter into the prepared tin and bake for approximately 1 hour 15 minutes, or until cooked (a skewer inserted in the middle should come out clean). Cool for 5 minutes in the tin, then turn out onto a wire rack. Ice the cake when cool, or sprinkle with cocoa powder or icing (confectioners') sugar.

If you are making the ganache, put the finely chopped chocolate into a heatproof bowl.

Warm the cream in a saucepan over a low heat, just until you see bubbles forming around the edges.

Pour the warm cream over the chocolate and stir until it's lovely and smooth.

Let it cool slightly before using as an icing. Alternatively, you can whip the ganache with beaters to make a fluffy ganache icing.

Utterly Awesome Chocolate Cake

Er, am I allowed to say things like that?!

I'm not blowing my own trumpet. I didn't create this recipe – I just tinkered with it.

Like it? It's a thing of beauty, right? Can we talk about recipe provenance?

Once, many years ago when we still lived in Sydney, my friend Anne-Marie made this cake for her son's birthday party and I begged for the recipe. It was, she said, her friend Carol's recipe. It was handwritten. Did Carol make it up? Was it a family recipe? Or did she find it in a book? I never even met Carol. And after you've reduced the sugar and the oil and upped the cocoa and baked it for every birthday in your family for ten years, does it count as yours? I don't even know. Here's what I'd like though: I'd like this to be *your* recipe. Please take it! Make it on a Sunday! Or for birthday cakes! It's delicious. And easy.

A gloriously chocolatey chocolate cake that doesn't actually use chocolate, which is convenient because it's a lot harder to snack on a box of cocoa powder in the pantry than on a block of 70 per cent. Or budget cooking chocolate. Everything that looks good at three in the afternoon.

Thank you, utterly awesome chocolate cake, wherever you came from.

SERVES 10

330 g (11½ oz/1½ cups) white sugar
185 ml (6 fl oz/¾ cup) grapeseed or rice bran oil, or other neutral-flavoured oil
2 free-range eggs
250 ml (8½ fl oz/1 cup) coffee, cooled
250 ml (8½ fl oz/1 cup) full-cream (whole) milk
300 g (10½ oz/2 cups) plain (all-purpose) flour
125 g (4½ oz/1 cup) unsweetened cocoa powder
1 teaspoon salt
1 teaspoon Baking Powder (page 24)
2 teaspoons bicarbonate of soda (baking soda)

Chocolate cream
2 tablespoons butter, softened
3 tablespoons full-cream (whole) milk
310 g (11 oz/2½ cups) icing (confectioners') sugar
60 g (2 oz/½ cup) unsweetened cocoa powder

METHOD

Preheat the oven to 165°C (325°F). Grease and line two 20 cm (8 in) round cake tins.

Mix together the sugar, oil, eggs, coffee and milk in a large bowl.

Sift together the flour, cocoa, salt, baking powder and bicarbonate of soda.

Add the dry ingredients to the wet mix and beat well until the batter is smooth (don't be alarmed, this is a very wet batter).

Pour into the prepared cake tins and bake for about 35 minutes.

Leave to cool in the tins for 10 minutes, then gently remove and cool on a wire rack. To do this, run a knife around the edge of the cake, place a plate on top of the tin and carefully flip the cake upside down onto the plate. Place the cake rack on top of the cake and carefully flip again to get it onto the rack the right way up.

For the chocolate cream, beat all the ingredients together well. Use approximately one-third of the mix to sandwich the cakes together and the remainder to ice the top of the cake. Awesome.

Passionfruit Shortcake

Shortcake is one of the things I don't make. I don't make it because my mum does.

And man, she makes a good shortcake.

I think in every family somebody specialises in something, right? Maybe you are the excellent birthday cake–maker. Or the beloved scone-bringer. Maybe you're known for your mimosas or champagne cocktails, or your perfect roast.

Mum has always made shortcake. Given that my aunts on my dad's side also make it, I suspect it was my grandma's recipe (she of the award winning sponge – next).

Anyway, Mum makes a terrific passionfruit shortcake. She always has a passionfruit vine growing somewhere, always has frozen fruit in sealed bags in the freezer. It's the passionfruit shortcake she makes for her adored sons-in-law. And for Dad, for super-special treats (when she has a house-full and can be sure he'll only get one piece, being diabetic and all that ...).

So, I really never make it. It's her thing. Except when I happen to have fresh passionfruit because they just happened to arrive in our weekly fruit and veg box and we are going to a friend's house for lunch, and no one needs to tell Mum, okay?

SERVES 8–10

300 g (10½ oz/2 cups) Self-raising Flour (page 25)
220 g (8 oz/1 cup) white sugar, plus 2 teaspoons extra for sprinkling
125 g (4½ oz/½ cup) butter, cubed
1 free-range egg

Filling
125 g (4½ oz/1 cup) icing (confectioners') sugar
60 g (2 oz/¼ cup) butter, softened
2 tablespoons fresh passionfruit pulp

METHOD

Mix the flour and sugar in a large bowl, then rub in the butter. Make a well in the centre and stir in the egg. It will feel really dry, but keep mixing until you can knead it well into a ball.

Push into a round 20 cm (8 in) cake tin, rough up the top with a fork and sprinkle with the extra white sugar. Cook at 160°C (320°F) for 35 minutes, or until golden. When cooled, split into two horizontally.

To make the filling, mix the icing sugar with the butter and passionfruit. (This works really well with finely chopped strawberries too.) Mix well to a cream, then spread onto one half of the shortcake and sandwich with the other half.

Slice, serve and enjoy!

Grandma's Sponge Cake

My grandma, my dad's mum, was a champion sponge cake–maker. Not a Royal Easter Show–type champion, but a local Berry Show regular First. A sponge beloved by all who ate it. And remembered today, for heaven's sake. Is there likely to be anything you make that people will remember forty years after you're gone? It's a sponge cake recipe I really, really, really wanted to find, and *no one* had it.

I didn't ever make a cake with Grandma. She wasn't really a cooking-with-kids lady. The cake itself I remember though: it was pale and very, very light. Sprinkled with icing (confectioners') sugar and filled with jam.

We don't have Grandma's recipe book – you know, the handwritten one that everyone's gran had? But I have some of her handwritten recipes among Mum's recipes.

I love the way she always signed things 'Grandma' in inverted commas, including books she gave me that I read to my kids when they were little. Like 'Grandma' was an identity she wore lightly, being Gladys, always, at heart. She was Geoffry's Gladys, in particular. My grandfather died before I was born, and she always missed him.

I found a sponge recipe that excited me for a second, but it wasn't Grandma's writing, and not my mum's either. Mum usually attributed recipes when she wrote them in her book.

I got distracted when I found another one – that's my nan's handwriting! I hadn't seen that spidery script for years now. Nan, my mum's mum, would have turned 105 last week. Scones, mmm. (And so, I stopped my investigation and made a batch.)

We found a recipe at the bottom of a scone recipe (that wasn't Nan's), which made it possibly Grandma's. Mum's handwriting, and she thought it *might* be The Sponge. Oh, my goodness the HOT WATER in the recipe. Yes, I thought I remembered the hot water! I made this one as a kid. But it uses self-raising flour and my Auntie Narelle, Dad's sister, always said that Grandma's recipe was based on cornflour (cornstarch). Still.

I looked up the *Gerringong Mayflower Village Cookery Book* sponge – it's quite possible they asked Grandma for her recipe; hers was the best-known at the time of publishing. It uses self-raising flour too! And hot water! This might be it!

And so, I baked the one we *thought* was Grandma's recipe. We gobbled it up over a couple of days. We agreed it was good, although it wasn't pale or incredibly light. I rang Auntie Narelle. She said she would remember it by taste and that she was virtually certain Grandma used the recipe from the side of the Fielders cornflour box, if they still print a sponge recipe there?

I said I'd find out, make her both sponges and bring them over for her to taste-test.

I thought I'd better take Dad too.

Auntie Narelle eventually located some of Grandma's recipes and copied and posted them to me, confirming the Fielder's sponge suspicion. Grandma's winning recipe was virtually a replica of the one printed on the side of a box of cornflour. Which is hilarious: imagine winning all the competitions with a standard recipe?! Perhaps that makes her an even more impressive baker.

Maybe one day in the faraway future, someone will turn up at my door with my mum's passionfruit shortcake a very long time after she'd last made it for me.

Food is evocative. I would cherish every bite. Because a cake is never just a cake, particularly when it's someone's signature. It's a sweet reminder of kitchen hours and bowl lickings and tea-time treats.

I hope you make this, and love it as much as we do.

SERVES 8

4 free-range eggs, separated
170 g (6 oz/¾ cup) caster (superfine) sugar
1 teaspoon vanilla essence
125 g (4½ oz/1 cup) cornflour (cornstarch)
1½ tablespoons plain (all-purpose) flour
1½ teaspoons Baking Powder (page 24)

METHOD

Preheat the oven to 180°C (360°F).

Grease, flour and line two 20 cm (8 in) round cake tins.

Beat the egg whites with a pinch of salt until soft peaks form. Gradually beat in the sugar, a bit at a time, then continue beating until thick and glossy.

Whisk the egg yolks together with the vanilla essence and slowly drizzle into the whites. Beat until combined.

Sift together your cornflour, flour and baking powder, then sift over the egg mixture.

With a light hand, fold the mixture together using a spatula. Don't stir it; you'll knock all the air out.

Divide the batter evenly between the two tins and bake for 18–20 minutes.

In the clipped-together recipes Auntie Narelle sent, there was a 'mock cream' recipe to fill the sponge sandwich with, of 90 g (3 oz) butter, 90 g (3 oz / ¾ cup) icing (confectioners') sugar and 1 tablespoon hot water. Dad confirmed this was *definitely* it.

To fill, soften the butter and whip together with the sugar and hot water. Spread onto the underside of one cooled cake, spread jam onto the underside of the other, join them together and sprinkle the top with more icing sugar.

Alternatively, this sponge is absolutely delicious joined together with a good layer of Lemon Curd (page 225) and whipped cream. I'm pretty sure Grandma would approve.

Happy days.

Easy Orange Cake

This is a terrific cake for a busy Sunday. I tell you, it's a winner. And super quick and easy. It's basically a simple butter cake with fresh orange juice instead of milk, and a bit of zest. And a smear of white chocolate icing. Yum.

SERVES 8–10

125 g (4½ oz/½ cup) butter, softened
220 g (8 oz/1 cup) white sugar
2 free-range eggs
300 g (10½ oz/2 cups) Self-raising Flour (page 25)
grated zest and juice of 2 oranges (about 250 ml/
    8½ fl oz/1 cup juice)
White Chocolate Icing (optional; see on right)

METHOD

Preheat the oven to 180°C (360°F). Grease and line a 20 cm (8 in) round or ring (bundt) cake tin.

Cream the butter and sugar together. Beat in the eggs, one by one. Stir in half the flour, then half your orange juice. Then the rest of the flour, then the rest of the juice. Stir through the zest.

Pop it into the prepared tin and bake for half an hour, or until golden and springy to the touch.

Turn out onto a cake rack to cool and then ice, if using. Or just sprinkle it with icing (confectioners') sugar. Or just eat it.

Orange and Almond Cake (Gluten-free)

It's rare for me to seek out a gluten-free recipe. I am a dedicated full-wheat bread baker (and eater). Pasta, too. And pizza. You could, in fact, call me Fiona Gluten Walmsley.

When I bake for a school cake stall though, the gluten-free options are big sellers.

The 'whole orange cake' with almonds is a pretty ubiquitous recipe now – some have more eggs, some have butter. This version is a good economic cake and is gluten- and dairy-free. When he was younger, Henry decided it was his favourite cake in the known universe, so I was known to knock out a three-egg version, which still worked, as four eggs was my entire weekly baking budget.

SERVES 10–12

2 oranges
4 free-range eggs
220 g (8 oz/1 cup) raw (demerara) sugar, or use
    white if that's all you have
200 g (7 oz/2 cups) ground almonds (almond meal)
1 teaspoon Baking Powder (page 24)

METHOD

Wash the oranges and cover them with water (skin and all) in a saucepan. Boil for 1½ hours, then set aside to cool.

Preheat the oven to 190°C (375°F). Grease and line a 20 cm (8 in) round springform cake tin if you have one. It's not going to fail if you bake it in a ring (bundt) tin. It'll work as cupcakes, too. Call them friands, if you fancy.

Crack your eggs into a big bowl. Use a hand-held blender, if you have one, and whiz. Or whisk. Add the sugar and whiz. Put the whole oranges into the bowl and whiz with the blender. If you don't have a hand-held blender, you'll need to process them in a food processor. Or normal blender. If you live in an Amish community and have no electric kitchen gizmos whatsoever, then bash up the oranges, taking out your frustration with these people who insist on publishing recipes requiring *equipment for heaven's sake*. Then chop as finely as you possibly can.

After the oranges and eggs and sugar are all beautifully combined, stir in the ground almond and baking powder. That's it. Too easy.

Pour into the prepared tin and bake for about 45 minutes.

White Chocolate Icing

This excellent icing recipe comes from my friend Anita Sheridan-Roddick, one of the best home cooks I've ever met.

MAKES APPROX. 450 G (1 LB)

175 g (6 oz/1 cup) white chocolate buttons (melts)
60 ml (2 fl oz/¼ cup) full-cream (whole) milk
250 g (9 oz/2 cups) icing (confectioners') sugar

METHOD

Melt the white chocolate buttons, then stir in the milk. Add this chocolate mix in dribs and drabs to the icing sugar until it's the right consistency. (If you add it all in at once it may be too runny, depending on your chocolate.)

OhmygoodnessSOyummy.

Cream Cheese Icing

This icing is delightful on a rhubarb cake, or carrot cake, or lemon cake, or orange cake. Super versatile! I like it spread thickly and smoothly just on the top of the cake, not down the sides (although that's entirely up to you), sometimes topped with shredded coconut (toasted or otherwise) or chopped nuts or pretty edible flowers.

MAKES APPROX. 375 G (13 OZ)

200 g (7 oz) cream cheese, softened
125 g (4½ oz/1 cup) icing (confectioners') sugar
50 g (1¾ oz) butter, softened
1 teaspoon Vanilla Extract (page 36)

METHOD

Beat all the ingredients together until smooth and spread onto a cooled cake.

Armenian Spice Cake

I love this cake. It's also a fika favourite. My mum gave me her recipe for 'Armenian Slice' many, many years ago and I always loved the cleverness of the crunch at the bottom and the softness on top. Mum always made it as a slice, with a recipe from her friend Pauline, who I think got it from the *Gerringong Mayflower Village Cookery Book*, but there it's called American Nutmeg Cake. I'm not sure there has ever actually been an American Nutmeg Cake — my suspicion is it's a transcription error. There is definitely a traditional Armenian Nutmeg Cake, which this is a variation on. I wanted the bottom crunch layer, but for the cake to also be tall with a lovely soft crumb, and with *all the spices*. I hope you make this, and love it, and eat it for fika with people you really like.

SERVES 10–12

125 g (4½ oz/½ cup) butter, plus extra for greasing
400 g (14 oz) Brown Sugar (page 28)
300 g (10½ oz/2 cups) Self-raising Flour (page 25)
½ teaspoon bicarbonate of soda (baking soda)
250 ml (8½ fl oz/1 cup) full-cream (whole) milk
2 free-range eggs, beaten
2 teaspoons ground or freshly grated nutmeg
1 teaspoon Garam Masala (page 31)
1 teaspoon ground cinnamon
1 teaspoon ground ginger
Cream Cheese Icing (optional; page 133)

METHOD

Preheat your oven to 180°C (360°F). Grease and line (including the side) a 20 cm (8 in) round cake tin.

Combine the brown sugar and flour. Rub in the butter. (Or do this in a food processor if you have one.) It will look like crumbs. Divide the mixture in half and gently pat half of the crumbs into the base of the prepared tin. (Don't press down too enthusiastically or it'll be too hard after baking.)

Dissolve the bicarbonate of soda in the milk and add to the other half of the mix, along with the eggs and spices. Mix together well, then pour over the base.

Bake for approximately 1 hour, or until a skewer inserted in the centre comes out clean.

Mum always made hers traditionally, with walnuts on top, but I leave them off. There are enough nuts in this house already. You can ice it if you like.

Lemon and Olive Oil Cake

We discovered lemon and olive oil cake via Brydie Piaf, who wrote a lovely blog called *City Hippy Farmgirl*. We started making Brydie's cake for workshop morning teas about eight years ago and it was always a favourite. It might even be better the day after it's made, I think. It settles into itself, it's denser and firmer and so, so delicious.

SERVES 10–12

4 free-range eggs
400 g (14 oz/1¾ cups) caster (superfine) sugar
250 ml (8½ fl oz/1 cup) olive oil
grated zest of 1 large lemon
juice of 2 large lemons
450 g (1 lb/3 cups) Self-raising Flour (page 25)

Syrup
juice of 1 lemon
115 g (4 oz/½ cup) caster (superfine) sugar

METHOD

Preheat the oven to 180°C (360°F). Grease and line a 24 cm (9½ in) round cake tin.

Beat the eggs and sugar together until pale, then drizzle in the olive oil. Tip into a large mixing bowl and add the lemon zest and juice. Fold through the self-raising flour.

Pour the mixture into the prepared tin and bake for 45–50 minutes.

Make the syrup on the stove. Mix together the lemon juice and sugar and cook until bubbling. When the cake is still warm, pierce it all over with a skewer and pour over the warm syrup.

Sultana Cake

I've made this cake A LOT. In fact, it was one of those things that I made intensely in the beginning, three times in a row with tweaks, to try and get it perfect. It's a lovely cake. I made it originally for Adam's father, Jim, who loves sultana cake, and now it's kind of a family challenge to see if we can improve it. (Brandy definitely improves it!) The cake is pictured opposite.

SERVES 8–10

- 400 g (14 oz/3¼ cups) sultanas (golden raisins)
- 125 ml (4 fl oz/½ cup) brandy
- 250 g (9 oz/1 cup) butter
- 200 g (7 oz) caster (superfine) sugar
- 4 free-range eggs
- 1 teaspoon Vanilla Extract (page 36)
- 250 g (9 oz/1⅔ cup) plain (all-purpose) flour
- 100 g (3½ oz/⅔ cup) Self-raising Flour (page 25)

METHOD

Put the sultanas and brandy in a bowl or jug to soak together for about an hour.

Preheat your oven to 160°C (320°F). Grease and line a 20 cm (8 in) cake tin.

Cream the butter and sugar. Add the eggs, one at a time, beating well after each addition. Add the vanilla extract.

Sift the flours together and add to the mixture alternately with the sultana/brandy mix.

Once combined, pour into the prepared tin and bake for 1 hour 10 minutes, or until a skewer inserted in the centre comes out clean.

Fruit Cake

How did fruit cake become a byword for twit? I'd really like to know. There is nothing stupid about a good slice of fruit cake. Perfect with a cup of tea. In fact, a small gathering of my old book club, Reading Between the Wines, could typically polish off an entire fruit cake with a selection of herbal tea, coffee and shiraz. It's the cake for every mood.

And THIS one. This one is particularly clever. This is an adaptation of a recipe my mum has used for years. It has no fat in it, and only the sugar from the fruit. So, it's kind of a noble cake. Plus, it's AWESOME.

Don't take my word for it, make it. Truly. It's so quick. And delicious. Obviously, it doesn't have the depth or the longevity of a good rich fruit cake, but did you see my earlier points about noble? And awesome?

SERVES 8–10

- 1 kg (2 lb 3 oz) dried mixed fruit, chopped
- 220 g (8 oz/1 cup) pitted prunes, chopped
- 1 big teaspoon mixed (pumpkin pie) spice
- 500 ml (17 fl oz/2 cups) pear juice
- 300 g (10½ oz/2 cups) Self-raising Flour (page 25)

METHOD

Soak all the fruit and the spice in the juice for at least 4 hours, or overnight if you've timed it right.

Preheat your oven to 150°C (300°F). Grease and line a 20 cm (8 in) square cake tin, or use a smaller tin for a taller cake.

Stir the flour through the fruit mix, pour into the prepared tin and bake for about 1¾ hours. It's ready when a skewer inserted in the middle comes out clean.

That's it. Enjoy!

Mum makes it with a mix of prune and orange juices, so you could always try that. I like pear. And I have multiple family members who are allergic to orange juice.

Sometimes when I make this, I add nuts. Because if you're going to be fruity you might as well go nuts. Amirite? Too much?

Torte Caprese

Torte Caprese is a traditional flourless chocolate cake (torte) originally from Capri, Italy. It is a recipe that we made every week for years and years as a dessert served at our on-farm workshop lunches.

We always made it in a Thermomix, and this recipe is heavily influenced by the version found in the Thermomix *Everyday Basics* cookbook.

It's straightforward and quick to make using a food processor, and a bit more complicated without one. You'll need to get the chocolate and almonds as fine as you can – try chopping both ingredients very finely, then separately bash them in a sealed bag with a corner still open (so it doesn't pop).

We typically serve this with Chocolate Sauce (page 215), Fancy Ice Cream (page 274) and edible flowers. We also sometimes top it with ganache (see on left).

SERVES 12–14

250 g (9 oz) dark chocolate
250 g (9 oz/1⅔ cups) almonds
250 g (9 oz) Brown Sugar (page 28)
150 g (5½ oz) room-temperature butter, cubed
6 free-range eggs
1 teaspoon Vanilla Extract (page 36)
1 tablespoon Baking Powder (page 24)
1 tablespoon unsweetened cocoa powder

METHOD

Preheat your oven to 170°C (340°F). Grease and line a 24 cm (9½ in) cake tin.

Grind the chocolate in a food processor until fine. Set aside in a bowl. Grind the almonds until fine too, then put them in the bowl with the chocolate.

In a large clean bowl, beat the sugar and butter until creamy, then add the eggs and mix well. Stir in the vanilla extract.

Stir in the baking powder and cocoa powder, then mix through the chocolate and nut mixture and pour into the prepared tin.

Bake for approximately 1 hour, or until a skewer inserted in the centre of the cake comes out clean. Leave to cool in the tin.

Chocolate Ganache

170 ml (5½ fl oz/⅔ cup) pouring (single/light) cream
200 g (7 oz) dark chocolate, chopped

METHOD

Warm the cream in a saucepan on the stove over a low heat.

Once warm – with bubbles showing around the sides – take off the heat and stir the chocolate into the cream. Keep stirring until it liquifies and the ganache becomes smooth.

Cool slightly before spreading over cake.

Rhubarb Cake

This cake was often on the morning tea table for cooking workshops. We've always had rhubarb growing here, and if you keep it well watered, mulched and give it a good feed of compost in autumn, you'll always have luxurious, large-leafed, thick-stemmed rhubarb growing.

When we first planted rhubarb crowns in the kitchen garden at the farm, Dad came round the corner with extra crowns he'd dug up from a corner of the garden that were *his* dad's. That's pretty cool. Heritage rhubarb. Note to self: don't kill it.

SERVES 10–12

- 250 g (9 oz/1 cup) butter, softened
- 250 g (9 oz) white sugar
- 2 teaspoons Vanilla Extract (page 36)
- 5 large free-range eggs
- 300 g (10½ oz/2 cups) plain (all-purpose) flour
- 2 teaspoons Baking Powder (page 24)
- 1 good bunch of rhubarb (approx. 8 stems) washed, trimmed and finely sliced

METHOD

Preheat the oven to 160°C (320°F). Grease and line the base and side of a deep 20 cm (8 in) round or ring (bundt) cake tin.

Put the butter, sugar and vanilla into a big mixing bowl and beat with an electric whisk until light and fluffy.

Beat in the eggs, one by one, then fold in the flour and baking powder.

Fold the rhubarb into the cake batter and scrape into the prepared tin. It's a thick mixture, so don't be alarmed!

Bake for 1 hr 15 minutes until a skewer poked in the centre of the cake comes out clean – you may need to lay a sheet of aluminium foil on top after an hour if the cake is browning too much. Cool for 15 minutes in the tin, then finish on a wire rack.

We often served this with Cream Cheese Icing (page 133), or sprinkled with icing (confectioners') sugar.

Apple Teacake

This recipe makes two cakes: one for today and one to freeze for later, or to give away to someone who is going to love you for ever and ever as a result.

MAKES 2 CAKES, OR SERVES 16

- 8 cooking apples, peeled, cored and sliced
- 250 g (9 oz/1 cup) butter, softened
- 250 g (9 oz) caster (superfine) sugar, plus 2 teaspoons extra
- 4 free-range eggs
- 1 teaspoon Vanilla Extract (page 36)
- 250 g (9 oz/1⅔ cups) Self-raising Flour (page 25)
- 3 tablespoons slivered almonds, for sprinkling
- 2 teaspoons ground cinnamon

METHOD

Preheat the oven to 170°C (340°F). Lightly grease and line two 20 cm (8 in) round cake tins and set aside.

Cook your apples in 2.5 cm (1 in) water in a saucepan over a medium heat for about 10 minutes until soft. Drain and set aside.

Cream the butter and sugar together, then add the eggs, one at a time. Add the vanilla and flour and mix well.

Divide the batter between the two tins and top with the reserved apple and slivered almonds. Mix the extra sugar and the cinnamon together and sprinkle over the cakes.

Bake for 30 minutes, or until a skewer inserted in the centre of the cake comes out clean. Serve warm or at room temperature.

Blueberry Teacake

Even when you bake for a living, you'll still stuff up the occasional batch of cakes. Unfortunately, when I stuff up a batch of cakes it's not usually, you know, one tray of twelve cupcakes.

Take blueberry teacake. I make lots of them. And then one day it all went horribly wrong. Bloody maths. When I was carefully explaining to my mother at seventeen years old that if I got 51 per cent in my final exams for maths, that was 1 per cent wasted effort because *I was never using maths again in my life*, I failed to see that I was not going to end up a medieval historian, but a baker, and then a cheesemaker, who calculates, uses percentages and multiplies every day.

Anyway, the arts degree that came with the medieval history encouraged imagination and so beyond the trays of failed cake there was ... trifle! The cake tasted fine, it just didn't rise at all. Or, inversely, sank to buggery in the middle.

But in the pantry, there were peaches preserved in January in syrup (see page 186). And with a bit of custard you could even make it look vaguely deliberate.

Cake + fruit in syrup + custard = trifle (see page 184).

That's *excellent* maths.

SERVES 8

220 g (8 oz/1 cup) white sugar
125 g (4½ oz/½ cup) butter, softened
1 teaspoon Vanilla Extract (page 36)
1 free-range egg
225 g (8 oz/1½ cups) Self-raising Flour (page 25)
155 g (5½ oz/1 cup) blueberries (frozen are okay!)
icing (confectioners') sugar, for dusting

METHOD

Preheat the oven to 170°C (340°F). Grease and line a 20 cm (8 in) round cake tin.

Cream the sugar and butter well, then add the vanilla. Beat in the egg and then gently stir through the flour.

Spoon the mix into the prepared tin and smooth down the top. Place the blueberries evenly over the surface of the cake, then bake in the oven for approximately 30 minutes, or until a skewer inserted in the centre of the cake comes out clean.

Serve dusted with icing sugar. This cake keeps well for at least 1 week in a sealed container, and it makes an excellent trifle base!

Carrot Cake

Oh my goodness, I love a good carrot cake. In fact, I'm not sure that it's not my favourite cake of all. I'm fussy though. Must contain cardamom, that's the secret. And oil, not butter, and pineapple. Every time I make it, I'm struck by what a fuss it is – so many ingredients! But then you slice into it, and take a bite, and it's 100 per cent worth the effort.

SERVES 8–10

105 g (6½ oz/1 cup, lightly packed) Brown Sugar (page 28)
100 ml (3½ fl oz) light oil, such as olive, grapeseed, rice bran or macadamia
3 free-range eggs
1 teaspoon Vanilla Extract (page 36)
300 g (10½ oz/2 cups) plain (all-purpose) flour
2½ teaspoons Baking Powder (page 24)
1 teaspoon bicarbonate of soda (baking soda)
1 teaspoon ground cinnamon
1 teaspoon ground or freshly grated nutmeg
2 teaspoons ground cardamom
1 teaspoon ground ginger
390 g (14 oz/2½ cups) grated carrot (I used 3 medium carrots)
45 g (1½ oz/½ cup) desiccated (shredded) coconut
1 × 440 g (15½ oz) tin crushed pineapple, drained
Cream Cheese Icing (page 133)
toasted walnuts, chopped, to decorate

METHOD

Grease and line either a 22 cm (8¾ in) round cake tin, or two 12-hole muffin tins, or two loaf (bar) tins.

Preheat the oven to 180°C (360°F).

Beat the sugar and oil together for a minute. Add the eggs, one by one, and beat well. Add the vanilla. Sift in the flour, baking powder and bicarbonate of soda and the spices. Stir to mix, then add the carrot, coconut and pineapple and combine well.

Put into the prepared tin and bake for approximately 30 minutes (less for muffins), or until a skewer inserted in the centre of the cake comes out clean.

This cake is excellent made with Cream Cheese Icing (page 133), spread cleanly over the cooled cake, and topped with toasted walnuts.

Lemon and Passionfruit Patty Cakes

This recipe is a minor variation on the good old butter cake, but the yoghurt makes it so moist and light, and the passionfruit flavour is delicious. They really don't need icing, but a Cream Cheese Icing (page 133) or lemon icing does nicely too!

MAKES 12

125 g (4½ oz/½ cup) butter, softened
220 g (8 oz/1 cup) white sugar
2 free-range eggs
2 tablespoons vanilla yoghurt
2 tablespoons passionfruit pulp
300 g (10½ oz/2 cups) Self-raising Flour (page 25)
125 ml (4 fl oz/½ cup) lemon juice

METHOD

Preheat your oven to 180°C (360°F).

Cream the butter and sugar. Add the eggs and mix well. Stir in the yoghurt and passionfruit, then sift in the flour and mix well. Add the lemon juice and that's it!

Divide the mixture between 12 cupcake cases and bake for about 20 minutes, or until golden and springy.

Alternatively, you can make this cake in a ring tin or bundt tin, or as a sandwich joined together with passionfruit and cream.

Occasionally I'll make this in loaf (bar) tins and serve one and freeze one.

Bikkie Baking

I have always had a very strong feeling for biscuits. I love them.
I'll take crunch over cake crumbs, and fingers over forks. I love the
versatility and I just love a bikkie with a cup of tea.

When we first moved to the farm and were trying to figure out cash
flow while everything was just getting going, I started a little biscuit-
baking business, Buena Vista Farm Bikkies.

I rented a commercial kitchen down the road in a conference
centre that was typically empty through the week and signed up to
run a stall at the Gerringong market. I got my head around insurance
and ordering ingredients in bulk, and labelling and all the things –
the easiest part of it was the biscuits themselves. Nothing made me
happier than showing up in a sun-filled clean commercial kitchen and
making crates of biscuits. What a dream.

We made some of the following biscuits commercially for about
three years until we decided to make fewer biscuits and more ferments
and wholefoods, and then cheese.

Brown Butter Bikkies

I'd been reading about brown butter cookies –
usually an American thing – for years and had
never really seen the point. Melt and brown the
butter then solidify it again before making biscuits?
Is it really worth the effort? OH YES. Yes, it is.
It is 100 per cent WORTH THE EFFORT.

When you brown the butter, it caramelises.
It gives the bikkies a wonderful crispness and
butteriness and caramelyness. SO GOOD. I played
around with this recipe for a while and now I'm
really happy with these. It may actually be my
favourite biscuit ever. What a treat.

MAKES APPROX. 30

280 g (10 oz) butter
375 g (13 oz/2½ cups) plain (all-purpose) flour
1 teaspoon Baking Powder (page 24)
1 teaspoon sea salt flakes
115 g (4 oz/½ cup, firmly packed) Brown Sugar
    (page 28)
110 g (4 oz/½ cup) white sugar
2 teaspoons Vanilla Extract (page 36)
2 free-range eggs
60 g (2 oz/½ cup) rolled oats
265 g (9½ oz/1½ cups) chocolate chips

METHOD

Place the butter in a small saucepan over a medium
heat and cook for about 2 minutes, stirring the
whole while, until the butter melts and turns a
caramel colour. Remove from the heat and scrape
the butter (including brown bits) into a bowl. Put it
into the fridge until it solidifies, effectively to room
temperature, about 1½ hours.

Preheat your oven to 180°C (360°F) and line three
baking trays with baking paper or silicone sheets.

In a medium bowl, whisk together the flour, baking
powder and salt.

To the bowl of a stand mixer fitted with the paddle
attachment, add the chilled brown butter and both
sugars and beat on medium speed for approximately
2 minutes, or until light and fluffy. Add the vanilla
and beat until smooth. Add the eggs, one at a time,
beating well.

Gently fold in the flour mixture plus the rolled
oats with a wooden spoon, then fold in the
chocolate chips.

Roll the balls to approximately the size of golf balls
(or larger, if you like) between clean wet hands and
place them on the prepared trays. Continue until all
the dough has been rolled.

Place the trays in the oven and bake for 13–
15 minutes, or until golden. If you prefer soft and
chewy biscuits, take them out earlier. I like them
crispy. They'll store well in a sealed jar for about
1 month (as IF!).

Gingerbread

I love the spice and nostalgia and versatility of gingerbread. Roll it out thin if you like it baked crisp, or if, like me, you like it soft and chewy, roll it out thickly. I cut these into Christmas tree shapes every December and decorate them with icing and powdered sugar as gifts. This is my son Henry's favourite biscuit, the one he hopes to see in a jar in the pantry when he goes looking.

MAKES APPROX. 20 (DEPENDING ON THE SIZE OF THE COOKIE CUTTER YOU USE)

- 125 g (4½ oz/½ cup) butter, softened
- 100 g (3½ oz) Brown Sugar (page 28)
- 350 g (12½ oz/1 cup) treacle (see Note)
- 1 free-range egg yolk
- 375 g (13 oz/2½ cups) plain (all-purpose) flour, plus extra for dusting
- 1 tablespoon ground ginger
- 1 teaspoon mixed (pumpkin pie) spice
- 1 teaspoon bicarbonate of soda (baking soda)

METHOD

Preheat your oven to 160°C (320°F).

Beat the butter and sugar together with the treacle until well mixed. Beat in the egg yolk.

In a separate bowl, mix together the dry ingredients, and then sieve or sift them into the butter mixture. Stir well to combine and then form the dough into a disc, cover in plastic wrap and rest in the fridge for half an hour.

After resting, roll the dough out on a floured board to 2 cm (¾ in) thickness and cut into circles with a 4 cm (1½ in) cookie cutter. (Note: The thicker you roll and cut the dough, the softer the gingerbread will be. For hard-crunch gingerbread cut thinner [1 cm/½ in thick] and cook longer, for softer chewy gingerbread, cut thicker and cook for slightly less time.)

When placing the biscuits on your baking tray, allow for spreading. Bake for 12 minutes.

Ginger Twirlys

Oh my goodness, I have made these in the thousands. It's just gingerbread (see on left) cut in a round and decorated with a white icing twirl. You want royal icing that pipes cleanly and sets hard.

MAKES 20

- 1 quantity Gingerbread (see on left)
- 125 g (4½ oz/1 cup) icing (confectioners') sugar
- 1 free-range egg white

METHOD

Make the gingerbread biscuits according to the instructions on the left.

Put the sugar and egg white in a bowl and mix with an electric mixer or using a stand mixer until the mix is quite stiff, glossy and firm (or use a balloon whisk and muscles). Spoon into a piping (icing) bag or a sealed bag with a very small corner cut off and pipe in a twirl on top of each round ginger biscuit.

Notes

If you don't have treacle you can use golden syrup (light treacle) instead. It works nicely, but the biscuit won't be quite as dark or soft. You can also replace the treacle with honey and you'll get something closer to a honey jumble.

These are best eaten in the first week; after that, they tend to go a bit soft.

Meringue

I make these bite-sized, but they're just as good as big generous puffs. They're very pretty coloured with a drop of pale pink food colouring (see Note), and they're an excellent use of leftover egg whites if you've been making ice cream (see page 274) or Gingerbread (page 146).

MAKES APPROX. 40 SMALL 2.5 CM (1 IN) MERINGUES

3 free-range egg whites
175 g (6 oz/¾ cup) caster (superfine) sugar

METHOD

Preheat your oven to 100°C (210°F) and line a baking tray with baking paper.

Beat the egg whites to soft peaks with an electric mixer or a stand mixer or balloon whisk.

Then very, very slowly add the sugar, little by little, while still beating, until all the sugar is added and the meringue looks glossy. Keep beating until you reach firm peaks, then spoon the mix into a piping (icing) bag or sealed bag with the corner cut off, and pipe little 2.5 cm (1 in) round meringues onto the prepared baking tray.

Bake for 1 hour, take them out of the oven and let them cool on the trays. Once cool, these meringues last well in an airtight container for about 5 days.

Note

To colour meringues, just add a few drops of food colouring at the end, before piping.

Shortbread

I'm judgy about shortbread. It must be very fine, buttery and crisp. It's one of those simple things that actually isn't that simple if you DON'T FOLLOW THE RULES!

The rules are:

1. Your rice flour must be FINE. No grainy flour, people! I'm begging you!
2. Sugar must also be fine! Like, icing (confectioners') sugar.
3. Butter must be cold. Sure, this is a boring rule. But if you don't use cold butter you'll have a slightly fatty-tasting shortbread with zero crispiness and LIFE IS SHORT! EAT FABULOUS CRISPY LOVELY SHORTBREAD! Because what else are we doing here, really? When life is uncertain, enjoy the certainty of excellent shortbread. It's in your reach.

MAKES APPROX. 30

125 g (4½ oz/1 cup) icing (confectioners') sugar
175 g (6 oz/1 cup) rice flour (as fine as you can get)
225 g (8 oz/1½ cups) plain (all-purpose) flour
250 g (9 oz/1 cup) cold butter
200 g (7 oz) salted, roasted macadamia nuts (optional)
1 free-range egg

METHOD

Preheat your oven to 180°C (360°F) and line two baking trays with baking paper.

The very best way to make this shortbread is in a food processor. Start by placing your icing sugar in the food processor and pulsing it for a few seconds to get rid of any lumps, then add the flours and then the butter. (You can add the macadamia nuts here for an extra nutty, crunchy kapow factor. Or leave them out – up to you.) Mix until it resembles breadcrumbs. Then add the egg and pulse until it forms a firm ball. Wrap in plastic wrap and chill in the fridge for half an hour.

Roll out to approximately 5 mm (¼ in) thickness and, using a small round circle-cutter, cut out circles. Bake for about 12 minutes, or until golden.

If you don't have a food processor, rub the butter into the flours and sugar with your fingers until combined and crumbly. Make a well in the centre of the mix and add the egg. Keep mixing until smooth and amalgamated and you can form it into a firm ball. Wrap in plastic wrap and proceed as above.

These shortbreads will keep in an airtight container for at least 3 weeks.

Marry Me Caramels

We made these commercially for many years and they still have a bit of a local cult following. Crisp shortbread bikkies sandwiched together with chewy caramel – *so* yum. The name was designed to make people giggle; you may love this biscuit so much you want to marry it, although feel free to use in any way you see fit. (Please report back.)

MAKES APPROX. 15

1 quantity Shortbread (page 149)
60 g (2 oz/¼ cup) butter
395 g (14 oz) tinned sweetened condensed milk, or 250 ml (8½ fl oz/1 cup) homemade (see page 28)
2 tablespoons golden syrup (light treacle)

METHOD

Make the shortbread according to the recipe on page 149. Roll the dough out to approximately a 5 mm (¼ in) thickness and cut the biscuits into approximately 3 cm (1¼ in) rounds.

For the caramel centre, you can use homemade Dulce de Leche (page 198) if you have it, or make it as follows.

Melt the butter with the condensed milk and golden syrup in a heavy-based saucepan and stir until golden and bubbling. Hold it at boiling point for at least 5 minutes, stirring continuously, until it thickens and sizzles off the side of the saucepan and turns a good caramel colour. Hold your nerve! And stir, stir, stir! If you take it off before it's properly caramelly it will be pale and will have no chew. Once ready, cool the caramel slightly, enough to spoon it into a piping (icing) bag.

Pipe a dollop of caramel onto the underside of a shortbread round, then press another round on top, creating a sandwich. The caramel will firm as it cools.

Lemony Snickets

These are a variation on the Marry Me Caramels (see on left) with zesty lemon shortbread and a lemon cream filling.

MAKES APPROX. 15

1 quantity Shortbread (page 149)
grated zest of 1 lemon
125 g (4½ oz/1 cup) icing (confectioners') sugar
juice of 1 lemon
3 tablespoons butter

METHOD

Make the shortbread according to the recipe on page 149, adding the zest of one lemon with the dry ingredients. Roll out to a 5 mm (¼ in) thickness and cut out with whatever cookie cutter you like. I like a 4 cm (1½ in) round cutter with a fluted edge for these. Bake as per the shortbread recipe.

Next, make the bikkie filling (do not assemble these until the lemon shortbread is completely cool). Make sure your icing sugar is really fine – whiz it in a food processor or blender if you need to.

Mix all the ingredients together, and ideally spoon into a piping (icing) bag or a sealed bag with a small corner cut off. Alternatively, just use two spoons to apply.

Pipe the lemon cream filling onto one lemon shortbread bikkie and press a second biscuit on top, making a sandwich.

Allow to set before transferring to an airtight container where they will keep for at least 2 weeks.

Currant and Spice Biscuits

If you pull these out of the oven when you have visitors over, don't expect any more than about one left on the plate. They're crunchy and spicy and yummo. And easy to make.

MAKES APPROX. 18

- 125 g (4½ oz/½ cup) butter, softened
- 115 g (4 oz/½ cup, firmly packed) Brown Sugar (page 28)
- 110 g (4 oz/½ cup) white sugar
- 1 free-range egg
- 150 g (5½ oz/1 cup) Self-raising Flour (page 25)
- 150 g (5½ oz/1 cup) wholemeal self-raising flour
- 1 teaspoon ground or freshly grated nutmeg
- 1 teaspoon ground cinnamon
- 1 teaspoon mixed (pumpkin pie) spice
- 75 g (2¾ oz/½ cup) currants

METHOD

Preheat the oven to 180°C (360°F) and line a baking tray with baking paper.

Cream the butter and the sugars together, then add the egg. Stir through the flours and the spices, then add the currants. Mix well. Spoon walnut-size balls onto the prepared tray and bake for approximately 12 minutes, or until golden brown. Cool on the tray.

These biscuits will keep in an airtight container for about 2 weeks.

Handsome Jam Sandwich

A little bit British, a frightfully decent treat, with a sporting chance of becoming a favourite.

MAKES APPROX. 25

- 1 quantity Shortbread (page 149)
- 315 g (11 oz/1 cup) strawberry or raspberry jam

METHOD

Make the shortbread according to the recipe on page 149. Roll out to a 5 mm (¼ in) thickness and cut into 5 cm (2 in) rounds with a hole cut in the middle of half your biscuits. Bake as per the shortbread recipe.

While your cooked biscuits are cooling, heat your jam in a saucepan on the stove until it boils. Boil for approximately 5 minutes, stirring constantly to make sure it doesn't stick. Spread the jam onto the large biscuits and place the biscuit with the hole on top to make a sandwich. The jam will harden as it cools.

These biscuits will keep in an airtight container for about 2 weeks.

Digestive Biscuits

Has there ever been a less attractive biscuit name? Terrific bikkie, terrible title. I've messed around with 'digestives' for years and this is my humble offering, as close to a bought one as I could make it, all crisp and crumble. This is a biscuit designed to make you happy, whatever you're called.

This bikkie is particularly delightful topped with a small teaspoon of Lemon Curd (page 225). Just saying.

MAKES APPROX. 24

- 130 g (4½ oz/1 cup) oats
- 200 g (7 oz/1⅓ cups) wholemeal plain (all-purpose) flour, plus extra for dusting
- ½ teaspoon bicarbonate of soda (baking soda)
- ½ teaspoon salt
- 80 g (2¾ oz/⅓ cup, firmly packed) Brown Sugar (page 28)
- 150 g (5½ oz) cold butter, cubed
- 80 ml (2½ fl oz/⅓ cup) full-cream (whole) milk

METHOD

Preheat the oven to 170°C (340°F) and line a baking tray with baking paper.

Blitz the oats in a food processor until they're fine. Add the flour, bicarbonate of soda, salt and sugar and blitz briefly to mix.

Add the butter and pulse until it resembles breadcrumbs. Add the milk and pulse until it comes together. Wrap in plastic or wax wrap and rest in the fridge for half an hour.

Roll out thinly on a floured surface until the dough is about 5 mm (¼ in) thick.

Cut out the biscuits with a cookie cutter and place them on the lined baking tray. Bake for about 12 minutes, or until the edges turn golden.

These biscuits will keep in an airtight container for about 3 weeks.

Note

I make these in a food processor. If you don't have one, you'll need to grind up the oats in a mortar and pestle and then rub the butter into the dry ingredients with your hands. Add the milk last and, once the dough is mixed, rest in the fridge and then roll out and bake as per the instructions.

Wagon Wheels

These are a bit of a fuss and a fiddle and super sweet, but such a delicious treat for a special occasion, and reminiscent of sticky-fingered childhood wonderment.

MAKES APPROX. 24

- 1 quantity Shortbread (page 149)
- 12 store-bought marshmallows, cut through the centre into round halves
- 45 g (1½ oz) strawberry jam, or flavour of your choice
- 400 g (14 oz) milk or dark chocolate, whatever your preference
- 2 teaspoons vegetable oil

METHOD

Make the shortbread according to the recipe on page 149. Roll the dough out to a 5 mm (¼ in) thickness and cut into 4 cm (1½ in) rounds using a serrated-edge cookie cutter. Bake as per the shortbread recipe.

Place cut marshmallow rounds onto half of the cooked biscuits and heat in the oven (at 170°C/340°F) for 2–3 minutes until the marshmallow is very soft and melty.

Spread jam on the other half of the biscuits, then sandwich them together and leave to cool and set.

Melt the chocolate with the vegetable oil in a bowl set over a pan of just-simmering water. Stir occasionally until thoroughly melted, then, using two forks, dip your biscuits into the bowl and cover with chocolate.

Allow to set. Totally wicked. They'll keep in an airtight container for about 2 weeks.

Note

You can also make wagon wheels using Digestive Biscuits (see on left) instead of shortbread.

Arrowroot Biscuits

Good old Arnott's Milk Arrowroots have a soft spot in my heart because for many years when I was a small child, they were the biscuit you had with Dad with a pre-dawn cup of tea before you went out to milk the cows.

Given my slightly maniacal need to attempt to make all the things from scratch, a number of years ago now I thought it might be fun to see if I could reproduce them.

I read the ingredients label: wheat flour, sugar, vegetable oil, condensed milk, salt, baking powder, arrowroot flour.

I experimented extensively using vegetable oil, trying butter instead, with varying amounts of sugar, flours and condensed milk.

It's terribly dangerous using less than a full tin of condensed milk in any recipe, I'd say. Just too tempting to dip in that spoon …*gargle in back of throat a la Homer Simpson*. But I digress.

If you want a perfect replica of a bought biscuit, you need to use oil and bake them low and slow. If you want a shortbready biscuit that tastes like an arrowroot but is made with the more socially acceptable butter, substitute the oil for 250 g (9 oz/1 cup) butter.

The kids love these. I kept making them and giving them away, and making them and giving them away, while the kids couldn't believe their luck: bikkies multiple days in a row while Mum experimented with recipes. Living their best lives.

MAKES APPROX. 20

225 g (8 oz/1½ cups) plain (all-purpose) flour
150 g (5½ oz/1 cup) arrowroot flour/powder
60 g (2 oz/½ cup) icing (confectioners') sugar
¼ teaspoon salt
1 teaspoon Baking Powder (page 24)
1 teaspoon Vanilla Extract (page 36)
125 ml (4 fl oz/½ cup) Condensed Milk (page 28)
170 ml (5½ fl oz/⅔ cup) grapeseed, canola or rice bran oil

METHOD

Preheat your oven to 170°C (340°F) and line a baking tray.

Mix all the dry ingredients together (I do this in a food processor). Add the vanilla, condensed milk and oil and mix well until it comes together as a dough. Wrap and rest on the bench for 30 minutes.

Break the dough into two and roll each into an 8 cm (3¼ in) round log. Slice with a sharp knife into 5 mm–1 cm (¼–½ in) rounds.

Poke holes in the bikkies with a skewer – very satisfying. Bake for about 15 minutes, or until pale golden.

Enjoy with a cup of tea right before you go out and milk the cows in the pre-dawn light.

Crazy Lady Bikkies

In Australia there was once a massive kerfuffle about a young lady with a huge social media following and a cooking app and cookbook who told and retold a very poignant story of successfully recovering from brain cancer by eating wholefoods. It eventually transpired that she had actually never had brain cancer and had defrauded a bunch of people through fake fundraising schemes. Her app was trashed and her cookbook was pulled, which was a shame because despite her questionable ethics there were some great recipes in it. One of them was a chocolate chip biscuit that was gluten, dairy and refined-sugar free.

We make a version of these biscuits every time we need a vegan bikkie, and we call them the Crazy Lady Bikkies.

MAKES 14

155 g (5½ oz/1½ cups) finely ground almonds (almond meal)
2½ tablespoons coconut oil, melted
35 g (1¼ oz/¼ cup) cacao nibs
2 tablespoons raw honey or maple syrup
1 teaspoon Vanilla Extract (page 36)
pinch of sea salt
¼ teaspoon Baking Powder (page 24)

METHOD

Preheat the oven to 170°C (340°F) and line a baking tray.

Combine all the ingredients in a bowl and mix thoroughly.

Form balls (about 1 tablespoon in size) from the dough and place on the baking tray, pressing down (they won't spread much while baking), and bake for 10–13 minutes until slightly golden.

Leave to cool completely – they will be too fragile to pick up when still warm.

Cookie Cutter Bikkies

Sometimes you just need a straightforward cookie-cutter recipe. One that you can roll and cut and re-roll and re-cut and that works every time.

You don't have to use this as a roll-and-cut recipe – you can totally make scoop biscuits and just press down with a fork. You can also roll it out flat, spread the dough with jam (or I've used Nutella too) and roll up like a jam roly-poly and slice and bake. They're very pretty.

The raw dough freezes well – if you don't need so many biscuits, just freeze the remainder until next time.

MAKES APPROX. 16 DEPENDING ON THE CUTTER YOU USE

250 g (9 oz/1 cup) butter, softened
170 g (6 oz/¾ cup) caster (superfine) sugar
1 free-range egg yolk
2 teaspoons Vanilla Extract (page 36)
335 g (12 oz/2¼ cups) plain (all-purpose) flour

METHOD

Preheat the oven to 180°C (360°F) and line two baking trays.

Cream the butter and sugar. Add the egg yolk and vanilla and beat well. Beat in the flour until the dough comes together. Knead a little bit, then wrap in plastic wrap and leave in the fridge for 30 minutes to firm up.

Roll out the dough to approximately a 5 mm (¼ in) thickness and cut out the biscuits with a cookie cutter. Place on the baking trays. Rework and roll out the leftovers until you've used up the dough.

Bake for 10–12 minutes, or until golden.

Biscotti

This recipe came to me from my sister Naomi, who got it from her friend Harriet, and it has sat in my recipe file with the title 'Harriet's Biscotti' for years. I'm not sure who Harriet is, but I'm grateful to her. We made these in commercial volumes for a few years, and I love them for their longevity and hardiness, versatility and variation and *how good they are dunked in coffee.*

MAKES APPROX. 30

375 g (13 oz/2½ cups) plain (all-purpose) flour, plus extra for dusting
230 g (8 oz/1 cup) caster (superfine) sugar (caster is ideal, but white is fine)
1 teaspoon Baking Powder (page 24)
½ teaspoon salt
3 large free-range eggs, lightly beaten
1 teaspoon Vanilla Extract (page 36)
80 g (2¾ oz/½ cup) almonds, chopped (optional)

METHOD

Preheat your oven to 160°C (320°F) and grease or line a baking tray.

In a large bowl, combine the flour, sugar, baking powder and salt. Add the eggs and vanilla until a dough forms (sometimes I add a tiny bit of water if the mix is particularly dry). Add the almonds, if using, and mix well.

Turn the dough onto a floured surface and knead several times. Halve the dough and then shape each half into a slightly flattened log. Place the logs on the baking tray. Bake in the middle of the oven until golden, about 25–30 minutes. Leave the oven on.

Take out and cool for 10 minutes, then cut each log diagonally into slices and return the slices, in a single layer, to the baking tray. Bake again, turning once, for about 10 minutes each side – just be careful as they can start to overcook very quickly.

Breakfast Biscotti

My seventeen-year-old hasn't had much appetite lately. I'll do anything for him, and that includes feeding him biscuits at breakfast if that's what we need to do! He has one coffee a day, which he loves, and so I invented Breakfast Biscotti, which he appreciates, and I get all the feelings watching him quietly dunk biscotti into coffee, and I wonder where the world will take him and whether he'll dunk biscuits into coffee in Italy one day and think of our breakfast table and his chattering sisters and his mother flapping around and his father coming in from milking, turning our precious coffee machine back on saying, 'There's BISCOTTI?!'

MAKES APPROX. 30

- 375 g (13 oz/2½ cups) plain (all-purpose) flour, plus extra for dusting
- 230 g (8 oz/1 cup) caster (superfine) sugar (caster is ideal, but white is fine)
- 1 teaspoon Baking Powder (page 24)
- ½ teaspoon salt
- 3 large free-range eggs, lightly beaten
- 1 teaspoon Vanilla Extract (page 36)
- 125 ml (4 fl oz/½ cup) full-cream (whole) milk
- 60 g (2 oz/⅓ cup) dried cherries, or cranberries
- 60 g (2 oz/⅓ cup) chocolate chips
- 40 g (1½ oz/⅓ cup) rolled oats

METHOD

Preheat your oven to 160°C (320°F) and grease or line a baking tray.

In a large bowl, combine the flour, sugar, baking powder and salt. In a separate bowl or jug, mix the eggs, vanilla and milk together. Add this to the dry mix and stir well until a dough forms. Add the cherries, chocolate chips and oats and mix well.

Turn the dough onto a floured surface and knead several times. Halve the dough and then shape each half into a slightly flattened log. Place the logs onto the baking tray. Bake in the middle of the oven until golden, about 25–30 minutes. Leave the oven on.

Take out and cool for 10 minutes, then cut each log diagonally into slices and return the slices, in a single layer, to the baking tray. Bake again, turning once, for about 10 minutes each side – just be careful as they can start to overcook very quickly. Store in an airtight container for at least 5 weeks.

Note

Other good 'breakfast' biscotti combinations include almonds and oats; pistachios and orange zest; walnut, cinnamon and hazelnut; white chocolate and cranberry.

Mum's Cornflake Cookies

Journal entry from late in 2008:

What you are proud of in your child says so much about you.
Some people are proudest of their children's good manners. Some of clever language. Some of inventive imaginative play.
I am intensely proud of the fact Henry, 4, can crack a series of eggs into a cake batter without a morsel of shell in the mix. Clever fellow. He knows the ingredients list for pikelets and can make a batch of cookies (with a bit of help). Yep. I am very proud.
Today we made cornflake cookies, my mum's recipe. We ate them outside for afternoon tea.

MAKES APPROX. 20

125 g (4½ oz/½ cup) butter, melted
220 g (8 oz/1 cup) white sugar
1 free-range egg
300 g (10½ oz/2 cups) Self-raising Flour (page 25)
2 tablespoons custard powder
30 g (1 oz/1 cup) cornflakes

METHOD

Preheat your oven to 180°C (360°F) and line a baking tray with baking paper.

Stir the melted butter and sugar together. Add the egg, then the flour and the custard powder and stir. Add the cornflakes. Stir. Ball into golf ball–sized cookies and press with a fork onto the baking tray. Bake for about 15 minutes, or until golden.

ANZAC Biscuits

Oh, the marvellousness of the ANZAC biscuit! The crunchy, oaty, golden-syrupy, coconutty FABULOUSNESS!

And all the while you're nibbling, you can think about the wonderful Australian and New Zealand women making them throughout World War I to send to the fellas in the trenches. A sensible bikkie, one with no eggs and not too much leavening that could spoil them on the trip to the Western Front/Middle East …

MAKES APPROX. 24

150 g (5½ oz/1 cup) plain (all-purpose) flour
110 g (4 oz/½ cup) white sugar
125 g (4½ oz/1¼ cup) rolled oats
90 g (3 oz/1 cup) desiccated (shredded) coconut
125 g (4½ oz/½ cup) butter
1 tablespoon golden syrup (light treacle)
2 tablespoons boiling water
1 teaspoon bicarbonate of soda (baking soda), dissolved in a little water

METHOD

Preheat your oven to 160°C (320°F) and line a baking tray with baking paper.

Mix together the dry ingredients.

In a large saucepan, melt the butter with the golden syrup then add the boiling water and the dissolved bicarbonate of soda. (It will froth up famously, hence the reasonable-sized saucepan!)

Mix it all together, roll teaspoonfuls of the mixture into balls, press the biscuits onto the baking tray with a fork and bake for 10–15 minutes until golden.

Don't forget they'll continue to cook on the hot tray for a minute once out of the oven.

Visitor Biscuits

Of all the recipes in this book, this one is the most tried and tested. Not only by me – and I must have made one hundred batches of these biscuits *before I even left home at eighteen years old* – but by all the people who attended the cooking school here. We made these in From Scratch, and in the Bikkie Baking class and, years later, I'm still seeing social media posts of people making and remaking them. They're a winner. They are, by a long shot, my youngest child Ivy's favourite biscuit of all time. I named them visitor biscuits when I was a kid, not because they were fancy and you only made them for visitors, but if random visitors showed up at your door, which they often did at our house, you could virtually get these into the oven by the time the hellos were over, everyone was sitting and the kettle had boiled.

My mum always made them with white sugar, but I make them with brown – it makes them softer and chewier. If you're looking for extra crunch, melt your butter and use white or caster (superfine) sugar instead of brown.

MAKES APPROX. 15

- 125 g (4½ oz/½ cup) butter, softened
- 230 g (8 oz/1 cup, firmly packed) Brown Sugar (page 28)
- ½ teaspoon salt
- 1 teaspoon Vanilla Extract (page 36)
- 1 free-range egg
- 300 g (10½ oz/2 cups) Self-raising Flour (page 25; see Notes)
- 90 g (3 oz/½ cup) chocolate chips or chopped pieces of chocolate (or more!)

METHOD

Preheat your oven to 180°C (360°F) and line a baking tray with baking paper.

Cream the butter and sugar with the salt and vanilla. Add the egg, then add the flour and chocolate.

Ball up into about 15 bikkies the size of golf balls, place on the baking tray with a bit of room for spreading and bake for about 17 minutes.

Notes

Replace the self-raising flour with spelt if you like, just make sure you add 1 tablespoon Baking Powder (page 24) too (2 teaspoons per 150 g/5½ oz/1 cup flour). Or try wholemeal (whole-wheat) or gluten-free flours.

You can also use unrefined sweeteners, such as honey or maple syrup in this recipe – just use 175 g (6 oz/½ cup) in place of the sugar.

You can also make these bikkies with many different additions instead of chocolate. Add in 60 g (2 oz/½ cup) sultanas (golden raisins) or dried fruit, or 90 g (3 oz) white chocolate and a good handful of macadamia nuts. We also like oat and cranberry and chocolate and zested orange.

We made a popular biscuit for many years called Choccy Choc Chocs which was a triple chocolate version of the Visitor Biscuit. Add in 2 tablespoons unsweetened cocoa powder plus 100 g (3½ oz) chopped white chocolate (or white chocolate chips) when you are adding in the other chocolate.

Slice of Wednesday

Slice of Wednesday started many years ago as a weekly blog post that included the slice I'd made for a special group of friends, who still meet together regularly to this day. In fact, this book can probably be largely attributed to Linda Evans, Lyndall Coulthart, Sarah Young and Heather Philpott, who pulled me into Gerringong like I belonged here, spurred me on for the formation of the bikkie business, held me together through little kids and a growing farm business and all the things, and were my biggest cheerleaders when this book finally came about. We've eaten a lot of slice together, we have an emergency group phone chat permanently set up and I love them dearly.

More recently, *Slice of Wednesday* became a farm newsletter that sometimes goes out on a Wednesday, and sometimes includes a slice recipe. Mostly, it's a slice of what's happening on the farm.

Anyway, for you: all the slices.

Brownie

A number of years ago when our first two children were very little and I was pregnant with the third …

Henry: (*to me, while in the car, Adam was driving*) How did the baby get in your tummy?

Me: *cough* Really? We're having that conversation?

Henry: (*steely-eyed*) But how?

Me: Daddy put it there.

Henry: Daddy, how did you do that?

Adam: (*straight-faced*) Mummies and daddies have special cuddles and that's how babies get into mummies tummies. (*yes, he used the expression 'special cuddles' – my takeaway coffee was coming out my nose*)

Henry: Do you cut a hole in the tummy to get the baby in?

Adam: A very reasonable question, Henry, but no, daddies make baby seed and put it in mummies.

Henry: Baby seed?

Adam: Baby seed.

Henry: Can I make baby seed? I want to make baby seed.

Adam: (*still straight-faced; I'd given up on my coffee as I was at risk of choking to death*) You can make baby seed when you're a grown-up.

Henry: Can I make baby seed with you, Daddy?

Adam: No, that's not how it works. Hey, Henry, look at that interesting car over there! Isn't it interesting?

Henry: I want to make baby seed.

Adam: I have to pull over. Your mother has inhaled her coffee. That's enough about baby seed.

Henry: Can we have more babies? We need a boy baby. There are three girls and two boys in this family. We need a boy baby.

Adam: No more babies, Henry. Get used to being outnumbered, dude. Honey, please just put the cup down. Take a deep breath. Here, take my hankie. Hey, everyone, let's just go home for a brownie. There are brownies at home. Brownies for everyone.

MAKES 24

185 g (6½ oz/1¼ cups) plain (all-purpose) flour
1 teaspoon salt
2 tablespoons dark unsweetened cocoa powder
300 g (10½ oz/2 cups) dark chocolate, coarsely chopped
225 g (8 oz) unsalted butter, chopped
1 teaspoon instant coffee powder
345 g (12 oz/1½ cups) caster (superfine) sugar
115 g (4 oz/½ cup, firmly packed) Brown Sugar (page 28)
5 large free-range eggs, at room temperature
2 teaspoons Vanilla Extract (page 36)

METHOD

Preheat the oven to 175°C (345°F).

Butter the sides and bottom of a 22 × 33 cm (8¾ × 13¼ in) brownie tin and line with baking paper.

In a bowl, whisk the flour, salt and cocoa powder together.

Put the chocolate, butter and coffee powder in a large heatproof bowl and set it over a saucepan of simmering water. Stir occasionally, until the chocolate and butter are completely melted and smooth. Turn off the heat but keep the bowl over the water and add the sugars. Whisk until completely combined, then remove the bowl from the pan. The mixture should be about room temperature.

Whisk the eggs together in another bowl, then add to the chocolate mixture and whisk lightly until combined. Add the vanilla and stir until combined. (Do not overbeat the batter at this stage or your brownies will be cakey.)

Sprinkle the flour mixture over the chocolate mixture. Using a spatula (not a whisk), fold the flour mixture into the chocolate until just a bit of the flour is visible.

Pour the batter into the prepared tin and smooth the top. Bake in the centre of the oven for 30 minutes, rotating the pan halfway through the baking time, until a toothpick inserted in the centre of the brownies comes out with a few moist crumbs sticking to it. Let the brownies cool completely, then cut into squares and serve.

The brownies will keep in an airtight cake tin or container at room temperature for about 2 weeks. In fact, they're actually better on day two than on the day they're made.

As if they'll last two weeks. Guffaw.

Cheat's Brownie ('Lazy Lady')

After I almost lost my hair one night in the fireball I created by spraying canola spray directly into a pan on the stove (a gas stove, yes, I know I'm an idiot), I am reflecting on the effects of my shortcutting, my quick-fixing and my life of interruptions.

I'd like to blame my mother. The master of the domestic shortcut. If there's a way to do a chore quicker and better she'll find it because when you finish doing whatever it is, you get to read. Or play in the garden. Or do something fun. And that's worth a shortcut.

So, no ironing. I grew up clothed exclusively in non-creasing polyester cotton, folded off the line. Hemming tape. Scuff stuff. Nail polish on a laddered stocking.

The slice we'd make for morning tea was actually called 'Lazy lady'. (It was EXCELLENT. Essentially, a speedy chocolate brownie. Recipe following.)

When I'm done blaming Mum for introducing me to aerosol canola I can consider the influence of my friends.

One of my dearest pals of all time doesn't even use pegs on her clothesline. She hangs the washing out and when it's dry it falls off the line and onto the ground. She and her children always look very clean, so this system obviously works. Love you, Nessie.

I shortcut every single day. Some days it's no underwear. No butter under the vegemite. And don't even get me started on the cleaning shortcuts I make. *Cough*

Maybe that's why, for many years, I was doubly killed by the occasional need to write 'home duties' next to 'Occupation'. I'm so unbelievably crap at home duties that I almost set myself and the house on fire. When young, my children frequently left the house with spectacular bed head and I would occasionally notice a child wearing pyjama bottoms while out shopping/visiting. I had a tendency to note appropriate top half and shoes but neglect the flannelette Elmo bottoms.

And it's not that I'm shortcutting and reading or gardening, greater the shame. Some days it feels like roller skates down a really steep hill. On concrete. Without the exhilaration (and the great early eighties perm and short skirt. And legs, for that matter).

Right now, I'm off to make a quick espresso, speed-read the *Sydney Morning Herald* headlines online and not do any cleaning. Again. No cleaning except for the big black smudge on the wall behind the stove, which is all that's left of my eyebrows.

MAKES 16 PIECES

125 g (4½ oz/½ cup) butter, melted
230 g (8 oz/1 cup, lightly packed) Brown Sugar (page 28)
1 free-range egg, beaten
2 tablespoons unsweetened cocoa powder
150 g (5½ oz/1 cup) Self-raising Flour (page 25)
45 g (1½ oz/½ cup) desiccated (shredded) coconut, plus extra to decorate
hundreds and thousands (sprinkles), to decorate (optional)

Icing
125 g (4½ oz/1 cup) icing (confectioners') sugar
2 tablespoons unsweetened cocoa powder
2 teaspoons softened butter
1½ tablespoons full-cream (whole) milk

METHOD

Make this in one saucepan – save the dishes.

Preheat your oven to 175°C (345°F). Grease and line an 18 × 28 cm (7 × 11 in) slice tin.

Stir the sugar into the melted butter, followed by the egg. Stir through the cocoa and then the flour and the coconut.

Spoon into the prepared tin and smooth it out. Cook for 15–20 minutes.

While the brownie's cooking, make the icing. Mix all the icing ingredients together and spread on the brownie while still hot. Sprinkle with coconut. Or hundreds and thousands.

Oh, those cut-off end bits! I grew up with these bits saved for the family while the rest of the slice was given away or taken to a function. The best bits.

Passionfruit Slice

Oh, humble slice, of church fetes and morning tea at Grandma's.

I've been so rude about slices. *Really*, I thought. *Slices? Why?* They have neither the crunch of a biscuit nor the wonderful texture of a cake. And then I moved to the country, where slices are *everywhere*, and they are EXCELLENT.

I made this one last weekend for a picnic. Passionfruit slice. Incredibly quick to make and so yummy. If you're Australian and outside of a major city (even then), you've probably tried it.

The bottom layer has crunch and chew and the top is a firm and creamy condensed milk and passionfruit combination. What is not to love?

Type 'passionfruit slice' into Google and you'll get this recipe twenty times. No one owns it. Not the Country Women's Association ladies. Not *Taste* and not *Gourmet Traveller*. Pfft.

My mum gave it to me, photocopied from the *Gerringong Mayflower Village Cookery Book*. We used that book for everything when I was growing up. It's more of a pamphlet than a book, I guess, and Mum's copy has almost disintegrated. A very well-loved friend. FULL of slices.

MAKES 16 PIECES

150 g (5½ oz/1 cup) Self-raising Flour (page 25)
90 g (3 oz/1 cup) desiccated (shredded) coconut
110 g (4 oz/½ cup) white sugar
1 teaspoon Vanilla Extract (page 36)
125 g (4½ oz/½ cup) butter, melted
395 g (14 oz) tinned sweetened condensed milk,
     or 250 ml (8½ fl oz/1 cup) homemade (page 28)
grated zest and juice of 1 lemon
2 fresh passionfruit or 3 tablespoons tinned pulp

METHOD

Preheat your oven to 180°C (360°F) and grease and line an 18 × 28 cm (7 × 11 in) slice tin.

Mix the flour, coconut, sugar, vanilla and melted butter together and press into the prepared tin. Bake for 15 minutes. Allow to cool.

Turn your oven down to 120°C (250°F).

Mix the condensed milk, lemon zest and juice and the passionfruit together. Spread on the cooled base and bake for 10 minutes. Allow to cool.

In some versions, you now spread it with cream, but if it's sitting in the fridge next to the apples, even without the cream, it's going to call and call me. Apples or slice. Apples or slice.

Put it in a container and take it to friends. The WHOLE slice, Fiona. *Cough*

Maybe there are just one or two pieces that don't quite fit into the container.

They're in the fridge. What apples?!

Chocolate Caramel Slice

This is not a fancy slice. Or a tricky one. It doesn't photograph particularly well and looks much the same on your friend's beaten up old chopping board as on a pretty plate. Because this one is not about appearances. It's the go-to. The old school. The one your eyes follow if someone carries it into morning tea. The one that sells out first at the fete.

I'm sure you've made it before. You probably even have the recipe handwritten in an exercise book in your fourteen-year-old handwriting. If you ever lose that book, you know you can come back to this one and find it. (Better still, commit it to memory. Really. A slice like this is important, I'm sure you'll agree.)

When we moved home and Mum and Dad built a new house on the farm, they moved out of the farmhouse and left behind some heirlooms like this: the tin I cooked my very first slice in. It's so beaten up, it's made countless slices, it's so awesome – see for yourself on the right ...

I made a grave error of timing last time I made this particular slice, though: it was not at all set when I needed to leave to take it to a friend's place.

I covered it with foil and put it on the passenger's seat and it still wasn't set when I arrived a full five minutes later. Darn it.

I stuck it in Linda's freezer and pulled it out forty-five minutes, two cups of tea and about sixteen serious belly laughs later. It did not look so pretty. But really, as I said at the beginning, no one cares what this one looks like. It's chocolate caramel slice – a happy-dance in a mouthful.

MAKES 24 PIECES

Base
150 g (5½ oz/1 cup) Self-raising Flour (page 25)
45 g (1½ oz/½ cup) desiccated (shredded) coconut
155 g (5½ oz/⅔ cup, firmly packed) Brown Sugar (page 28)
125 g (4½ oz/½ cup) butter, melted

Caramel
2 × 395 g (14 oz) tins sweetened condensed milk, or 500 ml (17 fl oz/2 cups) homemade (see page 28)
60 g (2 oz/¼ cup) butter
100 g (3½ oz/4 tablespoons) golden syrup (light treacle)

Topping
200 g (7 oz) milk or dark chocolate, melted

METHOD

Preheat your oven to 180°C (360°F). Grease and line an 18 × 28 cm (7 × 11 in) slice tin.

Combine all the base ingredients and press into the prepared tin. Bake for 10 minutes. Allow to cool.

Stir all the caramel ingredients together in a saucepan over a low heat until the butter is melted and everything is amalgamated. Keep stirring for about 6 minutes, or until the caramel changes colour to golden. Pour or spread over the cooled base and bake for another 10 minutes at 180°C (360°F).

When the caramel has cooked and had time to cool slightly, spread with the melted chocolate.

Allow at least 2 hours to set in the fridge, but heck, the freezer for 45 minutes worked for me. Best shared with girls you adore if at all possible.

Apple Slice

I love apple slice. I judge a bakery on its apple slice (after it passes the Vanilla Slice test, but that's another Wednesday).

Maybe you have a big pile of apples that are past their prime due to your key apple-eating kid having a wobbly tooth. For example.

Or maybe it's a day that feels like one long laundry day, and you just need to make apple slice.

A simple and delicious slice that works every time is a recipe for euphoria.

Of course, the converse *could* happen, if you were making something untested. Nothing wrecks my day like a baking failure. If you hear me snap at my children, look no further than the inedible gluten-free baking experiment poking out of the chook bucket. Oh yes, gluten-free baking and I – a battle of wills.

But not today. Today will be a high-five-the-oven day. With a piece of apple slice in the fridge to celebrate.

MAKES 16 PIECES

300 g (10½ oz/2 cups) plain (all-purpose) flour
2 teaspoons Baking Powder (page 24)
110 g (4 oz/½ cup) white sugar, plus extra for
    sprinkling
125 g (4½ oz/½ cup) butter, cold and chopped
1 free-range egg, beaten
400 g (14 oz) tinned cooked sliced apple, sold as
    'pie fruit', or 400 g (14 oz) home-cooked apple
    (3 large tart green apples; see Note)
full-cream (whole) milk, for brushing

METHOD

Preheat your oven to 180°C (360°F). Grease and line an 18 × 28 cm (7 × 11 in) slice tin.

You can make this recipe in a food processor if you have one: just whiz all the ingredients except the apple and milk together, give it a bit of a knead, then pop into the fridge for 30 minutes wrapped in plastic wrap/wax wrap.

Or, sift the flour and baking powder into a large bowl, stir through the sugar, then mix in the butter with a fork until it looks breadcrumby. Add the egg. Knead well until smooth, then pop into the fridge for 30 minutes wrapped in plastic wrap/wax wrap.

Break the dough in half and roll out the bottom slab as close to the size of your tin as you can. Press the dough into the bottom and trim if needed.

Spread the apple over, then roll out the top and place it over the apple. Brush with milk and sprinkle with sugar.

Bake for 20 minutes. Leave in the tin until it's cold, then carefully lift out and slice up. Store in the fridge. High five.

Note

Either use tinned pie fruit or cook your own, there's no judgement here. If you're cooking your own apples, peel approximately 3 large tart green apples, quarter and core them, and chop into small pieces. Put the apple into a saucepan with 250 ml (8½ fl oz/1 cup) water, put the lid on and simmer over a low heat for approximately 15 minutes until the apple is soft. Cool before using.

Helpful Hint

To make this slice really neat and tidy, particularly the top pastry, trace around your slice tin on a piece of baking paper, then roll out your pastry to fit perfectly within the tracing. You can lift up the baking paper with the pastry on it and flip it carefully into the tin, minimising the chance of it breaking in transition.

Chocolatey Whacko Bars

This slice is dead easy and quick, and awesome with an espresso! It's an echo of our 'Hairy Balls' treat (page 201) but in slice form, which makes it even quicker to throw together.

MAKES 16

250 g (9 oz) milk coffee biscuits, or other plain sweet biscuit
90 g (3 oz) Copha (vegetable shortening)
60 g (2 oz/½ cup) unsweetened cocoa powder
1 teaspoon Vanilla Extract (page 36)
395 g (14 oz) tinned sweetened condensed milk, or 250 ml (8½ fl oz/1 cup) homemade (see page 28)
60 g (2 oz/1 cup) shredded coconut, plus extra for the top

METHOD

Grease and line an 18 × 28 cm (7 × 11 in) slice tin.

Crush the biscuits to a fine consistency in a food processor. If you don't have one, you could bash them in a bag with a rolling pin until finely crushed. It might take longer but will be quite cathartic.

Melt the shortening in a small saucepan over a low heat. In a big bowl, mix the crushed bikkies, shortening, cocoa, vanilla, condensed milk and coconut. Mix well and use wet hands to press into the prepared slice tin.

Cover with shredded coconut and set in the fridge for about half an hour. Turn out and cut into bars. Whacko!

Notes

A note on 'Australian-ness'.

(a) BISCUITS: Most of these will work perfectly, whatever you can find: milk coffee, arrowroot biscuits, morning coffee, basically a plain sweet biscuit. When a Digestive Biscuit (page 155) is called for use them; the crumb is softer in texture than milk coffee or arrowroot.

(b) COPHA: Solidified coconut oil that stays solid at room temperature. It's white and comes in blocks, but turns clear when melted. Palmin is the German brand name of the same stuff we have in Oz. An alternative is two parts shortening or lard with one part creamed coconut.

(c) COCOA: as in the powdered chocolate stuff. It's different to cacao, which is raw, and not as dark.

(d) VANILLA: You can use vanilla essence if that's all you've got, but vanilla extract has better flavour. Make your own! (See page 36.)

(e) CONDENSED MILK, as in Nestlé sweetened condensed milk ... you can make this yourself too (see page 28).

(f) SHREDDED COCONUT: you can use desiccated if that's all you can find, but shredded has more texture.

No-bake Hazelnut Hedgehog Slice

This slice is quick and easy and generally kid-friendly (as long as they are not allergic to nuts).

It doesn't entirely need it, but you can drizzle melted white chocolate over it at the end unless you are surrounded by friends with sharp knives, which I regularly am when cutting a slice. Life in my hands, I tell you.

Its appeal to me is that it's no-bake. Not because turning on the oven and throwing a pan in for fifteen minutes is a problem, but because my oven often has something else cooking in it.

This is a melt-and-mix, with the incredibly evil involvement of lard.

Oh yes, lard. Obviously, I was without the supervision of Adam-I-draw-the-line-at-lard. I bought some once about twelve years ago to roast potatoes with (like his grandmother taught me) and he threw it in the bin.

He said he didn't care how freaking awesome his grandmother's roast potatoes were, no lard in our house, please. Then he made some creaking sound that was supposed to be the sound of his arteries hardening. Hilarious.

I bought lard because I wanted to try it in a medieval pastry recipe and so I snuck it into the fridge.

It does make this slice fudgy and delicious. You could, however, just use vegetable shortening, which will make the slice less fudgy and firmer. Swings and roundabouts. Sharp knives or sneaky lard — slice life is EXCITING.

MAKES 16–20 PIECES

- 110 g (4 oz) hazelnuts
- 250 g (9 oz/1 packet) Nice biscuits, or plain sweet biscuits
- 60 g (2 oz/½ cup) unsweetened cocoa powder
- 60 g (2 oz/1 cup) shredded coconut (half for the mix, half for the top)
- 395 g (14 oz) tinned sweetened condensed milk, or 250 ml (8½ fl oz/1 cup) homemade (see page 28)
- 2 teaspoons Vanilla Extract (page 36)
- 85 g (3 oz) lard
- 100 g (3½ oz) white chocolate, melted (optional)

METHOD

First, optionally, depending on what's going on with your oven, you can toast your hazelnuts on an unlined tray at 180°C (360°F) for 5 minutes. Bring them out, and if the skins are a little dark, rub the nuts between sheets of paper towel to remove the skins. (You don't have to do this, I've made it with and without toasting the hazelnuts.)

Crush the biscuits in a food processor until fine. Put into a large bowl. Run the hazelnuts through a food processor until finely chopped and add to the bowl.

Add the cocoa and half the shredded coconut, the condensed milk and the vanilla to the bowl.

Melt the lard in a saucepan over a medium heat. Pour it into the bowl and mix everything together well.

Press the mixture into an 18 × 28 cm (7 × 11 in) slice tin, sprinkle the top with the remaining shredded coconut and refrigerate until firm.

Drizzle the melted white chocolate over the top before cutting into bars, if inclined, and if your friends are better behaved than mine.

Creeeeeeeak

Easy Slice
('The Church Fete Killer')

Oh, life with small children. Some days are golden. And some days kick your arse.

I remember once when we were new in Gerringong, Adam was doing some work with IKEA in Melbourne and I was at home with a head cold and grouchy children. The house was a terrible mess, and a promised afternoon outing with friends to an animal park just felt like one long slog. Some days sail by, others you just feel like you Never. Stop. Working. You know?

When we drove in the driveway coming home, I saw feathers everywhere. I left everyone in the car and walked around the back of the house. I heard a chook in death throes. I saw at least two cadavers. And it was not a fox. It was not a stray dog. It was one of MY dogs. Escaped the yard somehow. About to end the life of another hen.

I got the hen away (and she survived for many years), but four hens were dead, which brought us down to a laying flock of fourteen (from twenty) which was no longer enough to supply my new bikkie business.

This day called for an easy slice, ultimately given away while still warm, to friends who'll prop you up and who know when to serve tea and when to serve sauvignon blanc. Or whisky.

This slice is not about fancy form and style, but super easy and quick, with lovely chewy caramelly edges.

And it's a slice that doesn't require eggs. I firmly believe there is always, always an upside.

MAKES 16 PIECES

185 g (6½ oz) butter
250 g (9 oz) Digestive Biscuits (page 155), finely crushed
200 g (7 oz/1 cup) chocolate bits
100 g (3½ oz) blanched almonds
45 g (1½ oz/¾ cup) shredded coconut
395 g (14 oz) tinned sweetened condensed milk, or 250 ml (8½ fl oz/1 cup) homemade (see page 28)

METHOD

Preheat your oven to 180°C (360°F). Grease and line an 18 × 28 cm (7 × 11 in) slice tin with baking paper, including the sides.

Melt the butter and pour it into the slice tin. (Even if this feels weird, trust me. Pour the melted butter straight into the tin.)

Sprinkle the crushed biscuits on top of the butter.

Next, sprinkle over the choc bits, then the nuts, then the shredded coconut.

Pour the condensed milk over the lot.

Cook for 20 minutes, then cool before slicing. Keeps in an airtight container for about 2 weeks.

Simple Lemon Slice to Soothe the Soul

Journal entry from mid 2011:

I'm pretty much a daily blogger, unless a day kicks my butt, which yesterday did.

There were so many moments, all put together, to remind me that while I may occasionally look collected and, you know, on top of it, I'm so not.

It started with me knocking over the whole bucket of expensive milk formula I'd carefully made up for the pigs. Followed by a long-wafty-skirt-and-electric-fence moment. Doofus.

It wasn't helped at all by not one but two sick children, the most miserable being the baby.

Three missing chickens.

Two dogs tearing up the lawn.

Same two dogs exuberantly jumping on top of an elderly neighbour up the lane as he tried to fix his fence. (He was so cool about it. Poor man. They're not little dogs. We did a bit more training today.)

No biscuit stock left. Orders waiting.

The record number of times I reheated a cup of tea in the microwave before I tossed it was four. Total number of hot cups of tea consumed: zero.

Kids underfoot. High winds. Forecast for higher winds.

And some small person left the net off the cabbages and the chickens had a field day.

However. That was yesterday.

Today, I found a very large steaming bucket of fresh cow's milk up near the pigs, left by a neighbourly dairy farmer who'd heard about them.

Today, I just carried the cranky baby in the backpack all day and got on with it.

Today, I cleaned up the kitchen. No small feat. And I feel so much better about the world.

And today is Wednesday. Which means there is a slice.

This one is particularly straightforward and simple. And today, simple was good.

MAKES 16 PIECES

Base
125 g (4½ oz/½ cup) butter, softened
55 g (2 oz/¼ cup) caster (superfine) sugar
1 teaspoon Vanilla Extract (page 36)
150 g (5½ oz/1 cup) plain (all-purpose) flour

Topping
4 free-range eggs
230 g (8 oz/1 cup) caster (superfine) sugar
2 tablespoons plain (all-purpose) flour
125 ml (4 fl oz/½ cup) full-cream (whole) milk
finely grated zest and juice of 2 lemons
icing (confectioners') sugar, for dusting

METHOD

Preheat the oven to 180°C (360°F). Grease and line a standard 18 × 28 cm (7 × 11 in) slice tin with baking paper.

Using an electric mixer if you have one, cream the butter, sugar and vanilla until creamy. Sift the flour into the butter mixture and stir until combined. (It'll look crumby.) Press the mix into the base of the prepared tin and bake for 10 minutes, or until just starting to brown around the edges. Let it cool.

For the topping, put all the ingredients, except the icing sugar, into a bowl and whisk well. Pour over the base and bake for 20 minutes at 180°C (360°F), or until just set. When cold, cut into squares and dust with icing sugar.

Wednesday: saved by a delicious lemony top and shortbread base.

Tomorrow's forecast: calm.

Oh, Sweet Lemon Slice

Adam does not have a sweet tooth in his head. (Pass him the olives and the feta any time of day.)

But some weeks he'll look up from his laptop and say, just ever so slightly forlorn, *that slice looked nice.*

Because mostly it's made, photographed and out the door before he's even sniffed it.

Not this one. Not because he's marvellous (although he absolutely is), or because I think he'll particularly love this one, but because I whipped it together at 9 am and was pressing it into the pan at 9.15 am when I needed to be walking out the door with it at 9.45 am.

This slice takes longer than half an hour to properly firm up. Just so you know. (I took biscotti instead.) Suddenly, there is a slice in the fridge.

This is not, for me, a particularly good idea and I think I'll carry it to a neighbour tomorrow. Less a piece or two for Adam.

It's super lemony and very sweet. A delicious treat.

MAKES 16–20 PIECES

200 g (7 oz) white chocolate
395 g (14 oz) tinned sweetened condensed milk
250 g (9 oz) Nice biscuits, or plain sweet biscuits, crushed
90 g (3 oz/1 cup) flaked almonds
60 g (2 oz/1 cup) shredded coconut
grated zest and juice of 2 lemons

METHOD

Grease and line an 18 × 28 cm (7 × 11 in) slice tin.

Gently heat the chocolate and the condensed milk together in a big saucepan on the stove, stirring constantly, until the chocolate melts.

Into this mix stir the crushed biscuits, almonds, coconut and lemon juice and zest. Mix well.

Press into the prepared tin and chill in the fridge for at least 1 hour until firm.

It's sweet and sticky and lemony and coconutty and altogether marvellous.

Sorry Adam, this one's leaving the house first thing in the morning. That, or I'm going to be up a dress size by the weekend.

Estelle's Insane Slice

My friend Estelle from Brisbane is involved in one of my favourite custard recipes (we put together her mother's recipe and my mother's recipe and got nirvana).

She's a marvellous foodie. She sent me a slice recipe, many years ago now, and I thought it sounded REALLY WEIRD. She admitted it sounded nuts too, but urged me to try it. She called it the 'most amazing nutty, brownie-like cakey slicey thing EVER'. (Direct quote.)

We might call it 'Estelle's Insane Slice'. And FAR OUT it's really good. Weirdly good.

MAKES 8 PIECES

250 g (9 oz/1 cup) crunchy peanut butter
90 g (3 oz/¼ cup) honey
1 free-range egg, lightly beaten
1 tablespoon unsweetened cocoa powder

METHOD

Preheat your oven to 180°C (360°F). Grease and line an 11 × 22 cm (4¼ × 8¾ in) loaf (bar) tin.

Mix all ingredients together and pour into the prepared tin. Bake for 20 minutes.

Estelle: *'I'm not joking, that's it.'* (Direct quote.)

Four ingredients. It takes approximately 2 minutes to make. You can double the recipe and put it in a larger (18 × 28 cm/7 × 11 in) slice tin too.

Snickery Snickeroonie Slice

Oh, my goodness, this slice. *Respectful silence*

My mouth is watering just looking at the photos of it. My fingers are itching to go get a piece out of the freezer. And you know what, I CAN'T. Because I had the foresight to give the entire thing away after sampling one (okay, two) pieces (yes, okay, maybe two and an edgy bit) and knowing that unless it was in someone else's freezer I was bound to nibble at least another three pieces while writing up a rhapsodising recipe.

I made it up, so this sounds totally egotistical, really. I am so besotted with my own slice I might give it its own webpage.

It's the combination of roasted, salted peanuts, dark chocolate and digestive biscuits. It's just a hedgehog-y thing – you've seen them before. No-bake. How wonderful. Keep this in the freezer; it holds together better when frozen and is frankly less likely to torment you every time you open the fridge for milk.

But you HAVE to try this. Then, seriously, give it to the canteen ladies or something, because if you have the self-control to just nibble a tiny piece at a time, you deserve to be canonised.

MAKES 24 PIECES

- 100 g (3½ oz) butter
- 100 g (3½ oz) dark chocolate
- 395 g (14 oz) tinned sweetened condensed milk, or 250 ml (8½ fl oz/1 cup) homemade (see page 28)
- 40 g (1½ oz/⅓ cup) unsweetened cocoa powder
- 140 g (5 oz) salted, roasted peanuts
- 200 g (7 oz) Digestive Biscuits (page 155)

Ganache
- 50 g (1¾ oz) butter
- 100 g (3½ oz) dark chocolate

METHOD

Grease and line an 18 × 28 cm (7 × 11 in) slice tin with baking paper, including the sides.

Make a base by melting the butter with the chocolate over a low heat. Stir regularly and don't walk away. As soon as the butter is fully melted you should be able to take it off the heat and finish melting the chocolate in the hot butter by stirring. Once the chocolate is melted, stir in the condensed milk until well mixed. Add the cocoa and the nuts, and roughly break up the digestive biscuits into the saucepan. Mix everything together well, then press into the prepared tin. Allow to set in the freezer for about 1 hour.

To make the ganache, just stir the butter and chocolate over a low heat for a couple of minutes until melted.

Spread over the cold slice. Set (again) in the freezer for about half an hour until hard.

Cut with a hot knife (run your knife blade under hot water) into about 24 small delicious pieces or, in my case, two and an edgy bit then into a container and out the door before I find myself eating the whole thing. Keep this slice in the freezer.

Oh, chocolatey biscuity peanutty slice. How I love you. I miss you. And without you, I am a lesser person (hopefully, say, two to three kilograms less).

Tuesday Night Dessert

When our kids were little, dessert night was always Friday. But then along came youth group, and their own social lives, and suddenly Friday night was often the one night of the week that we didn't all eat together. When we moved home to the farm, we started having my mum and dad over once a week on a Tuesday for an extended family meal, and that night kind of automatically became dessert night. In fact, most weeks now my mum brings dessert, the kids set the table with spoons in high anticipation, and each week my dad carries in something different and delicious in a box, sometimes destined for the oven, sometimes for the freezer. It's a total treat, all of it: the deliberateness, the tradition, the throwing back the tea towel to see what treat has arrived this week, and the sitting down with my parents on a weekly basis. I'm very grateful for it. And for dessert.

As Easy As (Apple) Pie

Okay. In a recipe for a super quick apple pie, you might think *making your own pastry* is ridiculous.

But seriously, this pastry is SO QUICK to make you'll have it rolled out quicker than defrosting a piece of store-bought stuff, I promise.

I had a moment's notice that Ad was bringing some friends home for dinner. One was a friend he worked with in Brisbane who I (and Adam) adore, so I wanted to whip up something quick and yummy.

I don't normally go in for tinned fruit (less nutrients and all that), but if you have a tin of apple in your pantry, or frozen berries in your freezer, go for it.

Try it. If you're not totally sold on homemade pastry after this, I'll ... I dunno ... eat my hat?

SERVES 8

ice cream or cream, to serve

Pastry
250 g (9 oz/1⅔ cups) plain (all-purpose) flour
125 g (4½ oz/½ cup) cold butter, cubed
1 free-range egg yolk
1 tablespoon icing (confectioners') sugar (optional)
80 ml (2½ fl oz/⅓ cup) iced water
full-cream (whole) milk, for brushing

Filling
800 g (1 lb 12 oz) tinned pie apple or 6 green or
        other tart cooking apples (see Note)
1 teaspoon ground cinnamon
½ teaspoon ground or freshly grated nutmeg
sugar, for sprinkling (optional)

METHOD

For the pastry, put the flour and butter in a food processor and whiz up. Add the egg yolk. Whiz.

Add the icing sugar, if using. Whiz.

Add the iced water (use tap water with ice added to it) until it binds together. This will depend a little on your flour, so apologies for not being precise.

When the pastry comes together as a ball, take it out, roll it in plastic wrap and refrigerate for 10 minutes, or until stiff when poked.

Preheat the oven to 180°C (360°F). Grease and flour a round 20 cm (8 in) pie dish.

Break the pastry into two pieces, one about two-thirds of the whole, the other about one-third. Roll out the larger bit of pastry on a large piece of baking paper. When the shape is right for your pie dish, up-end the baking paper over the pie dish and peel off the pastry. Much better chance of it coming off in one piece.

Fill the pastry with the pie apple. Or berries. Or apple and berries. DELICIOUS. If it's just apple, don't forget the cinnamon and nutmeg. A wee sprinkle of sugar over the fruit doesn't hurt either, but that's up to you.

Roll out the smaller piece of pastry and place it over the top of the pie. Crimp the edges together. Brush the top of the pie with milk and bake for about 20 minutes, or until golden.

Serve with ice cream or cream, or yummy vanilla yoghurt or custard. Oh. Yeah.

Note

Either use tinned pie fruit or cook your own. If you're cooking your own apples, peel six large tart green apples, quarter and core them and chop into small pieces. Put the apple into a saucepan with 250 ml (8½ fl oz/1 cup) water, put the lid on and simmer over a low heat for approximately 15 minutes until the apple is soft.

Our Whole-egg Custard

Custard is important to me. I grew up with it, and I think it might be my ultimate comfort food. I spent many years trying to find my perfect custard, and settled in the end on a crème pâtissière rather than a crème anglaise. The difference is primarily egg white. A crème anglaise, if you were being unkind, could be said to lack body. It's a lovely light custard (a custard sauce?), which is a perfect accompaniment to cake or pudding. It's runny and can hide a multitude of dry-cake sins as it can soak in, and it's lovely served with fresh fruit or meringue or a tart. But we are not here for crème anglaise, we are here for custard, and for me that's something rich and thick that has enough body to hold its shape on a spoon and coat your mouth with velvety goodness.

We have made whole-egg custard commercially on a small scale for many years here, running three Thermomixes at a time and filling up huge chest coolers with it to take to the farmers' markets each week. At Christmas time we'd make it with brandy, and Adam used to write a blackboard sign at the front of the stall 'best custard in the world', which perhaps, to be fair, should have said 'best custard in our world', because this is my ultimate, favourite version of my favourite comfort food.

This, first, is the volume I always make, and I use a Thermomix (totally not sponsored).

MAKES 1.5 LITRES (51 FL OZ/6 CUPS)

750 ml (25½ fl oz/3 cups) full-cream (whole) milk
250 ml (8½ fl oz/1 cup) fresh pouring (single/ light) cream
5 free-range eggs
170 g (6 oz) white sugar
2 tablespoons maize (gluten-free) cornflour (cornstarch)
1 teaspoon Vanilla Extract (page 36)

THERMOMIX METHOD

Put all the ingredients, except the vanilla, into the bowl of the Thermomix. Mix on speed 7 for 5 seconds.

Cook on speed 4 at 90°C (195°F) for 8½ minutes. Add the vanilla at the end and mix on speed 4 for 3 seconds.

Spoon into containers or a jug. It will keep well in the fridge for 1 week.

For a brandy version, add 1 tablespoon brandy at the end with the vanilla extract.

Below is a half-version for everyone who doesn't need a litre-and-a-half of custard, with stovetop instructions.

SERVES 6

375 ml (12½ fl oz/1½ cups) full-cream (whole) milk
125 ml (4 fl oz/½ cup) fresh pouring (single/ light) cream
½ teaspoon Vanilla Extract (page 36)
3 free-range eggs
85 g (3 oz) white sugar
1 tablespoon cornflour (cornstarch)

STOVETOP METHOD

Put the milk, cream and vanilla into a saucepan and heat over a medium heat until just simmering, stirring regularly.

Meanwhile, in a large, heatproof bowl, whisk the eggs with the sugar until light and creamy and then whisk in the cornflour and combine thoroughly.

Next, very slowly pour the warm milk and cream into the egg mix bowl and whisk very well. Leave it for a second while you quickly wash the saucepan out, then pour the whole lot back into the clean saucepan and cook, stirring constantly with a wooden spoon, until thick. The moment it thickens (it'll do it suddenly, and look kinda lumpy), take it off the heat and whisk, whisk, whisk. There's enough residual heat to finish cooking for the next minute, and you make it silky smooth by whisking. Easy.

Keeps refrigerated for 1 week.

My Mum's Custard

This is the custard of my childhood – a delicious, thick and pourable custard that calls for very unfashionable custard powder. It won't split, you don't have to hover with a whisk or a bowl of ice water, and it hits the spot of a custardy custard when custard is required and you have neither cream nor a surfeit of eggs.

MAKES APPROX. 1 LITRE (34 FL OZ/4 CUPS)

2 tablespoons custard powder
60 g (2 oz) white sugar
1 litre (34 fl oz/4 cups) full-cream (whole) milk
2 free-range eggs
1 teaspoon Vanilla Extract (page 36)

METHOD

In a saucepan, mix the custard powder with the sugar and 125 ml (4 fl oz/½ cup) of the milk.

Add the eggs and whisk together well. Add the vanilla.

Whisk in the remaining milk and then set the saucepan over a low heat until it almost comes to the boil and thickens, stirring fairly constantly.

As soon as it really starts to thicken, give it a good whisk to keep it lovely and smooth.

Serve warm or cold. When it's hot, it's pouring consistency; once it cools, it will be the consistency of a thick yoghurt.

This keeps in the fridge, covered, for 1 week.

Trifle

A mere trifle! It's nothing. No matter. Of no consequence. WHAAT? If you know how I feel about custard, you'll guess how I feel about its mathematically enhanced counterpart: custard + cake + fruit = trifle. Nothing trifling about it. This is important.

If you ever have a cake that doesn't cut the mustard, so to speak, add liquor, possibly fruit, definitely custard and optionally cream.

Trifle is a long-standing English favourite, and there's no question as to why. It's a champion dessert. It's quick to put together. It's better the next day, so it's great for occasions that need prepping. You can line up perfectly-cut sponge rolls around the edge of a glass bowl or you can dump in squares of less-than-perfect cake of most kinds and you've got trifle.

If you're deliberately making cake for this, I recommend Blueberry Teacake (page 142) with or without blueberries. But I've made trifle with Lemon and Olive Oil Cake (page 135), and it was lovely.

SERVES 8

1 teacake, compromised or otherwise (see page 142), or 8 jam rolls, sliced
250 ml (8½ fl oz/1 cup) sherry (or rum or brandy)
220 g (8 oz) fruit of whatever kind you like – we like Preserved Peaches (page 186), but fresh or frozen berries work well too
750 ml (25½ fl oz/3 cups) Whole-egg Custard (page 182)
250 ml (8½ fl oz/1 cup) fresh pouring (single/light) cream, whipped
cherries or grated chocolate, to decorate (optional)

METHOD

Slice your cake into pieces and arrange around the sides of a serving bowl, then pour the sherry over and let it soak into the cake.

Arrange the fruit over the cake and pour the custard over the top of everything.

Whip your cream until firm and spread over the top. Decorate with cherries or grated chocolate if you're being super fancy.

Note

A note on jelly – I don't like it so I don't use it. I never have. I think it wrecks a good trifle, but if you're set on it, absolutely no hard feelings, please go right ahead.

The Rose Blues Cheesecake

I have a proclivity to fixate on a food and make it repeatedly in varying versions until I get it right. I admit I have done this with brownies, and custard, and also cheesecake. I don't know how many cheesecakes I've made in my life. Many. Oh, so many.

The best one I ever tasted came from Rose Blues Cafe in Glebe, a cafe that no longer exists, where I worked as a cook about a hundred years ago, and I could never perfectly recreate it. I knew the head chef, Virginia, had given me the recipe, but I was nineteen and I was lucky if I could find my head, let alone a recipe on an index card from that time. Then, one day about ten years ago, it showed up. At Mum's place.

I don't mean to overstate it, but I don't think I've ever been so excited to see a recipe in my whole life. (I have a committed relationship to cheesecake, you have to understand.)

Anyway, for your enjoyment, here it is. Please make it, I hope you love it, and if you're looking for the recipe again you know where to find it.

SERVES 12

- 125 g (4½ oz) Tiny Teddy biscuits, or plain chocolate biscuits
- 125 g (4½ oz) shredded wheatmeal biscuits
- 135 g (5 oz) butter, melted
- 500 g (1 lb 2 oz/2 cups) cream cheese
- 3 tablespoons sour cream
- juice of 1 lemon
- 2 free-range eggs
- 165 g (6 oz/¾ cup) white sugar

METHOD

Preheat your oven to 100°C (210°F). Grease and line a 24 cm (9½ in) round springform tin.

Crush the biscuits in a food processor. Tip into a bowl and stir in the melted butter thoroughly. Press into the base of the springform tin and put into the fridge while you make the filling.

Soften your cream cheese really well, either in a microwave until you can really poke it, or at room temperature. This will make it smooth. Using a stand mixer (ideally) or an electric mixer, whiz in the sour cream, lemon juice, eggs and sugar and beat well until smooth.

Pour onto the cold base and bake in the oven for an hour. Turn off the oven and prop the door open slightly. Allow the cheesecake to cool and set for another hour in the oven. Chill in the fridge for at least another 2 hours before serving.

Preserved Peaches

Hello summer! If it's January, then I've been spending long days in a very hot kitchen, how about you? I try not to get horribly jealous of friends on holidays, in the long summer holidays, you know? Those who post photos of kids doing lots of fun things and going places and 'chillaxing', as Tilly used to say when she was seven.

Around here, we try to stop for ice cream, and trips to the beach, and chillaxing, and we try not to beat ourselves up about working and lobbing kids around and juggling schedules and events and farmers' markets and deliveries.

And every now and then I'll grab an hour and do something I really want to do, which some days is a bit of peach action.

A local farming friend drives to Araluen every January and picks up boxes of peaches and nectarines for his wife to preserve. She's an older lady, who shared lots of wisdom about preserving with me when I first moved home. They asked if I wanted some fruit, and I said YES PLEASE!

And so, I put up peaches. It's possibly way more fun than it sounds, and seriously, those glorious golden jars of summertime on the shelves in my pantry just make me happy. There's an earnestness about preserving, a feeling of won't-run-out or okay-if-the-zombie-apocalypse-comes. We can lock the door and eat through the pantry shelves before we're zombied. If that's even a verb.

I highly recommend it. It's pretty straight-forward. Sterilise some jars (see page 86), drop fruit into boiling water, peel the skins off, take out the seed, cut them up, pack them into jars and pour boiling sugar syrup over the top. Screw on the lids and process in a hot-water bath (I use my stockpot with a cake rack in the bottom) for 20 minutes.

Golden jars of sunshine; they make everything peachy.

MAKES 3 × 1 LITRE (34 FL OZ/4 CUP) JARS

880 g (1 lb 15 oz/4 cups) white sugar
1 litre (34 fl oz/4 cups) water
2 kg (4 lb 6 oz) fresh ripe peaches (Free-stone! Not cling-stone!)

METHOD

First, get a large pot of water on the stove to boil (this is to blanch your peaches in) and wash your peaches.

Preheat the oven to 150°C (300°F). Sterilise your jars (see page 86).

In a saucepan on the stove, stir the sugar into the water over a low heat. Let it simmer but not boil. The sugar needs to fully dissolve – this is your syrup. Take it off the heat and leave it aside for now.

Get a bowl of cold water ready – I use cold tap water and refresh it every couple of batches of peaches.

With a sharp knife, mark a cross at the bottom of each peach.

Blanch the peaches, five or six at a time, in the boiling water for 1½ minutes. Then transfer to the cold-water bowl.

Start the next five peaches in the boiling water while you peel the blanched peaches.

The skins should come off easily, unless they're unripe – that'll be trickier, use a knife if necessary. Place the peaches in a bowl once peeled and, once all are peeled, cut them in half, remove the pits, then cut again into quarters. Add the peach pieces to your jars and layer them tightly until the jars are full, leaving about 3 cm (1¼ in) of space at the top of the jars. If you've got a random half-jar at the end, I recommend just eating them rather than processing a half-full jar or a smaller jar in among larger ones.

Pour the syrup into your jars until the fruit is covered by 1 cm (½ in) or so, leaving about 2 cm (¾ in) between the syrup and the lid. Wipe the jar rims with a clean cloth dipped in boiling water.

Remove the air from each jar as far as possible. Gently bump the jar on the bench, or swish around a knife in the jars if needed. Fit the lids on, with Fowlers Vacola clips, or if using 2-piece Ball Mason jars, tighten each lid to finger tightness and place the jars in a water bath canner or large pot, sitting on a round cake rack off the bottom of the pot if possible, or on a folded tea towel (dish towel). You don't want the glass to be right on the bottom of the pot. You also want to avoid the water boiling too rapidly as it might knock the jars around and break them.

Bring the water bath to a boil and, once the water is boiling, process the jars for 15 minutes, making sure they are fully submerged.

Carefully remove the jars from the water bath using tongs and let them rest on a tea towel on your bench. Allow to cool for 12–24 hours before moving. If any lids are not concave and pressurised, keep that jar in the fridge and enjoy in the next 2 weeks. Your canned peaches will last well in your pantry for 1 year, at least.

Blueberry Baked Cheesecake

My dad (D.O.D., he always signs notes to me, short for Dear Old Dad), retired dairy farmer, coffee farmer, fit as an (83-year-old) fiddle: diagnosed with type 2 diabetes about twelve years ago.

He managed to shed about 15 kilograms in the blink of an eye, walking every day (not just running after cows) and completely changing his diet. And no insulin required until relatively recently. Excellent work.

Given that Mum keeps him on a super healthy diet, it's really VERY NAUGHTY of me to serve for dinner Thai noodles with fish and coconut cream, beef and Guinness pie with pea purée and cheesecake.

But it's because he's so good all of the time, that I'm allowed to spoil him some of the time.

And when it's that one time that there's eight adults at the table, logic is that everyone will only get a small portion, right?

SERVES 12

250 g (9 oz) Nice biscuits, or sweet plain bikkies
125 g (4½ oz/½ cup) butter, melted
500 g (1 lb 2 oz/2 cups) cream cheese, softened at room temperature
230 g (8 oz/1 cup) caster (superfine) sugar
½ teaspoon Vanilla Extract (page 36)
2 teaspoons grated lemon zest
1 tablespoon plain (all-purpose) flour
4 free-range eggs
300 g (10½ oz) sour cream
500 g (1 lb 2 oz) frozen blueberries

METHOD

Preheat the oven to 160°C (320°F). Grease and line a 23 cm (9 in) round springform tin.

Usually, I crush the biscuits to fine crumbs in a food processor, but you can also bash them enthusiastically in a big sealed bag with a rolling pin. Don't seal the bag right up though, otherwise it will pop.

Add the butter to the crushed biscuits, combine well and press into the tin very firmly, over the bottom and up the side. Put it in the fridge for 30 minutes to chill.

Use an electric mixer to beat the cream cheese, sugar, vanilla and lemon zest in a large bowl until combined. Beat in the flour then add the eggs, one at a time. Stir in the sour cream until combined. Stir in the frozen blueberries until combined.

Pour into the tin and place the tin on a baking tray (otherwise the butter from the base might run out and burn on the bottom of the oven – yep, this is learning from my mistakes). Bake for about 1 hour 15 minutes, or until just set in the centre. Turn off the oven, prop the door open slightly and leave the cheesecake inside for 2 hours or until completely cooled. This stops it cracking. Then put it in the fridge to chill for about 4 hours.

That's it. Cut into wedges and serve. Delicious. Make sure you go for a big walk the next day, and no other sugar for a week and everyone's fine. Marvellous.

Apple and Berry Crumble

Journal entry from 2010:

We do dessert one night a week: Friday-night-dessert-night we call it. One way of teaching the kids the days of the week.

Tonight, I made Apple and Berry Crumble.

I used up all my energy making dessert; it took freaking ages because my darling wee 5-week-old really didn't want to be put down today and I'm not prepared to cook with her in the sling – when she's bigger I think I'll get a backpack that I can put on my back.

Henry said, 'What's bloody crumble, Mum? You've said it two times.'

Anyway, all energy used up and so dinner was toasted Lebanese bread sandwiched with melted cheese and baked beans. From a tin.

But dessert was awesome.

SERVES 6–8

5 medium granny smith apples, or other tart cooking
    apples, peeled, cored and chopped
½ tablespoon white sugar
250 ml (8½ fl oz/1 cup) water
220 g (8 oz/1 cup) mixed frozen berries
vanilla ice cream, to serve

Crumble topping
150 g (5½ oz/1 cup) plain (all-purpose) flour
125 g (4½ oz/1¼ cup) rolled oats
230 g (8 oz/1 cup, firmly packed) Brown Sugar
    (page 28)
125 g (4½ oz/½ cup) cold salted butter, chopped

METHOD

Preheat the oven to 180°C (360°F) and grease an ovenproof dish or pie dish.

Put the apples into a saucepan set over a medium heat with the sugar and water and simmer until cooked. Put into the ovenproof dish. Sprinkle the berries over the top.

To make the crumble, mix all the ingredients in a bowl. Rub in the butter with your fingers until it's kinda evenly mixed. Fine if there are still butter lumps.

Spread the crumble over the top of the fruit and bake for about 20 minutes, or until golden brown on top and bubbling.

Some people insist crumble needs to be served with custard and I respect that. Any excuse for custard, I say.

But I believe, in an almost spiritual way, that crumble should be served with vanilla ice cream. Right on top so it starts to melt into the crumble. As good-quality ice cream as you can justify. Or make (see page 274).

Chocolate Self-saucing Pudding

If you've got this far in this book you'll be aware of my tendency to make stuff over and over until I find the *perfect* recipe. It's a personality flaw.

When I first met Adam, I made him chocolate self-saucing pudding. I think it was actually for our second date (chronology dependent on who you ask). He said he loved it. So I made it again. And again. And *sometime after we were married* (that would be SIX years later and heaven knows how many puddings) he confessed that he really didn't like chocolate self-saucing pudding. Any of them.

So, when Adam was out of town overnight recently, I made one, even though *it wasn't Tuesday night dessert night*. I know. Living large.

SERVES 6–8

100 g (3½ oz) butter
225 g (8 oz/1½ cups) Self-raising Flour (page 25)
230 g (8 oz/1 cup) caster (superfine) sugar
80 g (2¾ oz) unsweetened cocoa powder
250 ml (8½ fl oz/1 cup) full-cream (whole) milk
2 teaspoons Vanilla Extract (page 36)
230 g (8 oz/1 cup, firmly packed) Brown Sugar (page 28)
500 ml (17 fl oz/2 cups) boiling water

MICROWAVE METHOD

Place the butter in a microwave-safe pie dish and melt in the microwave. Stir in the sifted flour, caster sugar, half the cocoa powder and a pinch of salt, then the milk and vanilla, and beat until smooth. Combine the brown sugar and remaining cocoa powder and sift over the top of the batter. Pour the water over the top and cook on high for 12 minutes, or until just cooked in the centre. Stand for a few minutes before serving because it will be piping hot. Delightful with ice cream.

OVEN METHOD

Preheat your oven to 170°C (340°F) and grease a pie dish.

In a saucepan, melt your butter. Over the butter, sift in the flour, sugar, half the cocoa powder and a pinch of salt, and stir well to combine, then stir in the milk and vanilla. Scrape into the pie dish. Combine the brown sugar and remaining cocoa powder and sift over the top of the batter. Pour the boiling water over the top. Bake for 20 minutes, or until just cooked in the centre.

Now, I'm sure there is a spoonful left in the fridge, and given I know Adam will ignore it ... if you'll just excuse me ...

Lemon Sago Pudding

I soundly acknowledge that I am not a sophisticated cook. *So* not. You've probably gathered this already. I've catered long lunches and seasonal dinners and degustations for large numbers of people, but my menus were pretty simple.

I love truly skilful food. Clever chefs who use genius flavour and texture combinations, and restaurant plates that make you gasp.

But I also love really basic things.

Like the old lemon sago pudding. Right up there in sophistication terms with sausages and mash. Scrambled eggs on toast. Grilled cheese. I'm not knocking it. We're naming some of my favourite food here. Mmm … grilled cheese.

When I first moved to Sydney as a youngster, there was an Iku Wholefoods almost next door to the cafe I worked in. Iku made a *kick-arse* sago pudding. SO good. Dear me, I ate a few. Once, at the time, I kept the container with the ingredients list and tried to replicate it, and it was pretty good! Do you think I wrote down the recipe?

I'm an idiot.

Anyway, over the years I've made and remade it, and here it is: zesty and creamy and delicious. I tend to make it into several small containers, because the temptation of one big bowl might just spell disaster. Lip-smacking disaster. Multiple small containers feels like minimising the damage. And although it's delicious, I think what it's actually missing is the taste of 18-year-old freedom in the big smoke.

SERVES 6–8

130 g (4½ oz/⅔ cup) sago (tapioca) pearls
500 ml (17 fl oz/2 cups) water
400 g (14 oz) tinned coconut milk
165 g (6 oz/¾ cup) white sugar
2 tablespoons golden syrup (light treacle)
grated zest of 1 lemon
juice of 2 lemons

METHOD

Soak the sago in the water for 20 minutes or so.

Drain the soaked sago and pop it into a saucepan with the coconut milk, sugar and golden syrup and bring to a low boil, stirring constantly.

Once thickened, take off the heat and add the lemon zest and juice. Spoon or pour into containers or one big bowl and refrigerate until firm.

Special Treats

We have a Bad Day Baking tradition in this house. If someone has had a shocker day, what better way to attempt to rescue it than by putting on your favourite playlist in the kitchen and making something delicious with whoever can join in? The music is most regularly show tunes. And sometimes it's baking – brownies or a favourite biscuit – and sometimes, particularly as my kids get older, the day calls for something more special. Your favourite people, your favourite music, and a super-special handmade delicious treat. How wonderful to have days that can be rescued by Bad Day Baking. May it always be the case.

Killer Caramel

So, do you know that you can make kick-arse caramel with stuff already in your pantry?! That is: butter, sugar, milk? If this sounds just *too damn dangerous*, flick forwards to sauces or crackers now.

Right. It started like this.

I wander around the supermarket shunning bad food. No, not buying chocolate. No, not buying ice cream. Not even buying condensed milk, which will be turned into something naughty and, if I'm really lucky, I can use a recipe that does not use a whole tin and leaves remnants that need cleaning up.

You know.

And it's nine o'clock at night and it's been a lovely day and what would make it even more lovely would be some kind of chewy sweet marvellousness.

Dried fruit and nuts in the cupboard? Right now, they are just not going to cut it.

You know, you don't necessarily need condensed milk for caramel. If you cook sugar and butter and milk long enough it caramelises perfectly.

This is dangerous stuff. No nutritional value. If you have fillings, these will pull them out for sure. (And if you don't yet, eat a few of these.)

It's a good, solid, chewy caramel that you can cut in squares and wrap in pretty papers and give away. Which I highly recommend.

MAKES APPROX. 20

- 125 g (4½ oz/½ cup) butter
- 230 g (8 oz/1 cup, lightly packed) Brown Sugar (page 28)
- 110 g (4 oz/½ cup) white sugar
- 250 ml (8½ fl oz/1 cup) full-cream (whole) milk
- 1 teaspoon Vanilla Extract (page 36)

METHOD

(Caveat: If you like the precision of a candy thermometer, I'm afraid I'm going to disappoint you. You'll be able to do this without one, I promise.)

Grease a loaf (bar) tin and set aside.

In a heavy-based saucepan, melt the butter and the sugars over a medium heat. When melted, add the milk. Stir, stir, stir. It'll froth up. It won't look like caramel. Stir, stir, stir. It'll change colour (gradually go darker). The earlier you pull it off the stove, the softer and 'fudgier' it'll be. So be brave, leave it on and stir. The longer you leave it, the harder the caramel will set.

I can't tell you precisely how long this will take because it depends on the heat, gas or electric, whether you've got a window open and if you're wearing high heels. (Not really.)

It'll eventually start to thicken up nicely, the frothiness will subside by almost half and start to pull away from the sides of the saucepan. (Approximately 20 minutes.) Watch it closely.

Add the vanilla at the end, as you take it off the heat.

Pour into the greased tin and let it cool. Mark out the squares when cool then put it into the fridge. Depending on how long you left it on it might be rock-solid in the fridge, but it will soften up if you leave it out for an hour.

It truly rocks. (She says, licking her fingers.) Dip it in chocolate. Or enjoy it unadulterated.

Chewy Caramel

Do you have a signature dish? Something people ask you to make? Something people associate you with?

I wish my signature dish was a divine boeuf bourguignon, or breath-taking hand-rolled sushi, or an especially delicate lemon tart. Nope. I'm pretty sure this is my signature: caramel.

Now, before we get into Dulce de Leche (page 198), I HAVE to talk about caramel. This is one of those things I shudder to think of how many batches I made in my youth. SOOO many. I hardly ever make it nowadays as I have two girls with shocker sweet teeth who would inhale it, and Adam and Henry just don't really eat sweet stuff. (Leave the olives out on the table and it's all over, though.)

When I was eight years old, a neighbour of ours, Mrs Deasey, used to bring little foil pans of caramel to us, two doors down, as a treat. I'm not even sure we ever wrote the recipe down. I remember learning it very, very young, and it's still in my head.

I remember making it at college, in the college kitchen late at night, and a bunch of us would sit around and not even let it cool.

When my eldest nephew, Doug, was about to leave home for university, it was the thing he asked his mother, my beautiful sister Suzie, to make for him. Auntie Fi's caramel. Mrs Deasey's caramel. Or it can be yours, if you like. Here:

MAKES APPROX. 20

85 g (3 oz/⅓ cup) salted butter
155 g (5½ oz/⅔ cup, firmly packed) Brown Sugar (page 28)
395 g (14 oz) tinned sweetened condensed milk, or 250 ml (8½ fl oz/1 cup) homemade (see page 28)

METHOD

Grease and line a dinner plate with baking paper and set aside.

Start the butter melting in a heavy-based saucepan (a copper saucepan is great if you happen to have one) over a medium heat, then add the other ingredients and start stirring. Don't make this if you're likely to get interrupted – you can't stop stirring for a two-year-old bathroom emergency or five-year-old battery replacement drama. It'll burn in a breath.

Stir, stir, stir. The butter will melt and the sugar will dissolve and it'll be a pale caramel colour. Be very careful not to let it get too hot. Use a moderate heat on the stove. If you can see it starting to burn, pull it off the heat and stir, stir, stir! Basically, you stir it fast for 6–8 minutes over a moderate heat until it turns a deep golden colour. It'll get quite thick, too.

When it is a dark caramel colour and very thick, pour it onto the prepared dinner plate and leave to cool for a minute before putting in the fridge.

If you let it get too hot or take your eyes off it, you'll end up with bits from the sugar burning to the side of the saucepan. Start on a lower heat and cook it longer if you're feeling nervous.

Once cooled and hard, chop it up with a sharp knife, put it in a container and take it to work for everyone else to eat. Or keep it in your fridge if you have better self-control than me. Good on you. It's like the chewy inside of a Fantale. SO yummy.

Dulce De Leche

As I wandered around my kitchen late one afternoon in Sydney, many years ago, with a friend who was picking up her son who'd come around the corner to my place because he'd forgotten his keys, I was telling her that I was about to take Tilly to the doctor because she had a raging ear infection and a persistent temperature and I referred to the dulce de leche that was currently simmering on the stove and Yvette said, 'Today? Why would you do that today, with a sick toddler?'

Yes, a very good question.

Because when things get blue, I cook.

Because Tilly conked out around lunchtime and I looked at the tin of condensed milk in my cupboard and thought, *hello*.

Because when things are out of my control, I cook. Or better, make caramel.

Because I'm an extremely curious cook. Don't you just want to know what happens inside that can for three-and-a-half hours?!

And because it's really straightforward: one tin of condensed milk, label taken off, in your biggest stockpot, covered with water, and let it boil.

Yes, you *can* make this dulce de leche by pouring condensed milk into a baking dish, covering it and baking for 1½ hours. Better to LIVE ON THE EDGE, people.

Unless there's a real risk of boiling exploding tins, you're only half alive.

Do not make this half-heartedly and puncture the tin. You won't need to, and water will get in and crystallise the caramel. Yuck.

I also very strongly recommend letting the tin cool down before cracking it open, to avoid scalding molten caramel potentially geysering into your eye.

I also strongly recommend a 100 per cent covering of the tin with water at all times (like, don't doze off or go cuddle a sick kid because if there's boiling hot caramel inside the tin and no water outside because you've let it boil dry, I'm pretty sure the tin could explode. I've never tried this, please don't).

You know, I enjoy risk. But not of the it'll-take-me-three-hours-to-scrape-that-off-the-ceiling kind.

So please, a BIG stockpot, lots and lots of water. Three and a half hours and there we have it, folks. Dulce De Leche.

Now what do you *do* with it? Eat it by the spoonful and fall into a sugar coma?

Alternatively:

- Use it as the caramel in a Marry Me Caramel biscuit (page 150)
- Drizzle it over your tray of Brownies (page 163) before baking
- Spoon it over ice cream (page 274)
- Warm it up again and pipe it in skinny ribbons over the top of a baked cheesecake, again before baking (see page 188)
- Use it as the caramel in a slice (see page 163)
- Put it in shortcrust tart cases (see page 50)
- Roll it into balls, refrigerate, drop the cold balls into melted chocolate, refrigerate and enjoy something very close to a cobber or Fantale.

SO good. Not so good for you. But you're not here for diet tips, right?

MAKES 250 ML (8½ FL OZ/1 CUP)

1 × 395 g (14 oz) tin condensed milk

METHOD

Remove the label. Put the tin on its side into a large heavy-bottomed saucepan. (Putting the tin on its side stops it bouncing around quite so much.)

Cover the tin completely with water, with at least 10 cm (4 in) of water above the tin, and put the saucepan over a medium heat.

Let the water come to a boil and let it remain on a low boil for 3½ hours.

Check the saucepan at least every half an hour, and top up with boiling water from the kettle as often as required to keep the tin covered by 10 cm (4 in) water. Do not let the tin boil uncovered by water.

At 3½ hours, turn the heat off and leave the tin in the cooling water until the water is completely cold – for about 8–12 hours, or overnight.

Remove the cold tin, open and spoon out the dulce de leche into a jar or container. It keeps refrigerated for 6 weeks.

Note

Don't ever open a hot tin of dulce de leche, as this could result in burns. Always leave the caramel to cool completely in the tin before opening.

From Scratch Chocolate

No, I don't mean melting down milk chocolate and pouring it into moulds! I mean make it from scratch.

The first thing you should know is that unless you have a conching machine, your chocolate will not taste like Lindt. Conching removes the grit and makes chocolate silky and smooth. But it's still a delicious treat, and homemade, hooray!

MAKES 250 G (9 OZ)

60 g (2 oz/½ cup) icing (confectioners') sugar
140 g (5 oz) cocoa butter buttons or wafers
60 g (2 oz/½ cup) unsweetened cocoa powder
125 g (4½ oz/¼ cups) full-cream (whole) milk powder
small pinch of very fine salt
pure peppermint essential oil (optional)

METHOD

First, make sure your icing sugar is very finely powdered – ideally, blitz it in a food processor. Otherwise you'll have white sugar flecks in your chocolate.

Melt the cocoa butter to liquid in either the microwave or in a saucepan over a low heat.

Mix the four dry ingredients together first, then mix into the butter and stir really well.

Add five drops of pure peppermint essential oil if you are my children and peppermint chocolate is the answer to all the questions.

Pour into moulds and set in the fridge.

Raw Chocolate Balls

My kids won't eat these, which makes them a perfect after-dinner treat: chocolatey and satisfying and still in the fridge when I go looking for them.

MAKES APPROX. 16

50 g (1¾ oz/¼ cup) organic coconut oil
110 g (4 oz/½ cup) pitted organic prunes
180 g (6½ oz/1 cup) pitted fresh organic dates
½ teaspoon Vanilla Extract (page 36)
60 g (2 oz/½ cup) raw cacao powder,
    or unsweetened cocoa powder
45 g (1½ oz/½ cup) desiccated (shredded) coconut

METHOD

Melt the coconut oil to liquid over a low heat.

Whiz all the ingredients, except the desiccated coconut, in a food processor until completely amalgamated.

When smooth, roll into balls and then in the coconut.

Store in the fridge for up to 3 weeks.

Hairy Balls
(or Naked Balls, whatever you prefer)

Journal entry from 2010:

Ah well. When it falls apart it kind of makes sense for it to all fall apart.

I have a pretty solid habit of leaving things to the last minute. Er, make that everything. I know better. I do. I just never learn.

Here's what happened yesterday.

Yesterday was Henry's last day of kindergarten. The end of Summer Hill Public School for us, before the move to Gerringong. Very exciting. Un-freaking-believable in many respects.

Tilly and Ivy and I had a lovely day – a last-minute dash to IKEA for fabric for gift-making, and at 2.30 pm we were at home, both girls sound asleep. Need to leave at 2.45 pm for school pick-up. The last one.

I'd made a last-minute big chocolate slab cake to take to the park where Henry's class were gathering to celebrate the end of the year. I'd quickly finished balling up the chocolate brandy balls in a glass jar for the teacher.

It's 2.45 pm, and I transfer Ivy, asleep, to her car seat and wake Tilly, bribe her out to the car with a handful of smarties, and we're off. 'Cept we're not.

I'm turning the key in the ignition and nothing's happening. Turning over, not starting. Then it hits me. We are driving a Peugeot, and there's something about the fuel tank and parking on a slope and even at a quarter of a tank it will not start. *Cough* I may have done this before.

I could call the NRMA and I know (from experience) they will bring you $20 worth of fuel, enough to get you started and to the petrol station, and you have to pay them cash.

Except I gave my last $20 to my fifteen-year-old neighbour half an hour previously when he came in, cashless, needing a loan to get into the city.

I turn the key once more in desperation. The whole damn remote-locking thingo crumbles to pieces in my hand. There's a tiny bit of metal left stuck in the ignition. It's been threatening to do this for weeks. Of course it's today that it carks it.

It's almost 3.00 pm and it would take almost half an hour to walk up to school now, so I start calling my school

mum friends to pick up Henry. No one picks up their phones. I finally get onto my friend Nessie, who's not there but her husband is, and in a complicated series of mobile exchanges Henry gets collected by multiple people as the first messages filter through. I worried he'd fuss about me not being there with the gift for the teacher, but my friend Gaye managed to herd him down to the park with her tribe without incident.

Meanwhile I piled a very grumpy Tilly and woken-up Ivy out of the car and got Ivy into the pram and balanced the big slab cake on top. We walked to the park.

We met our friends, everyone had cake and biscuits and a big play and it was lovely.

The kids and I stopped on the way home at the ATM. I called the NRMA and the nice man arrived with his jerry can.

And even though I had sworn off chocolate (seems to affect breast-fed Ivy), I may have indulged in a couple of the teacher's chocolate balls. Now destined to be eaten by us. Sorry, Mrs Fisk.

My mum used to make these, but we made them into sausage shapes and always called them 'hairy sausages'. Then, when we were teenagers, we made them ball-shaped just for the sheer joy of serving around elegant plates of 'hairy balls'. Neither Tilly nor Ivy like coconut, so they invented 'naked balls' – just leaving off the coconut – which they think is hysterical.

They need just a little bit of Copha (vegetable shortening) to set nice and firmly; it also protects them a bit if they're gifts and they're not going to be refrigerated immediately. Mum's had sherry in them, I prefer brandy, but you can leave out the alcohol altogether and substitute Vanilla Extract (page 36) – 1 tablespoon is heaps.

CONTINUED >

Hairy Balls cont.

MAKES APPROX. 16

250 g (9 oz) arrowroot biscuits (see Note)
395 g (14 oz) tinned sweetened condensed milk, or
    250 ml (8½ fl oz/1 cup) homemade (see page 28)
3 heaped tablespoons unsweetened cocoa powder
2 tablespoons brandy, or use 1 tablespoon Vanilla
    Extract (page 36)
90 g (3 oz) Copha (vegetable shortening)
desiccated (shredded) coconut, for rolling (optional)

METHOD

Crush the biscuits very finely – I use a food processor
but have used a rolling pin in the past, which works
okay. In a large bowl, mix the finely crumbled
biscuits, the condensed milk, cocoa powder and
brandy.

Melt your Copha on the stove in a saucepan over
a low heat. Add to the rest of the ingredients
and stir to combine. Place in the fridge until firm
(approximately half an hour).

Using teaspoons, roll into balls slightly smaller
than a golf ball and roll the balls in coconut. Keep
refrigerated. These last well for weeks – if they're
really in your fridge for that long.

Notes

I use arrowroot biscuits, but you can use any crushed
plain biscuit you like.

    And you know what? Leave these to the last minute
to make. It's a safe bet. They take no time at all, and if
they're languishing in the fridge you run the risk of eating
them before you give them away.

    Or, do my trick and mess up your day so sufficiently
you fail to give them away at all. (I really wouldn't be
taking any planning advice from me.)

    You should see my Christmas gift sewing list *in the
week before Christmas*. Not very last-minute at all.

Chocolate Truffles

I make these every Christmas for my beloved
mother-in-law, Jennifer Jean Walmsley, who I
adore, because they make her close her eyes and lift
her shoulders and sigh with joy and say, 'Oooh, I
love Christmas. Ho ho ho.' I'm not making that up.
You would love her too.

MAKES 15

280 ml (9½ fl oz) pouring (single/light) cream
200 g (7 oz) plain dark chocolate
60 g (2 oz/½ cup) unsweetened cocoa powder,
    or drinking chocolate powder, for coating

METHOD

Pour the cream into a saucepan and heat gently to
just below boiling point – when there are bubbles
around the edges.

Remove from the heat and break the chocolate into
the warm cream.

Stir well until the chocolate melts and is totally
combined with the cream.

Transfer the mix to a glass or heatproof bowl, jug or
your stand mixer bowl and put into the fridge to cool
down for 30 minutes, then whisk, either by hand or
with a stand mixer whisk, for a few minutes until light
and fluffy.

Put the bowl back into the fridge for another
30 minutes, or until the mix is firm.

Sift the cocoa powder onto a tray and take spoonfuls
of mix, roll it into balls about the size of a walnut,
drop onto the tray to coat and pick up with a spoon.
Transfer to an airtight container in the fridge.

You need to work fast and not handle the mix for
longer than a few seconds or it will start to melt.

These store for about 1 week in an airtight container
in the fridge. They'll soften quickly out of the fridge
in warm weather.

Apricot Delight

Unless you buy organic apricots, you'll be using apricots with preservative 220 (sulfur dioxide), which can be dangerous for asthmatics and has been shown to cause hyperactivity and behavioural problems in children. Like many additives and preservatives, really.

I'll be honest: I don't always buy the preservative-free apricots, even though I know this. We have so few additives and preservatives around here that if I saw any effect of a handful of apricots served infrequently, I'd abandon them. But if you are all good with blackish organic apricots, then use those – they're better for you.

MAKES APPROX. 20

- 180 g (6½ oz/1 cup) dried apricots
- 55 g (2 oz/½ cup) ground almonds (almond meal)
- 2 tablespoons desiccated (shredded) coconut
- 2 tablespoons milk powder
- 2 tablespoons orange juice
- 85 g (3 oz) Copha (vegetable shortening)

METHOD

First, put the apricots in a heatproof bowl and pour boiling water over them. Leave to soak for 10 minutes.

Grease and line a loaf (bar) tin – about 20 × 10 cm (8 × 4 in).

Drain the liquid off the dried apricots and add the fruit to a food processor with the ground almonds. Pulse until finely ground.

Add the coconut, milk powder and orange juice and blend together well.

In a small saucepan, melt the Copha over a low heat, then add to the mix and blend again until a dough forms.

Press into the tin and refrigerate until firm. Cut into small squares and store in the fridge in an airtight container or jar for up to 4 weeks.

Chapter Seven

So Saucy

So Saucy

Over the years here on the farm, we've become increasingly and gratefully aware that we are not alone. We have my parents over the back fence. My dad is awesome in a crisis. And can find fox tracks in the grass like a magician, and has all sorts of solutions we'd never think of.

Many, many farmers feel like Robinson Crusoe or an afterthought to the rest of Australia. Like lonely solo worker bees, incredibly vulnerable to guilt and despair and a sense of failure.

Funnily enough, it was social media that really gave us a feeling of community. This really does ultimately affect all of us: every dairy farmer who stands over a cow down with milk fever, every market gardener looking at a crop of cabbages that were perfect yesterday and lie shredded after last night's hailstorm. Everything that affects the person trying to grow the food we eat affects all of us.

And THAT, friends, is the sound of the food revolution in motion.

No thinking person wants to eat industrially produced food that suppresses animals into systemic misery and ultimately poisons us all.

We don't want vegetables that have to be washed in bleach to remove the poisonous chemicals they've been doused in to reduce bugs and maximise shelf life.

The change is here. People are growing food differently, on small and large scales, and people are connecting with it.

Over here we are held up by friends and strangers offering help, advice, visiting for tours or buying whatever we produce. We're a tiny little farm. But it turns out people seriously care whether small farms fail or succeed, and this can only be a marvellous thing. And when it comes down to brass tacks, we feel like we've got the cavalry here.

Just when you think the sweetness has gone out of it and your heart is a drone, how about that, you find oranges on the orange tree at the back of the coffee grove.

Thankful for oranges. And chickens. And farm crew. And you. And sauces made from scratch.

The team (left to right, standing): Ellie Burke, Greg Thornton, Sarah Worboys, Stephanie Debeck, Oliver Stones; (seated) Annette Wright, Henry Walmsley, Adam Walmsley, Fiona Weir Walmsley.

Chilli Sauce

While I was recipe testing the Harissa (page 80) for this book, I kept trying it with capsicum (bell pepper) and ending up with chilli sauce, which I loved so much I've included it here too. This is now a fridge staple of ours, kept in a squeezy bottle, to drizzle on baked potatoes or pizza or to pimp a cheese toastie or top nachos or enchiladas. Pictured on page 212.

MAKES 600 G (1 LB 5 OZ/2½ CUPS)

2 red capsicums (bell peppers)
1 tablespoon ground cumin
1 tablespoon whole cumin seeds
1 tablespoon ground coriander
150 g (5½ oz/approx. 5) fresh long red chillies, de-seeded and chopped
5 garlic cloves, peeled
2 teaspoons salt
2 tablespoons olive oil

METHOD

Wrap your whole capsicums in foil and bake in a 200°C (390°F) oven for 35 minutes. Remove from the oven and leave in the foil to cool for 20 minutes. Once cooled, carefully peel off the capsicum skin, cut in half, scrape out the seeds and discard them.

Put all the ingredients in a food processor and blend to a sauce.

Store in the fridge with a layer of oil on top for up to 1 month.

Super Simple Tomato Sauce

When it's summertime and tomatoes are in season, this is a super low-effort dinner. Use homemade pasta (see page 34) if you're up for it, or keep a bag of nice pasta in your pantry for a quick meal.

MAKES 350 ML (12 FL OZ)

4 large ripe tomatoes, cut into quarters
handful of dried herbs
splash of olive oil

METHOD

Preheat the oven to 175°C (345°F).

Place the quartered tomatoes on a lined baking tray and sprinkle with herbs, olive oil and salt and pepper.

Bake for 25–30 minutes then whiz until smooth in a food processor.

Use stirred through pasta. Yummmm.

Ketchup

If you have children, you probably have some kind of relationship with tomato sauce. Mine is a bit fraught, and here is my alternative. I have been known to store it in an old tomato sauce bottle. No child has ever really been fooled.

MAKES 1 LITRE (34 FL OZ/4 CUPS)

2 brown or white onions, finely sliced
1 tablespoon olive oil or ghee
1 kg (2 lb 3 oz) tomatoes, chopped
100 g (3½ oz) Brown Sugar (page 28)
100 g (3½ oz/5 tablespoons) tomato paste
    (concentrated purée)
1 teaspoon mixed (pumpkin pie) spice
2–3 bay leaves
170 ml (5½ fl oz/⅔ cup) apple-cider vinegar

METHOD

In a large heavy-based saucepan, ideally stainless steel or cast iron, cook the onions in the oil over a medium heat until translucent.

Add all the other ingredients, season to taste with salt, and cook for at least 1 hour over a low heat, stirring intermittently.

Once thoroughly cooked and reduced in volume, remove the bay leaves and blend with a hand-held blender or in a food processor until really smooth.

Keeps refrigerated for 6 weeks.

Tartare Sauce

When I was little, on a Sunday there was Shakespeare on TV at lunchtime. My beautiful mum, theatrical to her bones and an educator at heart, said she'd buy fish and chips for lunch if we'd watch whatever Shakespeare was on that Sunday. (To the very end.) We watched just about every Shakespeare play, nibbling chips and dunking fish into the tartare sauce that came with it. I've had a strong feeling for tartare sauce (and *The Merchant of Venice*) ever since. Pictured on page 213.

MAKES APPROX. 400 ML (13½ FL OZ)

2 free-range egg yolks
1 tablespoon lemon juice or white-wine vinegar
250 ml (8½ fl oz/1 cup) grapeseed or rice bran oil,
    or other neutral-flavoured oil
¼ teaspoon white pepper
50 g (1¾ oz/¼ cup) pickled cucumber (see page 86),
    drained and finely chopped
1 tablespoon capers, drained and finely chopped
1 tablespoon flat-leaf (Italian) parsley, finely chopped

METHOD

Whisk the egg yolks with a pinch of salt and lemon juice for about 1 minute, or until smooth.

Very slowly and gradually whisk in the oil, taste for acidity and adjust with more lemon juice and salt. Add the pepper.

Add the chopped cucumbers, capers and parsley.

Refrigerate in an airtight container for up to 1 week, with plastic wrap pressed onto the surface to prevent a skin forming.

Béchamel

I make this a lot. It's a simple white sauce that I use for lasagne, mac and cheese, veggie bakes and fish or chicken pie.

MAKES APPROX. 500 ML (17 FL OZ/2 CUPS)

1 tablespoon butter
1 tablespoon plain (all-purpose) flour
500 ml (17 fl oz/2 cups) full-cream (whole) milk
½ teaspoon sea salt
½ teaspoon ground or freshly grated nutmeg

METHOD

In a saucepan over a medium heat, cook the butter and flour together until it bubbles.

Slowly add the milk, whisking until fully incorporated.

Add the salt and nutmeg and stir over a medium heat until the sauce thickens to coat a spoon.

Barbecue Sauce

This sauce is a great accompaniment to meat, or on a burger, but it comes into its own as a glaze for beef or pork, either cooked on a barbecue, or slow-cooked or roasted. Our favourite way to use this is to paint it onto ribs before and after slow-cooking them. It feels like a lot of ingredients and a fuss, but it's worth it. Yum.

MAKES APPROX. 500 ML (17 FL OZ/2 CUPS)

1 onion, finely chopped
4 garlic cloves, minced
125 g (4½ oz/½ cup) butter
¼ teaspoon cayenne pepper
2 teaspoons paprika
2 teaspoons mustard powder
1 teaspoon salt
½ teaspoon black pepper
100 g (3½ oz/5 tablespoons) tomato paste
  (concentrated purée)
185 ml (6 fl oz/¾ cup) apple-cider vinegar
75 g (2¾ oz) dark Brown Sugar (page 28)
375 ml (12½ fl oz/1½ cups) water

METHOD

In a saucepan, sauté the onion and garlic in the butter over a medium heat, then add the spices and cook for another minute. Add all the remaining ingredients and stir well to combine. Cook over a low heat for about 15 minutes, stirring intermittently.

Keeps well in the fridge for about 3 weeks.

Notes

You can make this gluten-free by using maize cornflour (cornstarch) instead of wheat flour. For the record, I've tried it with soy milk to make it dairy-free and it was not delicious.
  Quite often, I'll throw in a couple of handfuls of grated cheese at the end and stir until melted to make a simple cheese sauce.

Apple Sauce

This simple apple sauce makes the world a better place. If you have a huge amount of apples on hand you can make up a large batch and hot-water-bath-process the jars to keep on your pantry shelves for months. Alternatively, make it up as required and enjoy with pork in particular.

MAKES APPROX. 500 ML (17 FL OZ/2 CUPS)

4 green apples, peeled, cored and chopped
250 ml (8½ fl oz/1 cup) water
55 g (2 oz/¼ cup) white sugar
½ teaspoon ground cinnamon

METHOD

Place all the ingredients in a saucepan set over a medium heat and cook for approximately 10 minutes, or until the fruit is fully broken down. You can mash the finished sauce with a fork for a chunky version, or blitz with a hand-held blender for a smoother finish. Keeps refrigerated in an airtight container for 1 week.

Chocolate Sauce

For all the delicious uses: cold, on ice cream; warm, drizzled over cakes and dessert plates; or cooled and used as a ganache spread over a cake.

MAKES APPROX. 350 ML (12 FL OZ)

200 g (7 oz) cooking chocolate
250 ml (8½ fl oz/1 cup) pouring (single/light) cream

METHOD

Break the chocolate into a heatproof bowl, pour the cream over and place the bowl over a saucepan of simmering water. Stir frequently until the chocolate is melted and incorporated into the cream.

Use warm and fresh or refrigerate and gently heat again to liquefy.

Note

You can always stir in 1 tablespoon of liquor (try Grand Marnier or Cointreau) at the end to make it, as the kids say, *extra*.

Berry Coulis

My primary use for berry coulis is to serve with Torte Caprese (page 138), but you can use it in its own right over ice cream or to jazz up a pretty plate of summer fruit. I learnt to make coulis many many years ago at Rose Blues Cafe, where we served it drizzled over baked cheesecake (see page 188).

MAKES APPROX. 300 ML (10 FL OZ)

220 g (8 oz/1 cup) fresh or frozen berries
115 g (4 oz/½ cup) caster (superfine) sugar
1 tablespoon lemon juice

METHOD

Place all the ingredients in a saucepan and cook over a medium heat for approximately 5 minutes until the berries are broken down, stirring constantly.

Blend with a hand-held blender or in a food processor until very smooth.

Chapter Eight

Jams, Spreads, *and* Other Benefits *to* Toast

You Are My Jam

When I started dating Adam in 1997, he was a retailer. He was a friend of a friend and had been at college with my brother.

One night right at the beginning, my sister Naomi and I were both invited to a housewarming party at Adam's new share house overlooking the beach at Queenscliff. It was quite a pad.

Naomi and I rocked into the party a couple of hours early to help cook pizzas and set up the food. I was, I think, technically a might-be-girlfriend. And oh so hoped to be. He was so damned fine and I was a bit smitten. And hopeful. And there to make pizzas.

Naomi, an excellent cook, was responsible for cooking the bacon, and as she shook a frypan I stood in the kitchen with her and continued a flirting program with Adam, which seemed to be going quite well.

All of a sudden the fluffy white jumper Naomi was wearing went up in flames. Actually MY fluffy white jumper that she'd borrowed went up in flames. The floppy polyester totally fire-attracting sleeve must have dipped in the exposed gas flame as Naomie crispied the bacon. And whoosh. Fire raced up her back.

Without a breath of delay, Adam leapt across me, rolled her to the floor and batted the flames out with his hands.

Oh, my heart.

She was unharmed, let me rush in to say. A minor, minor burn on her abdomen and one of the other flatmates, a doctor, confirmed her all good, leaving me to my heart. In my mouth. And my hero. Washing his hands sheepishly.

And really, that was that.

What party? I don't really remember it. I remember sometime much later that night, as the party wound down, that Adam suggested we go for a walk on the beach (just out their back door for heaven's sake) that ended in our first kiss. And for it being so many years ago, I can remember clearly thinking: well, this is it then. This man, that chin, that smile, those arms, that chest – he is my jam. Still and always.

Bacon Jam

This is one of my favourite edibles to give as a gift to people who are not vegetarian.

If you've never tried it, it's like a bacon-y relish. It came about because I used to make a lot of onion jam as it went very well on a cheese sandwich, or on a cheese plate, or spread on the bottom of a blind-baked tart case before pouring a savoury custard over, making an excellent tart.

Then, once, I put our home-grown bacon into my onion jam, because it was in the fridge and I'd heard about bacon jam somewhere … and I never made onion jam again.

It's not a cheap jam to make if you buy proper bacon and use good maple syrup, which you should. But it's worth it when you spread it on toast underneath a poached egg, or use it instead of tomato pizza sauce on a pizza, or spread it on a blind-baked tart case before making a quiche or tart. Oh, my goodness.

MAKES 3 × 300 G (10½ OZ) JARS

500 g (1 lb 2 oz) sliced bacon, finely chopped
2 brown onions, finely diced
3 garlic cloves, finely chopped
1 tablespoon olive oil
125 ml (4 fl oz/½ cup) apple-cider vinegar
115 g (4 oz/½ cup, firmly packed) dark Brown Sugar (page 28)
60 ml (2 fl oz/¼ cup) pure maple syrup
185 ml (6 fl oz/¾ cup) black coffee

METHOD

In a cast-iron pot, if you have one, or a very heavy-based frying pan, cook the bacon, onion and garlic in the olive oil over a medium heat. Cook thoroughly until the bacon is browned and the onion is cooked through.

Add the vinegar, sugar, maple syrup and coffee, stir well and bring back to the boil.

Reduce the heat and cook for approximately 1 hour, stirring occasionally, until the jam is jammy and thick and viscous.

Let it cool, then store in jars in the fridge for up to 1 month.

Rhubarb Chia Jam

This is a nice refined-sugar-free jam, and although it doesn't have anywhere near the shelf life of a traditional jam, it's quick to make. For a completely raw alternative, use 500 g (1 lb 2 oz) of any fresh berry, for example raspberries, and in that case, no cooking is required.

MAKES 3 × 200 G (7 OZ) JARS

250 g (9 oz) rhubarb, washed and trimmed to 2 cm (¾ in) pieces
60 ml (2 fl oz/¼ cup) water
250 g (9 oz/1⅔ cups) fresh strawberries, hulled
2 tablespoons maple syrup
50 g (1¾ oz/⅓ cup) chia seeds

METHOD

Place the rhubarb and water in a saucepan and cook for 5 minutes over a medium heat.

Blend with a hand-held blender or in a food processor until smooth. Add the strawberries and the maple syrup and blend until smooth. Add the chia seeds and mix by hand until just incorporated.

Spoon into clean jars and allow to set in the fridge for at least 4 hours.

Keeps for about 3 weeks in the fridge.

Rhubarb and Strawberry Jam

Because we grow rhubarb and strawberries, this is the jam that we make most often. I love the tartness and the sweetness together. Rhubarb is delicious cooked all ways, but is particularly delicious in jam. We blitz this with a hand-held blender as part of the process because I like a smooth jam, without stringy rhubarb pieces. Of course, please interpret this as you like. It doesn't need to be blitzed, it's a personal preference. A bit like whether the scone needs butter as well as rhubarb and strawberry jam. Or just jam and cream. You choose.

MAKES 3 × 300 G (10½ OZ) JARS

650 g (1 lb 7 oz) rhubarb (one good-sized bunch), washed and trimmed to 3 cm (1¼ in) lengths
250 g (9 oz/1⅔ cups) strawberries, hulled
1 green apple, quartered and cored, skin left on
juice of 2 lemons
650 g (1 lb 7 oz/3 cups) white sugar

METHOD

Put the rhubarb, strawberries and apple in a large saucepan and add enough water to come about one-quarter of the way up the fruit (i.e. just a bit – don't drown it).

Add the lemon juice and simmer until the fruit is soft. Take off the heat and whiz thoroughly with a hand-held blender.

Add the sugar, then return to a medium heat and cook, stirring frequently, until it's 'jammy' and

1. hisses off the bottom of the pan when stirred, and

2. gels on a cold plate from the freezer.

Pour into sterilised jars (see Note on page 86).

To be certain about shelf life you would want to hot-water-process the jars by submerging them in a saucepan of boiling water for 10 minutes to create a vacuum under the lid, but as long as the jam goes into sterilised jars I've never had any trouble.

Apple Jelly Jam

There's a local family-run orchard near here, Glenbernie Orchard, that does lots of great things, including pick-your-own apples in apple season. Every autumn, we go and pick boxes of apples.

Sometimes I get busy, and after apple-picking day, an occasional box just sits around and sits around on the floor of my pantry.

I look at them every day and feel guilty about them ageing in the corner – all that work in a box. You know?

Once there was such a box, and my gorgeous sister Naomi, inherently a woman of action, showed up and peeled and cored the entire box for me (less five, which wouldn't actually fit in the stockpot) using our slightly addictive apple slinky machine.

I turned the whole pot into apple jelly. Apple jelly is not really that popular in Australia. I'd read about it, and I had occasionally seen it for sale at the Berry Sourdough Cafe, but I remember that pot of jam was a bit epic.

I followed my usual recipe, which was inspired by one of David Lebovitz's, except that after boiling the jam for over half an hour it was still not setting. At all. I considered passing it off as apple syrup, but instead poured it all into sterilised jars and left it for a few hours, blindly hoping it'd set. It didn't.

So, in the middle of making lunch for visitors, I poured it all back into the pot, washed and sterilised the jars again, and left it boiling until it had reduced by one-third. THEN it set.

OH MY GOODNESS, this JAM. It's an appley autumny burst of flavour. Light. Sweet. Glorious.

Afterwards, I remember Mum saying she thought something like apple jam would need the pectin in the skins of the apple to set. She said she'd never made jam but has been around a lot of jam makers. Oh my goodness, yes! In the hurry to clean up the box of neglected apples, I had fed the skins to the pigs and completely forgotten that, actually, I always included them.

It was kind of a testament that I am incapable of following a recipe properly, *even my own.*

You? Are you a recipe follower or a recipe general-sense-gatherer? A forget-the-recipe-let's-wing-it cook? Or are you I-LAUGH-in-the-face-of-recipes-ah-ha-ha-haaaaa?

Fruit skin. It's essential.

MAKES 3 × 300 ML (10 FL OZ) JARS

2 kg (4 lb 6 oz) apples
1 litre (34 fl oz/4 cups) water
600 g (1 lb 5 oz) white sugar
60 ml (2 fl oz/¼ cup) freshly squeezed lemon juice
2 teaspoons brandy

METHOD

Rinse the apples, cut them into quarters, remove the seeds, then cut them again into eighths and put them into a very large stockpot.

Add the water, cover and bring to the boil. Reduce the heat to a simmer and cook for about 20 minutes until the apples are soft.

Line a large mesh sieve with a piece of muslin (cheesecloth) and set it over another heavy-based saucepan, then carefully pour or ladle the apples and the liquid into the sieve.

Let it stand for a few hours and don't press the apples to extract juice or your jam will be cloudy.

You should have about 1 litre (34 fl oz/4 cups) apple juice at the end. Discard the solids.

Now add the sugar and lemon juice to the apple juice and bring it to a boil.

Cook the apple jam until it's thick and reduced in volume by approximately one-third. It's ready when you put a small dollop on a chilled plate out of the freezer, run your finger through it and the track you make stays clear. If the jam runs back together, cook it some more.

Once it's at setting point, take it off the heat, stir in the brandy and ladle it into sterilised jars (see Note on page 86), then put the lids on tightly.

You can follow the hot-water bath instructions on page 39 to make it shelf stable. Refrigerate after opening.

Note

I've made this with both red and green apples, but actually my preference is 1 kg (2 lb 3 oz) of each.

Lemon Curd

You know it's really lemon butter, right?
I mean, how dare it call itself a curd? That's a
cheese, surely.

It was always 'lemon butter' when I was
growing up, and it was delivered in precious jarfuls
by Lauris Buckman, a very special neighbour of
ours, who was friends with my grandma, who
bottle-fed me and my quad siblings when we were
one big stressful line of babies all needing feeding
at once, who taught me at Sunday school when
I was little and who walked my own children
around Gerringong in their pram while I was at
Sunday morning church services, so I could listen.
And rest.

Lauris would never call it lemon curd but
I wondered if you would turn to this page unless I
did? So let's, between us, call it Lemon Butter and
toast Lauris with it on a scone, or scooped into tart
cases, or piped into pastry, or, best of all, eaten
smeared on an Oatcake (page 249). Try it. The
crisp oatiness offsets the sharp sweet butteriness
absolutely divinely. Divinity a bit like Lauris's.

MAKES 1 × 500 ML (17 FL OZ/2 CUP) JAR

120 g (4½ oz) unsalted butter
grated zest and juice of 2 large lemons (about
    125 ml/4 fl oz/½ cup juice; see Note)
165 g (6 oz/¾ cup) white sugar
3 free-range eggs, lightly whisked

METHOD

In a heavy-based saucepan, combine the butter,
lemon juice and zest and the sugar.

Stir continuously over a low–medium heat just until
the sugar dissolves. Take the saucepan off the heat
and add the eggs, one at a time, beating well.

Return the saucepan to the stove and, over a
medium heat and stirring constantly, cook the curd
until it thickens. Be very careful not to let it boil,
it will curdle.

Pour the curd into a hot sterilised jar (see Note on
page 86) for storage in the refrigerator for 2 weeks,
or use immediately.

Note

I'm not sure that lime curd is not actually even more
delicious than lemon. Substitute the grated zest and
juice of 3 limes (about 125 ml/4 fl oz/½ cup juice) for the
lemon and proceed as per the recipe method.

Peanut Butter

Really, once you've made your own peanut butter I'd challenge you to ever go back to store-bought stuff. Homemade is just So. Much. Yummier.

Sadly, I have never really been able to try it out on anyone other than Tilly as everyone else in this household hates and detests the stuff.

Henry will actually move chairs at the breakfast table to get away from peanut butter on toast – mine or his sister's. But if you like peanut butter, give this a whirl!

Pre-roasted and salted peanuts make this very straightforward, but obviously you can roast and salt your own nuts.

MAKES 1 × 1 LITRE (34 FL OZ/4 CUP) JAR

640 g (1 lb 7 oz/4 cups) peanuts, roasted and salted

METHOD

Throw 480 g (1 lb 1 oz/3 cups) of the peanuts into the food processor and whiz for a good couple of minutes. It'll take that long for the nuts to break down and become oily. Add the last cup of nuts and whiz up to your desired chunkiness.

I don't want to overstate it but *this is the best peanut butter you'll ever eat,* which is why I'm suggesting you make a litre jar of it. Just halve the recipe if that feels excessive.

Peanut, Almond and Brazil Nut Butter

Journal entry from 2010:

It was Henry's first day back at school today and Tilly announced it would be her special day too. To qualify, it had to involve: making gingerbread men, picking flowers, painting a rainbow, and peanut butter sandwiches for lunch.

I've been feeling a bit guilty about my middle child this week. There's been a lot of requests for craft and a story here and there and play-with-me that have gone unrequited.

What the heck. The washing, the cleaning, the tidying up – it'll all still be there tomorrow. Why not have a day painting rainbows?

We flew through the list until I discovered we were out of peanut butter. I usually make our own, but I had a few different nuts on hand I wanted to try out.

So we made peanut, almond and brazil nut butter. PAB butter. No, not very catchy. Yummy though.

Here's how it goes.

MAKES 1 × 500 ML (17 FL OZ/2 CUP) JAR

160 g (5½ oz/1 cup) natural peanuts
80 g (2¾ oz/½ cup) raw almonds
80 g (2¾ oz/½ cup) raw Brazil nuts
1 teaspoon salt
2 tablespoons peanut oil

METHOD

Roast all the nuts either in a dry heavy-based frying pan or toast in a 180°C (360°F) oven for 5 minutes until golden. We used peanut kernels, which had a papery husk. We got most (okay, some) of the husks off after they'd cooled down, but got bored and just threw them in, husks and all. More fibre.

Put the nuts and the salt into a food processor and process for at least 5 minutes. It's clattering and loud and noisy but it takes at least this long for the oils to start coming out of the nuts and the mix to start clumping.

Then slowly add your peanut oil – you might not need 2 whole tablespoons. We like ours really spreadable, but you don't have to use oil at all if you like it thickish.

That's it.

Tilly likes hers on sandwiches. I think it's gorgeous on hot toast.

I could pretend we ate our sandwiches/toast nicely at the table. With placemats. Maybe even napery. We didn't.

Another essential Tilly-declared element to a *special* day? A tent in the middle of the kitchen.

Happy days.

To make straight almond butter, start with 310 g (11 oz/2 cups) raw almonds and proceed as above. All nut butter is better using nuts that have been toasted in the oven for 5 minutes first.

Chapter Nine

Snacka-roonies

Snackaroonies

If you are what you eat, then what are you?

I am not an apple, although I do love a sharp crunchy granny smith. (Better cooked, though. With a touch of sugar. And mixed with blackberries and topped with crumble. Mmmm.)

Maybe I am a kale chip, earnest, green, crisp when toasted.

I think I'd like to be a muesli bar – good for you, sweet, well intentioned – but suspect I am in fact a deeply uncool baked bean.

Snackaroonies are the in-betweeners that make days brighter and a long walk more interesting and lunchboxes worth opening.

If you are what you eat, make it delicious.

Hot Chips

The best potato to use for a hot chip is a floury potato. It'll hold its shape but will have a fluffy interior. You're looking for a potato with a thin white skin – Dutch creams are ideal, or I've often used sebago, and the other variety highly revered for chips (that you might have to grow yourself) is kennebec.

You can make these two ways. The first is deep-frying them, but it takes a lot of oil (which is then left over) and can be kind of messy. Also, oil. The second is in the oven. I make them both ways depending on my mood. So, I've included both here.

SERVES 4

In the oven
   1 kg (2 lb 3 oz) white-skinned potatoes
   80 ml (2½ fl oz/⅓ cup) olive oil

In oil
   1 kg (2 lb 3 oz) white-skinned potatoes
   1.25 litres (42 fl oz/5 cups) canola or grapeseed oil

METHOD

Scrub your potatoes thoroughly if yours are like mine and covered in dirt.

Peel them or don't – entirely up to you.

To make chips in the oven, cut the potatoes into 1 cm (½ in) chips. Put them in a bowl of cold water for 15 minutes (this helps remove the starch) while you preheat your oven to 200°C (390°F) and oil a baking tray.

Drain your chips thoroughly and dry by rubbing them in a clean tea towel (dish towel).

Toss them in a large bowl with the oil. Look, I know it's another bowl to wash up, but this will mean better oil coverage than putting them on the tray and sloshing the oil over.

Lift out of the bowl and put onto the baking tray.

Bake for 45 minutes, or until crispy.

Salt with sea salt after cooking, before eating.

The secret to hot chips in oil is cooking them twice. I never peel my potatoes when making chips, but you can if you're a purist.

Cut the potatoes into 1 cm (½ in) chips. Put them in a bowl of cold water for 15 minutes (this helps remove the starch) while your oil is heating up.

Place a heavy frying pan (I use a cast-iron 30 cm/ 12 in round pan) over a high heat and fill with the oil. Heat it until it reaches 160°C (320°F) on a candy thermometer. If you don't have one, just heat the oil until a chip sizzles madly immediately when you put one in it.

After soaking for 15 minutes, dry the chips thoroughly in a clean tea towel (dish towel) and carefully put into the very hot oil.

Cook all the chips until they are cooked and tender, about 5 minutes. I cook them in two batches to avoid overcrowding the pan.

Remove the chips with a metal slotted spoon (don't use plastic!) and drain on a tray while cooking the next batch.

Once the chips are all pre-cooked, reheat your oil to 185°C (355°F).

Cook the chips a second time until deep golden-brown and crispy. Remove with a metal slotted spoon and toss in sea salt.

Notes

If you're making these for a party or to serve with drinks, you can do the first stage of cooking earlier in the day and leave well-drained chips wrapped in paper towel ready to do the second fry right before they're served.

If your chips are browning in the oil but are not yet crispy, turn the heat down. They don't crisp up once out of the oil – you want to take them out crispy, so hold your nerve, leave them in until they're crunchy, and if they are cooking too fast for this, turn down your oil.

Potato Crisps

When Adam and I lived in London for two years, I loved the way the English call chips crisps. I love the way it differentiates them from hot chips, and the utter descriptiveness of 'crisp'.

We first made these out of purple potatoes many years ago, sliced finely and so perfect in their purple crispness. Some potatoes are better than others to make into chips. You want a waxy potato ideally, usually a red-skinned variety like a pontiac or desiree.

SERVES 4

3–4 waxy potatoes (ideally red-skinned)
splash of vinegar
500 ml (17 fl oz/2 cups) light oil for frying, like rice bran or light olive oil

METHOD

Leaving the skin on, carefully mandoline your spuds into thin slices. If you don't have a mandoline, just slice them as fine as you can. Don't make them paper thin, think chip-width.

Wash the chips well; it gets rid of starch.

Bring a pot of water to the boil, add a good splash of vinegar, and par-boil the chips for about 2 minutes.

Drain and dry the chips thoroughly with a tea towel (dish towel) or paper towel.

Put the oil in a frying pan over a high heat and heat until it reaches 160–180°C (320–360°F) on a candy thermometer. If you don't have one, heat the oil until a chip sizzles madly immediately when you put one in it. In batches, put your chips into the oil and fry until just golden.

Remove the chips with a metal slotted spoon (don't use plastic!). Drain on paper towel and toss with sea salt.

Eat immediately, or these store pretty well for a week or so in a sealed container.

Note

If your chips are browning but are not crispy, turn the heat down. They don't crisp up once out of the oil – you want to take them out crispy, so hold your nerve, leave them in until they're crunchy, and if they are cooking too fast for this, turn down your oil.

Baked Beans

Beans, beans, good for your heart.

What kid doesn't love baked beans? Well, actually, I didn't. I don't think I even tried them until I was about nineteen and at university and when baked beans and two-minute noodles seemed to be adequate nutrition. In total. Maybe with vegemite toast as a backup. Been there? Anyone?

Anyway, I now love them. The smallies loved them. The teenagers still love them. So, I make them. Here's my recipe.

A note on beans: Navy beans are the traditional and best beans for baking. They're also sold as Great Northern Beans in Australia. Cannellini beans are good too. If you happen to live near an awesome Italian grocery, you'll usually be able to find big, very economically priced bags of dry navy beans. Wish I knew THAT when I was nineteen.

SERVES 4

- 375 g (13 oz) dried beans, or 800 g (1 lb 12 oz) tinned beans, drained
- 2 onions, finely diced
- oil, for frying
- 6 tomatoes, puréed in a blender, or 400 g (14 oz) tinned tomatoes
- 1 tablespoon dijon mustard
- 1 tablespoon worcestershire sauce
- 2 tablespoons tomato paste (concentrated purée)
- 1½ tablespoons Brown Sugar (page 28)
- 2 teaspoons smoked paprika
- 1 teaspoon salt
- ½ teaspoon pepper

METHOD

If using dried beans, soak your beans all day or overnight, then rinse and cook over a medium heat for about 30 minutes on the stove, covered with fresh water, until tender.

Preheat your oven to 160°C (320°F).

Sauté the onion in a little oil in a heavy-based ovenproof saucepan, then add your tomatoes, mustard, worcestershire sauce, tomato paste and brown sugar. Cook for a minute then add the beans plus the paprika, salt and pepper and bake in the oven with the lid on for 45 minutes.

Loving those beans. Optional: For extra smokiness, add in a tablespoon of chipotle peppers with the beans if you happen to have chipotle on hand.

Kale Chips

Kale chips don't really need a recipe, more like some general guidelines.

I absolutely love kale chips, so does my dad, and my middle child, Matilda.

We sprinkle them over salads or eggs, or snack on them, or have them on the side of dinner plates.

If you've ever eaten a really good kale chip you know they should be salty, crunchy and crispy.

We grow curly kale mainly for kale chips, and for Ivy's pet guinea pigs who truly love it, and if you know of a better way to eat kale – flaky, crunchy and salty – please tell me.

Here's how you make them:

SERVES 2–4

- 1 bunch curly kale (curly kale works much better than cavolo nero)
- 2 tablespoons good olive oil
- 1 tablespoon good sea salt flakes (see Note)

METHOD

Preheat your oven to 170°C (340°F).

Strip the kale off its stems and tear into pieces. Put onto an unlined baking tray.

Drizzle the olive oil over, sprinkle on the salt and smoosh it all together with clean hands.

You're trying to cover all the kale with oil, but not so much that it's soggy. You want a single layer of kale only. If there's kale on top of kale it won't crisp up properly.

Bake for 10–15 minutes. THIS IS THE IMPORTANT BIT. Start checking at 10 minutes and anything that's turning from dark green to brown TAKE OFF THE TRAY and set aside while the rest cook. (Use tongs. It'll be tempting to pick one up with your fingers and eat it, don't do it, they will be the temperature of the sun.)

Once they're all crispy, remove from the oven. The crisps will store for about 3 days max in an airtight container – good luck keeping them for that long.

Note

Of course, you can use ordinary granulated salt, but if you haven't discovered sea salt flakes you should get among it – you'll never look back.

Beef Sausage Rolls

Quite an unattractive food, really.

But oh so yummy. Homemade sausage rolls. With tomato sauce. An Australian kid's birthday party is *incomplete* without them.

I remember when my godson Sebastian turned six (he's now eighteen), and he had a spectacular Star Wars–themed party complete with R2-D2 cupcakes and a Darth Vader piñata.

I made sausage rolls for him, and they ate them slathered in tomato sauce, supervised by his mother, Nessie, dressed extremely convincingly as Princess Leia.

So, Beef Sausage Rolls. If you've never made them you won't believe how easy they are, particularly if you shortcut and use store-bought puff pastry.

MAKES 16 SMALL SAUSAGE ROLLS, OR 8 LARGE

500 g (1 lb 2 oz) minced (ground) beef
1 large onion, finely diced
1 large carrot, grated
2 free-range eggs, lightly beaten
big handful of flat-leaf (Italian) parsley, finely chopped
1 teaspoon dried mixed herbs
4 sheets frozen puff pastry, partially thawed, or 1 batch Rough Puff Pastry (page 51)
approx. 60 ml (2 fl oz/¼ cup) full-cream (whole) milk, for brushing
sesame seeds, for sprinkling

METHOD

Preheat the oven to 200°C (390°F) and line a baking tray with baking paper.

Combine the mince, onion, carrot, egg, parsley and dried herbs and season with salt and pepper in a large bowl. Mix well.

If using frozen pastry, cut the pastry sheets in half into rectangles (so you have eight pieces in total).

If using a batch of homemade rough puff, cut it into four pieces, roll out each piece to roughly a 30 cm (12 in) square and cut in half so you have eight pieces.

Shape a solid sausage of mince mix along one long edge of pastry. Brush the edges with milk and roll up the pastry to enclose the mince in a sausage.

Brush the top with milk and sprinkle with sesame seeds. Trim the ends of the rolls and cut each roll into two if making small sausage rolls. Put onto the baking tray.

Bake for 20–25 minutes or until puffy, golden and deliciously oozing.

Serve with tomato sauce and Princess Leia ear-muff hairdo.

Vegetarian Sausage Rolls

Really! So good. You totally get the sense of a sausage roll and they're perfect for vegetarians.

I invented these for my own kids' birthday parties before we moved to the farm, when the whole family was vegetarian.

They're delicious and you won't miss the meat.

I served them with sweet chilli sauce or tomato sauce at little kids' parties all those years ago, but for dinner I would serve them with steamed veggies. A rocket (arugula), pine nut and haloumi salad would go perfectly, too.

MAKES 16 SMALL SAUSAGE ROLLS, OR 8 LARGE

150 g (5½ oz/1½ cups) Breadcrumbs (page 26)
60 g (2 oz/½ cup) rolled oats
1 large zucchini (courgette), finely grated
2 carrots, finely grated
1 onion, finely grated
150 g (5½ oz/1 cup) chickpeas (cooked or tinned and drained)
2 free-range eggs
1 tablespoon tahini
1 teaspoon salt and a few good grinds of black pepper
1 tablespoon tomato paste (concentrated purée)
2 teaspoons dried mixed herbs
4 sheets puff pastry, partially thawed, or 1 batch Rough Puff Pastry (page 51)
1 tablespoon full-cream (whole) milk
sesame seeds, for sprinkling

METHOD

Preheat the oven to 180°C (360°F).

This recipe is easiest if you have a food processor, but you can easily do it without. If you have a processor, whiz your breadcrumbs and oats until fine. Otherwise, make your breadcrumbs and bash up your oats in a mortar and pestle.

Add your zucchini, carrot and onion to the processor and whiz, or add to the breadcrumbs and oats in a big bowl and mix well.

Add the chickpeas to the mix and process well until smoothish. Add the eggs, tahini, salt and pepper, tomato paste and mixed herbs and process again, or just stir up well in the bowl.

If using frozen pastry, cut the pastry sheets in half into rectangles (so you have eight pieces in total).

If using a batch of homemade rough puff, cut it into four pieces, roll out each piece to roughly a 30 cm (12 in) square and cut in half so you have eight pieces.

Spoon some mix down one long side. Paint the edges with milk (to help the pastry stick) and roll up into a long sausage. Cut into two if making small sausage rolls and paint the top with milk. Sprinkle with sesame seeds.

Bake for about 20 minutes, or until golden.

Hide them from the kids unless you want them all eaten (note to self). Also hide from Adam. In fact, make an extra batch because they freeze beautifully (uncooked) and you can take them out and cook from frozen for a snack. Add 10 minutes to the baking time, but make sure to check so they don't burn.

Because it's all about *satisfying* snacks. Or any excuse to crack out the tahini, really.

Muesli Bars

Do you know, my very first blog post – in May 2009 – was a muesli bar recipe. In fact, this very one. It was before I'd thought about actually including photos of the food, and unless you are either of my two sisters you probably never read it.

There's something else about these little bars: before there was Buena Vista Farm, there was Buena Vista Farm Bikkies, and before the Bikkies there was Grub Organics. I never actually got to the retail stage, but I put way more time into the recipe testing phase than I ever did with the bikkies. It was a little organic snack food company for kids that I was building with my friend Anita Sheridan-Roddick, one of the best home cooks I've ever met, and my muesli bars were probably the product I was most proud of.

I am extremely serious about muesli bars. They have to be hard, solid, seedy, not too sweet, a bit chewy and have lots of toasted oats.

What I love about this one is that it's very flexible, depending on what is in your cupboard. The original recipe had wheatgerm and pepitas (pumpkin seeds). Include them if you're inclined. Just sub in whatever you like. Chuck in apricots. Dates. Swap out the quinoa for rolled barley or whatever you have. GO CRAZY. No, don't go crazy. Follow the recipe relatively closely and it'll work. If you go totally freestyle you may end up with fabulous granola, who knows. The bars are pictured opposite.

MAKES 12

125 g (4½ oz/1¼ cups) rolled oats
60 g (2 oz/½ cup) sunflower kernels
75 g (2¾ oz/½ cup) linseeds (flax seeds)
190 g (6½ oz/1 cup) quinoa flakes
80 g (2¾ oz/½ cup) sesame seeds
125 g (4½ oz/1 cup) sultanas (golden raisins)
60 g (2 oz/½ cup) dried cranberries
125 g (4½ oz/½ cup) butter, melted
175 g (6 oz/½ cup) honey

METHOD

Grease and line a 17 × 28 cm (6¾ × 11 in) slice tin. Or really, whatever size you've got that's not in the dishwasher.

Cook the oats, sunflower kernels, linseeds, quinoa flakes and sesame seeds in a frying pan over a medium heat, stirring until golden or you start to lose your sense of humour about it.

Transfer to a bowl. Put it somewhere to cool where the baby won't tip it over her head. Stir in the sultanas and cranberries.

Cook the butter and honey in a small saucepan over a medium heat for a few minutes. No, your stirring arm should not be fatigued yet. Bring to a boil and reduce the heat to low. Simmer, without stirring, for a few minutes until the mixture is really golden. Let's say bronzed. Add to the dry ingredients and stir until combined.

Spoon into your pan and use a large metal spoon to press everything down firmly. Cool and cut into bars. If you store them in a foil-lined container they'll be good for 7 days.

Good luck keeping them in the cupboard that long. Now insist someone else do the washing up. You did the cooking and it's a very tasty, healthy snack.

AND you just made something with sunflower kernels in it. You are awesome.

Kamut Crunch

This Kamut Crunch is my own evil invention. Such a smackerel, it's a good hiking snack and a terrific picnic food. Kamut is a relative of durum wheat. I buy an organic brand of kamut, so I can kid myself this is a healthy snack. Er, you decide.

You can substitute any puffed cereal for the kamut here.

MAKES APPROX. 250 G (9 OZ)

90 g (3 oz/⅓ cup) butter
75 g (2¾ oz/⅓ cup) white sugar
1 tablespoon honey
40 g (1½ oz/4 cups) kamut or other puffed cereal

METHOD

Preheat the oven to 150°C (300°F) and grease and line a slice tin

Melt the butter, sugar and honey together in a saucepan over a medium heat until a bit frothy. Add the kamut and stir well. Dump the mix into the tin, but don't pack down.

Cook in the oven for about 10 minutes. When you pull it out, break it up with a fork.

When it cools it'll be more stuck together. Break it up, or sneak a whole nice chunky bit if no one's looking, or if you've just hiked 5 kilometres. This stuff is delicious. And life's too short to have a picnic with just fruit and raw almonds, surely.

Chapter Ten

Obviously Crackers

Obviously Crackers

What do you do to feel normal? When everything is out of whack, what's your protocol? For me: I make crackers. They go with everything, they're quick and easy, and so tasty.

I love making wheat crackers, rice crackers and oatcakes, and I love them most because, at a pinch, they can be dinner. Certainly lunch. They're terrific vehicles for cheese, perfect for entertaining and so satisfying lined up in jars in your pantry.

Life-changing Wheat Crackers

These are the crackers we have taught for years in From Scratch, and they are the quickest, simplest and most customisable crackers ever.

This is the cracker that just might make you completely evangelical about homemade food over store-bought. It's the one that is quicker to make than to buy, and cheaper, and exponentially tastier.

I've always hoped that these crackers were not just crackers but a hook. The gateway from-scratch recipe. The thing that most people buy and that once they start to make their own, never go back.

The canary in the coalmine of home food prep: once people start making their own crackers, we know the tide of supermarket stranglehold over home food production is over.

Can a cracker really be all those things? Why not?

MAKES APPROX. 20

300 g (10½ oz/2 cups) plain (all-purpose) flour
125 ml (4 fl oz/½ cup) water
185 ml (6 fl oz/¾ cup) olive oil
2 teaspoons sea salt
herbs and/or seeds, to taste, such as finely
    chopped rosemary

METHOD

Preheat your oven to 180°C (360°F) and find two baking trays.

Put all the ingredients together in a bowl and mix well until it resembles dough.

Divide the dough into two balls and roll between two sheets of baking paper until it's very thin (2 mm/⅛ in), or use a pasta maker for this job, if you have one.

Remove the top sheet of baking paper and cut the dough into squares or strips with a sharp knife or pizza cutter (I use a ridged ravioli cutter). Lift the whole sheet of paper onto the first baking tray.

Repeat with the other dough ball so you've got two trays of rolled out and cut crackers.

Bake for 12 minutes, or until crisp and pale golden. Allow to cool on the trays before transferring to an airtight container.

These crackers stay fresh for about 4 weeks. At least.

Brown Rice Crackers

Making rice crackers is a big deal for me. We go through A LOT in this house, and processed crackers are really very highly processed. None of my kids do well eating too many. I was shocked, many years ago, to discover that rice crackers were kind of *the worst* for kids' digestion. You think a rice cracker is a healthy snack, but actually, in some kids, highly processed white rice crackers can really mess with their intestinal function. Anyway, they're simple to make, your homemade version will contain good amounts of fibre, better flavour and no nasty chemicals. This is a great thing to do with leftover rice.

MAKES APPROX. 40

75 g (2¾ oz/½ cup) linseeds (flax seeds)
125 ml (4 fl oz/½ cup) cold water
370 g (13 oz/2 cups) cooked brown rice (see Note), cooled completely
2 teaspoons tamari or soy sauce
2 tablespoons sesame seeds
2 tablespoons sesame oil, or olive oil
3 tablespoons brown rice flour
1 teaspoon salt

METHOD

Preheat the oven to 170°C (340°F) and line two large baking trays with baking paper.

Combine the linseeds with the cold water and set aside to soak for 15 minutes.

Combine the soaked and gelatinous linseeds with the remaining ingredients in a food processor and blend until the rice is entirely broken down and the mix is a sticky dough.

Using a wet ½ tablespoon measure or teaspoon, scoop the dough into balls and place on the trays. It's super sticky, so keep a cup of water handy to dip the spoon into if it gets too awkward to handle.

Put a piece of baking paper over the top of the dough balls and smoosh each ball flat with the underside of a glass or cup. This process is immensely satisfying. Smoosh all the balls as flat as you can – about 2 mm (⅛ in) thick – always using a barrier piece of baking paper, otherwise you'll have sticky rice everywhere.

Remove the top sheet of baking paper and bake in the preheated oven for 20–30 minutes, rotating the trays midway, until the crackers are completely dry and crisp.

Cool completely, carefully crack to separate and store in an airtight container for up to 5 days.

If they lose their crispiness after a few days, pop into a hot oven for 5 minutes to refresh them.

Note

If you're cooking the rice especially for this recipe, begin with 200 g (7 oz/1 cup) uncooked rice to yield 370 g (13 oz/2 cups) cooked rice. Cook your rice and let it cool.

Homemade Seaweed Crackers

I love seaweed crackers, and I love the fact we can make our own.

Like most crackers, you can buy them so cheaply it's a hard sell to convince people that it's worth their time to make them. Homemade seaweed crackers are so satisfying though, it's worth a crack. This is a great thing to do with leftover white rice, and it is the most umami snack ever, in my humble opinion.

MAKES 40

2 nori seaweed sheets (see Note)
370 g (13 oz/2 cups) cooked white rice (short-grain is best, but anything will work; see Note)
1 tablespoon sesame oil, or olive oil
1 teaspoon salt
2 tablespoons brown rice flour

Glaze
1 tablespoon soy sauce
2 teaspoons mirin

METHOD

Preheat the oven to 170°C (340°F). Line two baking trays with baking paper.

Shred the nori sheets very finely with a sharp knife, or cut with scissors.

Place all the ingredients in a food processor and blitz until it comes together like a dough.

Using a wet ½ tablespoon measure or teaspoon, take a ball of the rice dough and put onto the lined tray. Repeat with the rest of the mix, leaving room between each ball for spreading. Put another piece of baking paper over the top.

Smoosh the balls flat with the bottom of a cup or glass.

Remove the top sheet of baking paper and bake for 20 minutes or until golden and crispy. (Don't do the glazing step until they're thoroughly cooked and crunchy.)

Take out, combine the glaze ingredients and brush with the glaze, then return to the oven to bake until lightly browned (this will take 2 minutes only).

Cool completely before eating.

Store in an airtight container for about 5 days. After that, they'll lose their crispness, but can be revived in 3 minutes in a hot oven – put them in upside-down so the glaze doesn't burn.

Notes

Make sure the nori is cut as finely as you can get it – big pieces of seaweed in your crackers send them soggy within a day or two.

If you're cooking the rice especially for this recipe, begin with 200 g (7 oz/1 cup) uncooked rice to yield 370 g (13 oz/2 cups) cooked rice. Cook your rice and let it cool slightly.

Totally Seedy Crackers

I love the simplicity of seed crackers – how the chia and linseed (flax seed) act as the glue so there's no need for oil. These are pretty, and popular on a cheese plate or grazing platter.

MAKES APPROX. 24

- 125 g (4½ oz/1 cup) sunflower kernels
- 65 g (2¼ oz/½ cup) pepitas (pumpkin seeds)
- 75 g (2¾ oz/½ cup) linseeds (flax seeds)
- 40 g (1½ oz/¼ cup) chia seeds
- 2 teaspoons salt
- 1 teaspoon smoked paprika
- 250 ml (8½ fl oz/1 cup) water

METHOD

Mix all the ingredients together in a bowl, then leave aside for about half an hour, or until the water is absorbed and the mix is gelatinous.

Preheat your oven to 160°C (320°F). Prepare two large baking trays with baking paper.

Take half of the mix out and put onto a baking tray. Spread it out with a spatula (an offset spatula works perfectly here if you have one) to a 2 mm (⅛ in) thickness. Spread out the other half on the other tray.

You can score it with a knife if you like, or bake as a sheet and break into large shards once cooked.

Bake for about 50 minutes, or until golden brown and crispy.

The crackers will store well for about 2 weeks in an airtight container.

Sourdough Crackers

I wonder how many hundreds of these crackers I've made? Many. It's such a good thing to do with sourdough starter that you're about to throw out because you're refreshing it (see page 61). The yeasty starter lends a cheesiness to this cracker that is delicious. They're simple and quick, and they last in a jar in your pantry for weeks. This is the favourite cracker on the farm, the one everyone reaches for first for farm team lunches, on the side of your salad plate, to pile pickles and cheese and relish on, or just as a crispy mouthful to go with leftover Lentil Dahl (see page 116). A favourite.

MAKES APPROX. 20

- 250 g (9 oz/1 cup) un-fed sourdough starter (see page 61–2)
- 225 g (8 oz/1½ cups) bakers flour
- 2 teaspoons salt
- 125 ml (4 fl oz/½ cup) olive oil
- 1½ teaspoons sesame seeds (optional)

METHOD

Preheat the oven to 180°C (360°F).

Mix all the ingredients together until they form a dough. Break the dough into four pieces.

Lightly knead one piece at a time and roll out thinly – about 2 mm/⅛ in) or so – with a rolling pin, into a rectangle.

I cut the messy edges off and re-incorporate them in the next bit of dough, and transfer the whole piece to an unlined stainless steel baking tray (they won't stick) and then cut the crackers on the tray with a wheel knife. Repeat with the remaining dough.

Bake for 16–18 minutes, or until golden. Make sure they're crispy when they come out of the oven, and put them back in if at all cardboardy. These store well in the pantry in an airtight container or jar for up to 4 weeks.

Oatcakes

These are something I worked hard on to get right because I really love eating them and because oatcakes are my mum's very favourite thing to eat with cheese.

I've messed around with sunflower kernels and cooking some of the oats and leaving some whole, and butter or no butter – anyway, here is my recipe for our oatcakes. These are, if I may say so, spectacular with some fresh goat's cheese and beetroot relish. Or for lunch with a slice of tomato, a crumble of feta and flakes of smoked salmon. Or, for a life-altering snack of pure divinity, with a good smear of Lemon Curd (page 225).

MAKES APPROX. 24

- 280 g (10 oz/2¾ cups) rolled oats
- 150 g (5½ oz/1 cup) whole spelt flour
- 75 ml (2½ fl oz) olive oil
- 150 g (5½ oz) butter
- 3 tablespoons full-cream (whole) milk
- a good pinch of salt and three grinds of a pepper grinder

METHOD

Preheat your oven to 170°C (340°F) and line two baking trays.

Next, whiz your oats in a high-speed blender or food processor for a few seconds until they are finely ground.

Pop all the other ingredients into your food processor or blender and mix until it all comes together.

Pull the mix out of the processor and make sure it all holds together in a ball. Break the dough in two and put half on a big square of baking paper, then top with another square of paper.

Roll out the dough with a rolling pin between the sheets of paper until it's about 5 mm (¼ in) thick.

Discard the top sheet of paper and cut out the oatcakes with a round cookie cutter or whatever you have. Re-roll the off-cuts until you've used it all up, then do the same with the second half of the mix.

Bake for 20 minutes.

They will keep in an airtight container or jar for at least 4 weeks.

Chapter Eleven

Dairy Beloved

Dairy Beloved

A few years ago now, I found myself Googling 'symptoms of a heart attack'.

This was after ignoring left-side chest pain for three days, increased shoulder pain for two and tingling down my left arm when I woke up. Hmm.

I don't generally over-dramatise things or make a fuss, but there's some bad hearts in my family history (medically speaking, let me rush to add, BIG hearts if we're talking metaphorically). So, I Googled it and panicked just a little, and wondered how on earth the world would go on without me, and I shed a small tear imagining my little family doing just that, and would it be a quick death?

I spent another day worrying about whether someone else would be able to untangle the farm accounts and pay the plumber because, surely, no one would think to do that in the days right after my death. The left-side chest pain got worse and my fingertips started to go numb. I picked up the kids from school and dropped them at youth group and spoke to my dear friend Fi Clare as I ran out the door to the doctor's surgery.

She made me stop. She had had the EXACT same symptoms six months before. And she had some specific advice for me. Breathe. Breathe really deeply. Fi had already self-diagnosed multiple sclerosis before she took herself to the doctor, who apparently *actually laughed* and said: you're not breathing deeply enough. Your circulation is not working properly.

Fi made me take ten deep breaths. I felt immediately better, mostly because I really didn't want to die with the house in the state it was in. No one will ever find anything. I really must get it sorted out.

Breathe in, breathe out. Sit and have a cup of tea.

Taking nice deep breaths. Big deep breaths right down to your belly.

Then go and make homemade butter, because your heart is fine and just having a jar of this wonderment on hand is enough to spark joy.

Butter

I think I just heard my sister, maybe both of them, slap their foreheads with the palms of their hands. There was a muttered, 'Will you just BUY the damn butter?' along with the head slapping.

They're right. It's ridiculous. I have three children, a clean washing pile that takes up a double-seater sofa and some of the floor. A diabolical kitchen, and I'm truly not exaggerating. The bathwater may still be in the bath, I can't remember. There's a dinner plate or two still on the table. Whatever was stuck on the door of the fridge is currently all over the kitchen floor, and there's a huge, unstable pile of paper (some very important, I'm sure), cut-out recipes, old cheese room hats and the pants with a missing button my daughter asked me to repair all over my desk.

And yet, here I am. It's late at night and all I want to do is make butter.

Because in a day that was pretty much hell in a handbasket, the fifteen minutes it takes to make butter may just be the highlight.

Butter.

There's something about the science of it that is terribly attractive.

You take cream, you whip it until it splits magically into solids and buttermilk, you squish it, you salt it and you have butter.

A note on cream: use the best-quality fresh cream you can find. Not thickened (whipping) cream, ideally, as it has various stabilisers and gums added to it (although it will work and if that's all you have, don't stress about it).

I buy fresh cream in bulk from our local dairy co-op because I like to make butter, sour cream and ice cream all in one big dairy extravaganza (some days, not always, and mostly in a happy fifteen-minute window).

MAKES APPROX. 500 G (1 LB 2 OZ)

1 litre (34 fl oz/4 cups) pouring (single/light) cream
½ teaspoon salt

METHOD

Whip the cream in a food processor until it separates into solids and liquid.

It will go right through the whipped cream stage and out the other side. Once it splits into liquid and solid you'll see yellow butter sloshing in the cream buttermilk. It takes about 4 minutes in my processor depending on the freshness of the cream.

Take out the butter solids and let them stand in a sieve for about 5 minutes to drain out the buttermilk. Strain the buttermilk again and save for another use.

Put the butter into a bowl and run water over it until the water runs clear.

Drain off the water and mash the butter with a wooden spoon (or with paddles) to press out as much of the liquid as possible. Keep kneading until it's dense and creamy, knead in the salt and, hey presto, you've got amazing-tasting butter.

And at least when I get up in the morning and the house still looks like a tip, I'll have gorgeous fresh butter to spread on toast.

Fifteen minutes. Day saved.

Cultured Cream/ Sour Cream

Sour cream is a useful and tasty cultured product containing about 20 per cent butterfat, with a delicious sour flavour. (Crème fraîche is a cultured cream product containing more butterfat, with a milder flavour, technically fermented for less time.)

With all finished cultured cream, stir to blend and refrigerate for 24 hours before using. Keeps for 2–3 weeks, refrigerated.

Culturing cream using yoghurt

Add 1 tablespoon yoghurt per 250 ml (8½ fl oz/ 1 cup) pouring (single/light) cream in a glass jug or bowl. Mix well and cover with plastic wrap or wax wrap. Culture for 12–24 hours at room temperature.

Culturing cream using buttermilk

Add 1 tablespoon cultured buttermilk per 250 ml (8½ fl oz/1 cup) cream in a glass jug or bowl. Mix well and cover with plastic wrap or wax wrap. Culture for 12–24 hours at room temperature (see page 258 for how to make your own buttermilk).

Culturing cream using milk kefir

Add 1 teaspoon milk kefir grains (see page 287) to 250 ml (8½ fl oz/1 cup) pouring (single/light) cream in a glass jug or bowl. Mix well and cover with plastic wrap or wax wrap. Culture for 12–24 hours at room temperature. Remove the grains from the cream before using.

If using finished milk kefir, add 1 tablespoon finished milk kefir per 250 ml (8½ fl oz/1 cup) cream.

Culturing raw cream

Leave raw cream in a glass jug or bowl or jar to culture at room temperature for 12–48 hours, covered with plastic wrap or wax wrap or a lid. (Don't try this with pasteurised cream.)

Cultured Butter

Cultured butter is made using cream that has been cultured.

In the old days, all butter was cultured because raw cream left to its own devices at room temperature contains naturally occurring lactic acid–producing bacteria and will perfectly enculturate over time.

You can make your own cultured cream and then churn it to make cultured butter a number of different ways.

In an acidic environment such as cultured cream, potentially harmful microorganisms are discouraged, so the shelf life of the cream, and the butter, is increased.

METHOD

Take 250 ml (8½ fl oz/1 cup) cultured cream and whiz in a food processor (or a stand mixer or with an electric mixer) until butter is formed, following the recipe opposite.

Press all the buttermilk out of the butter (or it will go rancid quickly) with a spatula and add salt to taste (half a teaspoon makes a nicely flavoured butter).

Buttermilk

Originally, buttermilk referred to the liquid left over from churning butter from cultured or fermented cream. Traditionally, before cream was skimmed from whole milk, the milk was left to sit for a period of time to allow the cream and milk to separate. During this time, the naturally occurring lactic acid–producing bacteria in the milk fermented it. This facilitates the butter-churning process because fat from cream with a higher acidity (that is, cultured cream) coalesces faster than the fat in fresh cream.

In modern times, cultured buttermilk is usually milk that has been pasteurised and homogenised and then inoculated with a culture to simulate the naturally occurring bacteria in the old-fashioned product.

To make traditional cultured buttermilk at home, you need to start with fresh cream, add a mesophilic starter culture to it, which you can get from a cheesemaking supply store online, churn the cultured cream and voilà, cultured buttermilk is the by-product.

Alternatively, add a mesophilic culture directly to your milk, and you'll end up with thick cultured milk, which is pretty close.

I know you can make a 'cheat's' version by which you add 1 tablespoon lemon juice or white vinegar to 250 ml (8½ fl oz/1 cup) room-temperature full-cream (whole) milk and let it stand for 5–10 minutes before using, but I've never found this very satisfactory.

Here's a better way without fussing around with culture.

This is a simple 'backslop' process: use a small amount of cultured buttermilk to make a new, refreshed larger amount.

Once you've made this once you can keep a 'starter' amount of your own homemade buttermilk to make the next batch of buttermilk. Freeze your starter amount if you're not going to use it within three weeks, and let it defrost before using again.

MAKES 250 ML (8½ FL OZ/1 CUP)

2 tablespoons store-bought cultured buttermilk
250 ml (8½ fl oz/1 cup) full-cream (whole) milk

METHOD

Stir the buttermilk and the milk together, cover and leave at room temperature for 24 hours to culture.

Stir it and check for thickness. If it's still completely runny (maybe the room is cold?), leave it out for another 12 hours.

Refrigerate and use within 3 weeks, including using it to make your next batch of buttermilk.

Yoghurt

Yoghurt is such an old food.

I thought about it for a long time as a committed from-scratcher (or is it a from-scratchie?) before diving in, as I balked at the idea of leaving milk to incubate on the bench. I'm the daughter of a dairy farmer. You do not leave milk on a bench, especially not to incubate.

However, people have been leaving milk on benches forever, safely, producing amazing cultured dairy products and *not killing people with it*.

And once I got going, I never looked back.

There are many, many things I love about yoghurt, not least that it's full of probiotic cultures, great for the gut microbiome, and one of the things that centenarians often say they've been eating regularly for their happy healthy hundred years.

I also love the 'backslop' way of making it – so economical. And such an attractive term. You 'backslop' some of the last batch into the new batch, therefore transferring the culture. Clever. And simple.

I made it for years this way, but could never make the yoghurt last beyond about seven generations. By that I mean I'd use my current batch of yoghurt six or seven times as backslop culture for the next, before the resulting yoghurt would become thin and runny.

I realised, after learning about milk kefir and how cultures work, that the yoghurt I was using as starter culture – yoghurt made on modern freeze-dried starter culture or using yoghurt from the supermarket – was yoghurt containing only a few types of specific bacteria, not a lovely robust swathe, the way milk kefir does. What I needed was an *old* yoghurt starter, an original, that had beautiful, rapidly reproducing, sturdy and long-lasting bacteria in it.

And then, one day, at a cheesemaking course in Sydney, I met a fabulous woman called Pam, from Kangaroo Valley, who mentioned she had an heirloom yoghurt culture. I nearly fainted with joy when she casually offered me some.

Pam's friends had been the National Parks caretakers on Deal Island off the north coast of Tasmania when a yacht sailed in, crewed by enthusiastic Aussie yachties who had been sailing around the world. While travelling, they'd been given some yoghurt by the crew of a boat called *Barnacle B*. The *Barnacle B* crew had recently been in Turkey and had met a Turkish sailing family who had a very old family yoghurt on board their boat, which had been in the family for hundreds of years. They made fresh yoghurt every week with it, and they shared it with the *Barnacle B* crew, who shared it with the Aussie yachties, who shared it with Pam's friends on Deal Island. Pam and her friends christened the yoghurt starter 'Barnacle B', and that's how it came to be in my kitchen.

It's a robust, rich yoghurt full of wildly active bacteria that will make it almost inedibly sour after two weeks, so it needs to be remade regularly, and incubated or cultured for six hours maximum.

Most heirloom starter cultures can be successfully frozen and defrosted, or dried on fabric or paper then scraped into the warmed milk to be restarted.

I love Barnacle B, it never, ever, ever gives up; it stays thick always, and it's full of crazy busy bacteria – I hope that means my family will all live to be a hundred.

CONTINUED >

yoghurt cont.

MAKES 1 KG (2 LB 3 OZ)

1 litre (34 fl oz/4 cups) full-cream (whole) milk
90 g (3 oz/⅓ cup) plain yoghurt with live cultures
    (or ⅛ teaspoon freeze-dried yoghurt culture)

METHOD

Bring the milk up to 95°C (203°F) in a saucepan, stirring constantly.

At 95°C (203°F), take off the heat and let it cool to 45°C (115°F).

Add the yoghurt – this can be from your last batch ('backslopping'), or from any plain yoghurt with live cultures – and stir well or whisk into the cooled milk.

Either put into a yoghurt-maker and follow the setting instructions, or leave in another temperature-regulated environment for approximately 6–8 hours, or until set (e.g. a chest cooler with 15 cm/6 in water at 45°C/113°F works very well).

After culturing, refrigerate your yoghurt for at least 2 hours before consuming (it will set more firmly).

Notes

You can add thickness to your yoghurt by draining additional whey out of it once finished. You do this by pouring the yoghurt into a strainer lined with muslin (cheesecloth) and leaving to drain for 1 hour.

For a sweet yoghurt, add to the warmed and cooled milk:

    90 g (3 oz/⅓ cup) yoghurt with live cultures
        (or ⅛ teaspoon freeze-dried yoghurt culture)
    75 g (2¾ oz/⅓ cup) white sugar
    1 teaspoon Vanilla Extract (page 36)

Stir well and either put into a yoghurt-maker and follow the setting instructions, or leave in another temperature-regulated environment for approximately 5–6 hours, or until set. Refrigerate for at least 2 hours before consuming.

TROUBLESHOOTING

If you want to cool your milk quickly because, you know, you have a life to get back to, don't pour it into another container from a height – you'll end up with too much aeration. Just sit the saucepan in a sink of cold water until the temperature comes down to 45°C (113°F).

Don't stir the yoghurt as it is setting or you'll break up the structure and it will be too runny. You can stir it after it is set (stir honey or maple syrup into it at this point if you choose – if you want to keep using the yoghurt for future batches, make sure you retain an unsweetened jar for backslopping), but the yoghurt will be thinner and may need to be strained through muslin (cheesecloth) to thicken it up a bit.

If you check your yoghurt at 6 hours and it's still runny, you can safely leave it incubating for up to 24 hours and it will usually thicken. (That is unless you're using a bacteria-rich heirloom starter culture, which after 24 hours would have curdled your yoghurt into an unfortunate grainy mess.)

The less 'messed with' the milk is, the thinner the yoghurt. This has to do with how pasteurisation rearranges the proteins in the milk. What this means is that UHT milk actually makes the thickest yoghurt – I'm not advocating for using UHT milk but just so you know, you can!

You can incubate yoghurt a hundred different ways. We like the chest cooler method, but I've seen people incubate yoghurt in dehydrators, in Thermomix Thermoservers, in water baths in an oven with a pilot light on, and a friend of a friend made it in prison in a rice cooker set on warm. Perhaps some unfortunate life decisions, but excellent gut health.

Homemade yoghurt is cheap, it's easy, it's *delicious* and it's probiotic.

And you *can* just incubate it on a kitchen bench wrapped in a blanket if you don't suffer the dairy girl genetics that I have that make me smell every bottle of milk every time I make a cup of tea. What *is* that?

Labneh

The origin of labneh, a drained yoghurt-cheese, is held tight by many cultures. Is it Lebanese? Is it Palestinian? Is it Greek? It's delicious, that's for sure, incredibly versatile and so straightforward to make. Adam and I lived in Israel for a couple of months when we were younger, on our way home from England. We worked on a friend's moshav in the Negev desert, picking cherry tomatoes and grapes. I was fired after a few days because the furry spiders living in the vines kept making me shriek, and I kept making everyone else jump, and it was way too hot for theatrics and how about I just wait back at the house? Perhaps because of our (wonderful apart from those vine spiders) time spent in Israel, our preference here on the farm is to eat labneh the Israeli way: smooshed onto a plate, sprinkled with Za'atar (page 31), drizzled with good olive oil and eaten with Flatbread (page 57). Yum.

MAKES 250 G (9 OZ)

500 g (1 lb 2 oz) natural yoghurt, or as much as you like
½ teaspoon salt (optional)

METHOD

Add the salt, if using, to the yoghurt, either in a bowl or straight into the jar or container.

Pour or spoon the yoghurt into a muslin (cheesecloth)-lined colander.

Drain at room temperature for up to 24 hours, and then in the fridge for up to an additional 4 days, depending on how dry you want it. For spreadable labneh, one day is sufficient. For ball-able labneh (see page 262) drain for a minimum of 2 days, first day at room temperature and, after that, in the fridge until it feels really firm when poked. If you live in a very hot climate, I'd recommend only leaving the labneh out at room temperature for 12 hours, not a whole day.

Notes

After meeting David Ashar, natural cheesemaker extraordinaire, we started to employ his trick of using white nylon 'du-rags' (which we buy on eBay) to drain our yoghurt in. They have convenient long ties, which makes securing it to a long spoon (for hanging and draining) very simple.

Sweet labneh: You can sweeten your labneh with honey or maple syrup before draining, if you choose. A teaspoon of honey or maple syrup to 500 g (1 lb 2 oz) yoghurt works well. Stir into the yoghurt, then put into the lined colander to drain.

Marinated Labneh

Golden jars of balled cheese. So good. Such a fantastic gift. It's such a good way of lengthening the shelf life of yoghurt. Once you drain whey out of yoghurt, it lasts longer anyway, and then when you submerge it under oil, it lasts about twice as long again. All cheese is really milk's leap towards immortality – cheese under oil exemplifies this deliciously.

MAKES 2 × 300 G (10½ OZ) JARS

    2 garlic cloves, peeled
    1 teaspoon black peppercorns
    dried thyme leaves
    250 g (9 oz) pre-drained Labneh (page 263) from
        500 g (1 lb 2 oz) yoghurt drained for about
        3 days
    240 ml (8 fl oz) olive oil
    360 ml (12 fl oz) rice bran oil (or any other seed
        or vegetable oil)

METHOD

Divide the garlic, peppercorns and thyme between two jars.

Form the very firm labneh into balls with wet hands.

Place the balls into the jars.

Cover the cheese with oil at a ratio of about 40/60 olive oil to rice bran – straight olive oil will set solid in the fridge, but with a split of oils it should stay liquid. If it doesn't, just allow half an hour for the jar to come to room temperature before serving.

Labneh stored under oil keeps, refrigerated, for at least 6 weeks (longer, really).

Yoghurt Maple Balls

Yoghurt maple balls. *sigh*

I'm finicky about recipe provenance. I always try to credit anyone and any recipe that has influenced one of mine. This one is a wee problem though.

Adam and I stayed at a friend's weekender in the Blue Mountains one weekend many years ago and I found this recipe in a magazine. I wrote the recipe down but didn't think to write down which magazine it was in. So, I'm sorry to the original inventor of this recipe, whoever you are, you creative genius. I've been making and teaching this recipe for ten years, so I feel vaguely proprietary about it, but the original idea was not mine. I'm reproducing it here because it is perfect and needs to be shared.

These little yoghurty nutty mapley things are *gorgeous*. Enjoy.

SERVES 4–6

    1 kg (2 lb 3 oz) thick Greek-style yoghurt
    125 ml (4 fl oz/½ cup) maple syrup
    1 tablespoon ground cinnamon
    2 tablespoons caster (superfine) sugar
    70 g (2½ oz/½ cup) hazelnuts, roughly chopped
        and toasted

METHOD

Combine the yoghurt and the syrup in a bowl and stir together well.

Pour or spoon the yoghurt onto a large square of doubled muslin (cheesecloth) (do this over a bowl) and gather together tightly with string (or use a du rag, with convenient long ties).

Loop the ties around a chopstick and suspend over a bowl or container in the fridge for 4 days to remove the liquid.

Form tablespoon-sized balls with wet hands and roll in the mix of cinnamon and sugar, then toss to coat in the hazelnuts.

Aaahhh… *gargle in back of throat*

They are fabulously dense and not too sweet and totally delicious.

You can omit the maple syrup and the sugar to make a perfectly keto version, and you can also substitute whatever nuts you like.

Ricotta

It's easy to make crappy ricotta. You warm milk to just under boiling point, throw in a good splash of vinegar and, voilà, it splits into curds and whey. It's magic. Except the resulting ricotta is *not* delicious. It's a seized curd – if you use it immediately it's okay, but as soon as it cools it's pretty rubbery.

Proper ricotta is made from the whey left over from cheesemaking – not lactic or fresh cheesemaking (such as the cheese recipes in this book), but rennet-set hard cheeses, ideally an Alpine or Tomme.

Traditionally, the whey would be left at room temperature and all the lovely bacteria still in the whey would get to work acidifying it, and then if you heat it just a bit, you'll get gorgeous soft clouds of ricotta billowing to the top of your pot.

Alternatively, you can gently acidify whole milk and then heat it, in the closest resemblance of this process.

MAKES APPROX. 250 G (9 OZ/1 CUP)

1 litre (34 fl oz/4 cups) full-cream (whole) milk (see Notes)
250 ml (8½ fl oz/1 cup) buttermilk (see Notes)
salt, to taste (see Notes)

METHOD

Combine the milk and buttermilk in a heavy-based pot and heat until it reaches 90°C (194°F). Remove from the heat and let it sit for up to 10 minutes to allow the curds to form. Don't stir, or the ricotta will be grainy.

If it hasn't split, you can add 1 tablespoon white vinegar to help it along. You can also add vinegar to 'firm up' the curds if you'd like to.

Ladle the curds into a colander and let them drain for up to an hour, depending how dry you want your ricotta.

When it has drained, transfer it to a bowl, break it up and stir. Add salt to taste. Use immediately or refrigerate for up to a week.

Baked Ricotta

I think it's worth making your own ricotta just to make this dish.

Alternatively, buy the ricotta and whip this up in a flash as a side dish to a roast or a barbecue, or to serve as an entrée with homemade crackers, or as part of a delicious vegetarian extravaganza.

MAKES 250 G (9 OZ/1 CUP)

250 g (9 oz/1 cup) fresh Ricotta (see on left)
handful of fresh herbs (thyme and oregano, ideally)
grated zest of 1 lemon
2 tablespoons olive oil

METHOD

Preheat the oven to 180°C (360°F).

Mix the ricotta with the herbs and lemon zest and season well with salt and pepper. Place into a casserole or baking dish and drizzle with the olive oil. Bake for 15–20 minutes, or until golden. Serve warm. Yum.

Notes

A note about milk: while it is the very best for cheesemaking, you cannot buy unpasteurised milk in Australia, it's illegal. Use non-homogenised milk if you can get it. This will work with homogenised milk if that's all you can find. If you are using lovely fresh milk, particularly if it's non-homogenised milk, and it starts to split before 90°C (194°F), sometimes as early as 70°C (158°F), just take it off the heat and leave it alone for 5 minutes to form the curd.

Buttermilk: you can buy cultured buttermilk in most supermarkets, and it will work perfectly. Alternatively, you can make your own (see page 258).

The salt ratio is approximately ½ teaspoon to 1 litre (34 fl oz/4 cups) milk.

Ghee

Ghee is clarified butter, revered by cooks for its high smoke-point and long shelf life. It smells like caramel, is essential if you like cooking Indian food and is fun to make purely to see the transformation from butter to shelf-stable liquid gold.

Ghee has none of the milk solids of butter left in it, only the fat. Used to cook homemade popcorn, it's transformative. Delicious.

MAKES 1 × 250 ML (8½ FL OZ/1 CUP) JAR

250 g (9 oz/1 cup) good-quality unsalted butter

METHOD

Place the butter in a stainless steel saucepan and melt over a medium–high heat, bringing it up to the boil.

When it reaches the boil, reduce the heat to low–medium, and watch for foam appearing on the surface. The initial foam will disappear and come back a second time, then you'll get nice big bubbles on the surface (this is the water evaporating).

Watch carefully now for milk solids sinking to the bottom and forming a caramel-coloured crust on the base of the saucepan – you don't want to let these burn.

The butter should look clarified (under the bubbles) and smell caramelly. Once you see the big bubbles appear, take it off the heat and strain through muslin (cheesecloth) into a bowl or jug, or directly into a glass jar for storage.

It does not require refrigeration and lasts at least 6 months.

Mozzarella

This quick version of this cheese has none of the complex buttery acidity of a longer-fermented mozzarella cheese, but it's so satisfying to make, can be made using milk from the supermarket, and can be made fresh to put on homemade pizza, which is so much fun.

You can order liquid rennet online at www.cheesemaking.com.au. I usually order citric acid online from bulk wholefood stores.

MAKES APPROX. 450 G (1 LB)

4 litres (135 fl oz/16 cups) full-cream (whole) non-homogenised milk
1¼ teaspoons citric acid
1¼ ml liquid rennet diluted in 60 ml (2 fl oz/¼ cup) unchlorinated water

Salted brine
35 g (1¼ oz/¼ cup) salt dissolved in cold water

METHOD

Pour the milk into a large heavy-based pot and add the citric acid, stirring for 2 minutes. Bring the milk to 31°C (88°F) then remove the pot from the heat.

Add the rennet mix to the milk and stir for 30 seconds. Cover the pot and let it stand for 15 minutes.

Using a long sharp knife, cut the curds into 2.5 cm (1 in) cubes and let stand for another 5 minutes.

Heat the curds over a low heat, stirring very gently to keep them separated. Slowly heat to 42°C (108°F). Turn off the heat and continue stirring every few minutes for another 15 minutes.

Spoon the curds into a colander lined with muslin (cheesecloth) and drain for about 15 minutes.

Heat another 1 litre (34 fl oz/4 cups) water on the stove to approximately 65°C (149°F). Remove from the heat.

Cut the curds into medium-sized pieces and, using a spoon, place them into the hot water until they are stretchable. Lift them, one by one, out of the hot water (using a spoon) and, using your hands (wear rubber gloves), stretch and knead the cheese lightly until it begins to get shiny and stringy. Squeeze until any excess water is removed. Roll the pieces into balls.

Place the cheese balls into the bowl of cold brine to set and acquire salt.

The mozzarella can be eaten immediately or kept refrigerated for up to 1 week.

Fresh Goat's Cheese

This is a simple fresh goat's cheese using a balance of cultures from my original cheesemaking teacher Graham Redhead, listed below and available within Australia at www.cheesemaking.com.au.

It's very difficult to get your hands on fresh unpasteurised goat milk unless you milk your own goat (which I highly recommend) and, for the record, I've tried this recipe with goat milk from the supermarket, out of curiosity, and it didn't work particularly well. That would have to do with the complete structural change of proteins in the milk that pasteurisation causes, and also the calcium lost every day in the milk past its milking date.

I've included it here on the off-chance you ever have access to a milking goat. Alternatively, you can make this using ordinary cow's milk, non-homogenised, which you can find at the supermarket.

MAKES APPROX. 500 G (1 LB 2 OZ)

4 litres (135 fl oz/16 cups) unpasteurised goat's milk
  (or non-homogenised cow's milk)
1/32 teaspoon (a 'smidgen') M235 aromatic mesophile
  culture (see Note)
1/64 teaspoon (1 'drop') MA315 culture (see Note)
2 drops liquid rennet
salt

METHOD

Sanitise everything – all equipment, spoons, pots, etc. – with either an iodine solution, or, at the very minimum, extremely hot soapy water.

DAY 1	Warm your milk to 25°C (77°F) over a low heat in a large heavy-based saucepan. Check the temperature with a thermometer.
	Add your culture (powdered or milk kefir) and stir well.
	With a dropper, drop the rennet into the milk and stir for 30 seconds.
	Cover and let stand for at least 16 hours to coagulate. A solid curd will form and sink below the surface of the whey.
DAY 2	The next day, gently scoop out the curd and place into cheese forms. Fill the forms to the top and let them drain. Let the curd settle. Top up the forms as necessary.
	After approximately 4 hours, flip the cheeses in their forms.
	Flip again at least once more today.
DAY 3	The following day, take the cheeses out of their forms and salt them by applying salt directly to the outside of the cheese, a good pinch of salt per surface. The cheese is now ready to refrigerate and eat, or ash, or age, or put under oil. Refrigerate as soon as possible. We 'cure' our cheese by leaving it uncovered in a cool room for at least 24 hours, then package it.

Note

You can replace these cultures with 60 ml (2 fl oz/¼ cup) milk kefir (see page 287).

Cheesy Chive Crack

The simplest way to make this is to buy fresh goat's cheese and whip it in a food processor with fresh chives.

Alternatively, make your own goat's cheese using the recipe on the opposite page.

MAKES 250 G (9 OZ)

250 g (9 oz/1⅓ cup) fresh goat's cheese, drained of any brine or oil (see Note)
1 teaspoon fresh chives, finely snipped

METHOD

Beat all the ingredients together well and put into an airtight container.

It will last in the fridge for approximately 2 weeks – or 4 if you have used your own freshly made cheese.

Goat's Milk Ice Cream

I think this might be my dad's favourite Tuesday Night Dessert Night treat. (Possibly accompanied by apple pie.) You can make goat's milk ice cream perfectly well with supermarket-bought goat's milk, and it's terrific if you're serving someone who doesn't do so well on cow's milk (because the proteins in goat's milk are quite different, sometimes people with lactose intolerance can tolerate goat's milk).

MAKES 1.25 LITRES (42 FL OZ/5 CUPS)

1 litre (34 fl oz/4 cups) fresh goat's milk
pinch of sea salt
220 g (8 oz/1 cup) white sugar
1 teaspoon Vanilla Extract (page 36)
4 large free-range egg yolks

METHOD

Beat all the ingredients together and cook over a low heat in a heavy-based saucepan, stirring constantly and scraping the bottom with a heat-resistant spatula, just until the custard thickens enough to coat the spatula. Remove from the heat, put into a jug, cover and refrigerate until cool, about 2 hours.

Whiz in a food processor or with a hand-held blender to aerate before putting into an ice-cream maker and churning according to the manufacturer's instructions, or placing into a container in the freezer with a lid or foil over it.

If not using an ice-cream maker, partially freeze for 3–4 hours, take out, whiz thoroughly in a blender or food processor and put back into the freezer for another 4–5 hours to set firm.

Note
Commercially bought goat's cheese would usually be salted. If it's not, add ½ teaspoon very fine salt.

The Simplest No-churn Ice Cream

TWO ingredients. THAT'S IT! Apart from being dead-easy to make, it's so creamy and delicious, and you know exactly what's in it. Even if one of the ingredients is slightly evil condensed milk.

My mum now makes this ice cream as a Tuesday Night Dessert Night treat, and she adds three chopped chocolate bars to make it super Evel Knievel.

She puts a layer of Malt 'O' Milk biscuits into a lined 21 × 31 cm (8¼ × 12½ in) slice tin, smooths the ice cream on top of the biscuits, then puts another layer of biscuits on top of the ice cream.

What you have there is grandkid-thrilling ice-cream sandwiches. Genius.

MAKES 1.5 LITRES (51 FL OZ/6 CUPS)

600 ml (20½ fl oz) thickened (whipping) or fresh cream
395 g (14 oz) tinned sweetened condensed milk, or 250 ml (8½ fl oz/1 cup) homemade (see page 28)

METHOD

Pour the cream into a large bowl and, using an electric mixer or a hand-held blender, beat until soft peaks form.

Very slowly drizzle (or spoon) in the condensed milk, beating well as you go until it's thick.

An electric mixer or a stand mixer are best for this job, but a wooden spoon and some good elbow grease works too. Think about those burning calories. Or not.

Store it in the freezer (obviously).

Mum keeps ice-cream sandwiches in her freezer in sealed bags for emergencies. (May we all have emergencies that can be solved with one of those.)

Just a quick note: this ice cream doesn't actually store very well for long periods. It's great when you first make it but after a few days it seems to get a slightly floury texture. This appears to be mitigated by adding extra ingredients à la my mother, and making it into ice-cream sandwiches. No one has ever complained of a floury ice-cream sandwich.

Simple Chocolate Ice Cream

I remember the day my friends Megan and Darren Collins first brought this over, many years ago, and we stood in my kitchen eating spoonfuls of it while Megan gave me the recipe off the top of her head. It doesn't contain eggs, which at the time I remember being helpful because my chooks had been significantly reduced in numbers by a fox. You don't have to have an ice-cream maker to make this, but you do need to do a second whip after partially freezing it in order to get good aeration and creaminess.

MAKES 1.5 LITRES (51 FL OZ/6 CUPS)

115 g (4 oz/½ cup, firmly packed) Brown Sugar (page 28)
110 g (4 oz/½ cup) white sugar
125 g (4½ oz/1 cup) unsweetened cocoa powder
375 ml (12½ fl oz/1½ cups) full-cream (whole) milk
600 ml (20½ fl oz) pouring (single/light) cream

METHOD

The easiest and best way to make this is to whiz it all up well in a blender. Wait until it's thick and creamy then put it in the fridge for at least 20 minutes.

I've found that if you thoroughly chill your ice-cream mix before you process it, it's lighter and fluffier and processes up easier.

Once chilled, put into an ice-cream maker, if you have one, and churn for at least half an hour.

Alternatively, whip the cold mix really well in a stand mixer or with an electric mixer, partially freeze the mix in a container, then scrape back into a big bowl and whiz with a hand-held blender. Put back into the freezer to fully freeze.

Notes

1. I have more than triple-checked this recipe. Like, a hundred times over.
2. Ice cream texture is vastly improved by an ice-cream maker. Maybe think about putting one on your Christmas list if you can, if you're at all serious about homemade ice cream.
3. When you are lying on your deathbed in many years' time, you will not remember the virtuous sultana muffin you gave yourself as a treat today. Or the righteous omission of treats altogether. THIS, though, this you will remember.
4. You're very welcome.

Fancy Ice Cream

I went through a semifreddo phase in the early nineties, but I haven't been as loyal to any dessert recipe as I've been to this one.

I think ten years or so ago, this recipe was inspired by one by David Lebovitz. He is the king of the scoop, after all, but we've made it so often now that it feels like ours. That's how recipes work, I think.

This is a proper, custard-based, creamy ice cream without the cloy of condensed milk and with no tiny frozen icicles. If we didn't call it 'fancy ice cream' it would be 'grown-up ice cream' or something along those lines. You get my drift.

This is joy in a mouthful.

MAKES 1.25 LITRES (42 FL OZ/5 CUPS)

250 ml (8½ fl oz/1 cup) full-cream (whole) milk
220 g (8 oz/1 cup) white sugar
2 teaspoons Vanilla Extract (page 36)
5 large free-range egg yolks
500 ml (17 fl oz/2 cups) pouring (single/light) cream

METHOD

Heat the milk, a pinch of salt, the sugar and vanilla in a saucepan over a medium heat until the sugar dissolves. Remove from the heat.

In a separate bowl, whisk the egg yolks. Gradually pour some of the warm milk into the yolks, whisking constantly as you pour. Scrape the warmed yolks and milk back into the saucepan.

Cook over a low heat, stirring constantly and scraping the bottom with a heat-resistant spatula, until the custard thickens enough to coat the spatula. Take off the heat, pour into a jug, cover and refrigerate until cool, about 2 hours.

Whip the cream until stiff peaks are formed, then whip the cooled custard into the cream.

Either put the mix into an ice-cream maker (one with a pre-frozen bowl or one that freezes as it churns) or a container with a lid or foil over it, in the freezer.

If you're not using an ice-cream maker that freezes as it goes, this ice cream will need at least 8 hours to really freeze through, and ideally you will pull it out and whip it again when semi-frozen (after 3–4 hours). That's optional though; it's pretty light and creamy even without that second whip.

The ice-cream maker we use at the farm is a Cuisinart Ice-cream Maker with a compressor that makes 1.5 litres (51 fl oz/6 cups) at a time. It was my Christmas present a few years ago and I admit that I love it with a deep, deep love not usually reserved for appliances.

Frozen Yoghurt

So, we have a bit of yoghurt in the fridge here – I'm in the habit of making it but my family goes in and out of the habit of eating it. Once you get the hang of making yoghurt, it's dead-easy and makes itself, mostly. Culture and all that (see page 259).

Anyway, one day long ago we ran out of ice cream, so I thought – I wonder what happens if you churn yoghurt? It turns into a delicious frozen dessert. DELICIOUS, I tell you! So straightforward.

Now we tend to make it deliberately and not as an afterthought. It's particularly terrific as an after-school afternoon tea on hot summer afternoons.

Strawberry Frozen Yoghurt

MAKES 1 LITRE (34 FL OZ/4 CUPS)

115 g (4 oz/½ cup) caster (superfine) sugar, or substitute white or organic raw or whatever you have
250 g (9 oz/1⅔ cups) strawberries, hulled and chopped
500 g (1 lb 2 oz/2 cups) plain Yoghurt (page 259)

METHOD

In a bowl, stir the sugar through the strawberries and leave for an hour to soften the fruit.

Then stir through the yoghurt and put into an ice-cream maker and churn for half an hour or so, then freeze.

Alternatively, carefully whiz up with an electric mixer or a hand-held blender, or in a food processor (or with a whisk if you are totally insane and have stronger arms than me) and semi-freeze, then whiz again after half an hour.

The yoghurt I use is my homemade version (see page 259), but any nice thick yoghurt would work. Steer clear of low-fat though – too icicle-y.

So simple. So yummy.

Passionfruit Frozen Yoghurt

MAKES 1 LITRE (34 FL OZ/4 CUPS)

500 g (1 lb 2 oz/2 cups) plain Yoghurt (page 259)
115 g (4 oz/½ cup) caster (superfine) sugar
pulp of 4 fresh passionfruit

METHOD

Proceed as per the recipe above, substituting the strawberries for passionfruit, which does not need to be softened with the sugar.

Freeze and enjoy. It's better for you than ice cream!

Chapter Twelve

Fermented Goodness

Fermented Goodness

We've been fermenting things here at the farm since the day, many years ago, that the amazing Victoria Royle came to stay. Tori was a graduate of the Whole Foods Chef Training Course in Perth, run by two women who I have admired for years, Jude Blereau and Holly Davis. Tori came to us to do a month of practical work as part of her course, and stayed for an extra couple of months because we just couldn't let her leave! Tori brought with her jars of SCOBYs and starters, and some of what we make today still uses those original starters.

There's nothing quite like learning all about fermentation under the eye of a resident wholefoods chef, and I'm very aware of what a gift that was. By the time Tori left, we'd pivoted the business from biscuits to wholefoods and ferments, so her impact on Buena Vista, and our long-term gut health, can never be underestimated. To this day, I'm still grateful that Jude and Holly thought of us and pointed Tori in our direction.

Fermentation is a food preservation process that has been used by most cultures, in some form, for thousands of years. It is a metabolic process that converts sugar to acids, gases or alcohol. Grains and fruit are fermented to produce beer and wine, milk is fermented to produce yoghurt, cheese is fermented, sourdough bread is fermented.

One of the main barriers for home fermenters is a concern about *encouraging* bacterial growth in food. How on earth can that be safe? How do you know whether the *right* bacteria are growing? Are you going to make someone you like, or yourself, sick?

We tend to leave microbial transformation to the 'experts', somehow assuming that industrial-scale food production is safer. Which is weird. Because people have been fermenting food for centuries in homes less sanitary than yours, and with less information. You're going to make splendid fermented foods, all safe, and you just might live to be one hundred with all that marvellous probiotic goodness in your gut.

When making fermented foods and drinks, always use filtered water or unchlorinated water. Chlorine is an antibacterial agent that will compete with the useful bacteria in your ferments. If you don't have access to a water filter, leave a bowl or jug of tap water out on the bench overnight and the chlorine will evaporate.

A jar of homemade kimchi.

Sauerkraut

One of the first things Tori taught me to make was sauerkraut, and it was the beginning of a long-time love affair with cabbage. Good sauerkraut is just a perfect balance of salt and cabbage and time. We know it's safe because we're creating favourable conditions for the microorganisms and bacteria to preserve and transform the food while out-racing (and smacking down) putrefying bacteria, which would cause it to spoil.

Salt, too, is key in slowing down pathogenic bacterial growth, long enough for lactobacillus and the 'good' bacteria to build up and be self-protective.

An important note: you HAVE to keep ferments like krauts and kimchi under their own liquid to prevent mould spores from attacking the food. If you are running out of liquid, make a 1–2 per cent brine solution to top it up.

MAKES 1 × 1 LITRE (34 FL OZ/4 CUP) JAR OR 2 × 500 ML (17 FL OZ/2 CUP) JARS

1 kg (2 lb 3 oz) cabbage (see Notes)
1 tablespoon sea salt

METHOD

Clean and dry all the jars (see Note on page 86).

Thinly slice the cabbage and sprinkle on salt according to its weight (we're using a 2 per cent ratio; or 1 tablespoon of salt to 1 kg/2 lb 3 oz cabbage). You can mix it roughly with your hands, and then go do something else for 15–30 minutes. (We never do this, we start 'krauting' straight away, but I thought it was friendly to tell you that you could.) The combination of salt and time will start drawing the juices out of the cabbage.

Massage the salt into the cabbage and massage or pound the vegetables until they begin to release liquid and look like they're in a small cabbage juice pond.

Fill each jar to within 3 cm (1¼ in) of the top, compacting the cabbage as much as possible with a spoon or your fist so you squeeze as much into the jar as you can. The cabbage should be covered in liquid. Top up each jar with the remaining sauerkraut juice from the bowl.

Fold the halved external cabbage leaves and push into the jar, providing a means to keep the contents below the water line. You may also like to place a plastic bag filled with brine solution or wedge a carrot between the cabbage leaf and the lid to keep the vegetables submerged.

Put the lids on tightly.

After approximately 3 weeks – a typical time frame based on room temperature – taste the sauerkraut for the desired sourness. The cooler your home, the slower it will ferment; the warmer your home, the faster it will ferment.

Refrigerate when it's done, and enjoy with those you love! It'll last for at least 6 months in the fridge. (Except it won't – you should eat that stuff! YUM!)

Notes

Select green and red cabbages that are heavy for their size to ensure high water content. Reserve half a cabbage leaf per jar for submerging the kraut.

Red cabbage is colour-dominant, so if you use half red and half green cabbage, your kraut will turn red.

You can add 1 tablespoon caraway seeds (in the same proportion as the salt) for a traditional sauerkraut flavour. The longer you leave it at room temperature, the sourer it gets.

You should see bubbles running up the side of the glass jar after a day or two when it first starts. It may push the vegetables up and liquid might squeeze out from under the lid and spill onto your bench. This indicates good bacterial activity, and the natural production of carbon dioxide. Put the jar on a plate to catch spillage.

You can add whatever you like to kraut: carrot, grated apple, beetroot, spices such as ginger, turmeric, garlic, mustard seeds or juniper berries; just ensure that you keep a ratio of 80 per cent cabbage, as it's the bacteria on this vegetable that's the most effective as the starter for fermentation.

Beet

Cloud Pickles

We make large volumes of these traditionally fermented pickles in summer when the pickling cucumbers are on and plentiful. We call them cloud pickles because the lactic-acid fermentation creates an obvious cloudiness in the clear brine.

MAKES 1 × 1 LITRE (34 FL OZ/4 CUP) JAR

- 6 small pickling cucumbers (approx.) or 1–2 large cucumbers, sliced
- 1 tablespoon pickling spice mix (1 teaspoon each of coriander seeds, mustard seeds, celery seeds and juniper berries)
- 2 garlic cloves, ends removed and smashed
- fresh dill sprig (optional)
- 50 g (1¾ oz) large-granule sea salt
- 1 litre (34 fl oz/4 cups) filtered water

METHOD

Properly clean a 1 litre (34 fl oz/4 cup) jar.

Gently clean and remove the flower ends from the cucumbers (there's an enzyme in the blossom end of cucumbers that can make your pickles soggy. There's nothing worse than a soggy pickle).

Stack the bottom of your jar with as many cucumbers as you can fit, then add the pickling spice to the jar, along with the garlic.

Add the dill, if using, to the jar, then fill the jar with as many more cucumbers as you can fit. Do not allow the cucumbers to go up into the band/twist-top area. Make sure there's at least 1 cm (½ in) of headspace between the top of the liquid and the lid.

Dissolve the salt in the water by stirring vigorously. Add the brine to the jar.

Add something to the top of the cucumbers to keep them submerged under the brine, such as ceramic fermentation weights, or a small lid, or a sealed bag full of water, or a folded leaf of grapevine or horseradish or oak leaf (see Notes on right).

Place the jar in a cool, dark place for approximately 1 week (in warm weather) and 2 weeks (in cold weather).

The liquid in the jar will turn cloudy. Do not be alarmed.

Refrigerate when the cucumbers are sour and crunchy and pickled (refrigeration stops the fermentation process). The pickles will keep in the fridge for up to 6 months.

Kimchi

Of all the fermented foods, kimchi is my favourite and I'm proud of this recipe. We make this kimchi commercially at the farm, and I made it and made it and made it in the beginning until my kimchi-mad bestie Nessie approved it. It was my other bestie Kirsten who taught me how to eat it. She puts it on *everything*, and it was the day I watched her put it on a pizza that I understood. Kimchi improves your life. It really does. That spice and flavour and crunch and heat, it just makes everything taste better: scrambled eggs. Salad. Sausages. Pizza. No kidding.

MAKES 1 KG (2 LB 3 OZ)

- 1 kg (2 lb 3 oz) Chinese cabbage (wombok)
- 1 tablespoon salt
- 3 garlic cloves, finely chopped
- 2–3 cm (¾–1¼ in) piece ginger, peeled and finely chopped
- 3 red chillies, finely chopped
- bunch of spring onions (scallions), finely chopped
- 2 teaspoons sugar
- 2 tablespoons fish sauce
- 1 tablespoon soy sauce

METHOD

Wash the cabbage really well, then shred finely. Add all the ingredients to a large bowl with the cabbage. Massage, knead or pound the ingredients together until a good brine is formed.

Press the kimchi into a jar until it is completely submerged in its own brine. Press a small plate or lid onto the veg to ensure they stay submerged while fermenting.

Put the lid on, make sure no air can get to the kimchi, and leave to ferment for at least 2 weeks, or longer in colder weather. Check for sourness and deliciousness, and as soon as it is ready, keep it in the fridge. It'll last for up to a year refrigerated.

Note

On using 'sacrificial' leaves on top of your ferment:
You can add a grapevine, horseradish or oak leaf to the top of the jar if you have one; it can work to keep the vegetables submerged. These leaves are particularly high in tannins and will help keep your pickles crunchy.

Alternatively, when these summer leaves are not available, there are some winter leaves you can use: cabbage leaf, kale or broccoli leaf works well too.

Water Kefir

'Water kefir is a probiotic fermented drink. It's full of electrolytes, it's enzyme-rich, effervescent, and filled with active live cultures that help balance your body's inner ecosystem.'

Adam has probably said this, or something very like it, approximately seventy-hundred times at the farmers' markets, every time someone asks, 'What's water kefir?'

Thanks to Tori, we now make A LOT of kefir. We didn't start with kilograms of culture and huge drums and bottles that arrive by the pallet-load, but we got there after a few years, and water kefir is now one of the main products of our farm's commercial kitchen.

Water kefir is made with a SCOBY (a symbiotic culture of bacteria and yeast) and you cannot make kefir without this starter, called kefir 'grains'. These grains are colonies of wild bacteria and yeast living in crystal cribs made of sugar. The microbes inside all have different jobs – some of them fix and build structure for the community, others exist to defend against enemies, and, as the colony takes in sugar, some of the microbes use the sugar to reproduce. As these communities of microbes get bigger and more complex, they become visible to the naked eye. SO COOL, right?

MAKES 1.5 LITRES (51 FL OZ/6 CUPS)

55 g (2 oz/¼ cup) unrefined raw (demerara) sugar
¼ teaspoon blackstrap molasses (optional)
1.5 litres (51 fl oz/6 cups) filtered or unchlorinated water
60 g (2 oz/¼ cup) water kefir grains

METHOD

Stir the sugar, molasses, if using, and water in a large (2 litre/68 fl oz/8 cup) jar until dissolved. (Make sure you leave enough room for your grains and a few centimetres/inches of extra space at the top of the jar to allow for the build-up of fermentation gases.)

Add the grains and cover with the lid.

First ferment: Leave the grains to ferment at room temperature for 48 hours. If you taste a spoonful of the drink at 48 hours, it will still be quite sweet. We're going to fix that in the second ferment. Don't let your grains culture longer than 48 hours, as they'll start to weaken and shrink.

Second ferment: Strain the grains out of your finished water kefir and bottle the liquid with a tight-sealing lid. Leave it on the bench to fizz up for another few days. Once it's fizzy and as tart as you like, drink immediately or store in the fridge for up to 6 months. (Note: This second-ferment stage can take up to 2 weeks in really cold weather.)

Meanwhile, remake your grains into another batch of kefir and repeat.

Notes

Once you are comfortable with your grains, and if they are multiplying well, you could try some second-ferment experiments! I don't put anything in with my actual grains; I do all the flavouring after I've strained off the grains after the first fermentation, when it's bottled and capped and waiting for effervescence in the second-ferment stage.

Try adding 125 ml (4 fl oz/½ cup) juice to just under 750 ml (25½ fl oz/3 cups) finished (first-ferment) kefir, in a 1 litre (34 fl oz/4 cup) bottle. Leave room at the top for gas build-up and, for the record, I like milk and juice bottles for this, not a skinny-necked wine-shaped bottle. There seems to be too much gas build-up in the neck. The only kefir explosion I've ever seen was in a strawberry second-ferment in a long-necked swing-top bottle. THAT was spectacular.

We also love adding ginger, and lemon, or ginger and lemon together. We like blackberry and blueberry and raspberry kefir. Grape juice is fun.

Variations

Coconut Water Kefir: Follow the instructions using coconut water instead of filtered water. You will not need any sugar or molasses. Add the grains right in. The fermentation is MUCH faster. Check it in 6 hours and don't let it go for much longer than 12–15. Some may like the taste, but you might not. It is dry (unsweet) and pretty yeasty. But try it, maybe you'll love it.

Cultured Herbal Teas: With 'spare' or extra grains, make your favourite herbal tea and let it cool before following the basic recipe. Rosehip and hibiscus is delightful. I recommend doing this with spare grains as they will take on the flavour and colour of whatever you put them in, and it's best to keep your everyday grains flavour-free.

Milk Kefir

Dairy kefir, or milk kefir, is the fermented dairy drink you would have grown up with if you are from Eastern Europe. It's not as common in Australia as we're suspicious of fizzy milk. Milk kefir, though, reportedly consists of over thirty different strains of live bacteria and yeasts, more than either water kefir or kombucha, so you're getting excellent bang for your probiotic buck.

No one has a clear handle on the origin story of kefir, but it's thought to have originated in the Caucasus Mountains in the former Soviet Union, thousands of years ago.

Milk kefir is a fermented dairy product similar in many ways to yoghurt and buttermilk. It's *how* kefir is cultured that makes it really unique – instead of heating the milk, adding a culture, and keeping it warm as you do with yoghurt, all you need to make milk kefir are kefir grains.

Milk kefir grains are not 'grains'; there's no gluten involved. They are actually tiny, rubbery, knobby-looking cell structures that are home to the bacteria and yeast that ferment the kefir. Milk kefir grains are white and look like cauliflower florets, they're also a SCOBY (symbiotic culture of bacteria and yeast) and are a matrix on a surface of a complex polysaccharide with a casein core. They are, more or less, the equivalent of the grains we use to make water kefir, or the SCOBY used to make kombucha. All cultured foods and drinks, but most powerfully milk kefir, contribute to a lively bacteria-rich microbiome, which is useful when you consider about 90 per cent of a human body's serotonin is made in the digestive tract. Happy little knobbly things.

Making milk kefir is a lovely and simple thing. You add about 1 teaspoon milk kefir grains to 250 ml (8½ fl oz/1 cup) milk, cover the glass/jar, and let it sit out at room temperature for about 24 hours. During this time, the healthy bacteria and yeast in the kefir grains will ferment the milk, preventing it from spoiling while transforming it into kefir.

When done, the kefir will have thickened to the consistency of buttermilk and taste noticeably tangy, like yoghurt. Strain out the grains so you can use them in another batch, and the kefir is ready to drink.

You can make a new batch of kefir roughly every 24 hours (the temperature of your kitchen can affect the exact time) just by putting the kefir grains in a fresh cup of milk. Over time, the grains will multiply and you can either discard the extra or share them with friends. You can also take a break from making kefir by putting the grains in a new cup/jar of milk and storing in the fridge.

Kefir grains work best with full-cream (whole) milk from cows, goats and sheep. You can successfully make kefir with reduced-fat milk, but if you notice that your grains are behaving sluggishly or taking longer and longer to ferment the milk, put them back in a jar of full-cream (whole) milk to refresh them.

If you're looking for a non-dairy option, try making the kefir with coconut milk. Since coconut milk has totally different proteins and nutrients than animal milk, the kefir grains will lose their vitality after a little while. To refresh them, put them back in some animal milk for a batch or two. Milk kefir grains don't ferment almond milk, soy milk or other dairy-free milks very well, but you can experiment, as long as you 'refresh' them in cow's milk, to revive them.

CONTINUED >

Milk Kefir cont.

MAKES 250 ML (8½ FL OZ/1 CUP)

250 ml (8½ fl oz/1 cup) milk, preferably full-cream
    (whole) milk
1 teaspoon active dairy kefir grains (see Notes)

METHOD

Pour the milk into a clean glass jar and stir in the kefir
grains. The milk can be cold or room temperature,
either is fine.

You can cover the jar with muslin (cheesecloth),
a paper towel or a clean napkin and secure it with a
rubber band, but actually, for years, I have just put
a lid on the jar. Typically, we are advised not to do
that due to gas build-up in the jar, but it's a short
fermentation and I've never ever had a problem.

Ferment for 12–48 hours. Store the jar at room
temperature away from direct sunlight and check it
every half day or so. When the milk has thickened
and peels off the side of the jar when you tip it,
it's ready. This will usually take about 24 hours at
average room temperatures; the milk will ferment
faster at warmer temperatures and slower at cooler
temperatures. If your milk hasn't fermented after
48 hours, strain out the grains and try again in a fresh
batch (this sometimes happens when using new kefir
grains, when refreshing dried kefir grains, or when
using grains that have been refrigerated).

Place a small strainer over the jar in which you'll store
the kefir and strain the kefir into the jar, catching the
grains in the strainer.

Stir the grains into a fresh batch of milk and allow to
ferment again. This way, you can make a fresh batch
of kefir roughly every 24 hours. To take a break from
making kefir, place the grains in a small jar of fresh
milk, put the lid on and refrigerate.

The prepared milk kefir can be used or drunk
immediately, or covered tightly and stored in the
fridge for up to 1 week.

Notes

When buying kefir grains, your first port of call should be
contacting your local food co-op or online community
forum – you will more than likely find someone locally
with grains to share. Alternatively, grains can be bought
online and are either sold fresh (recommended) or
dehydrated.

Activating dried kefir grains: If you bought your kefir
grains in a dried form, rehydrate them by soaking them
in fresh milk at room temperature. Change the milk every
24 hours until the grains begin to culture the milk and
make kefir. It may take 3–7 days for the kefir grains to
become fully active.

Making more or less kefir: You'll need about
1 teaspoon grains to ferment 250 ml (8½ fl oz/1 cup)
milk. You can also ferment less milk than this, but
fermentation will go more quickly. Your grains will start to
multiply over time, allowing you to ferment more milk if
you like. Maintain a ratio of about 1 teaspoon grains to
250 ml (8½ fl oz/1 cup) milk.

What to do if your kefir separates: The kefir will
separate into a solid layer and milky layer if left alone.
This is fine! Shake the jar or whisk the kefir to recombine
and carry on. If this happens regularly, start checking your
kefir sooner.

Kombucha

Kombucha is fermented tea made with a starter culture called a SCOBY (symbiotic culture of bacteria and yeast), sometimes also known as a 'mother', or mushroom.

This drink is tangy, sweet and tart, with a touch of effervescence and loaded with probiotics, like its kefir counterparts.

Once the microorganisms in the SCOBY act on the sweetened tea, there really is nothing overly tea-like about this drink. It's reported to be rich in B vitamins for energy, capable of boosting metabolism, loaded with active enzymes to aid in digestion, and rich in polyphenols, super-charged antioxidants that fight degenerative disease. That's a lot of claims for one floppy unattractive SCOBY.

I love kombucha straight, but again, like water kefir, you can flavour it however you like.

Making your own means you control the sweetness, and you can leave it fermenting until the sugar has all been eaten up.

MAKES 2 LITRES (68 FL OZ/8 CUPS)

- 2 litres (68 fl oz/8 cups) filtered or unchlorinated water
- 110 g (4 oz/½ cup) raw organic sugar, or ordinary white sugar
- 4 teaspoons loose organic black tea (or 4 tea bags)
- 125 ml (4 fl oz/½ cup) kombucha tea (from your last batch or that your SCOBY arrived in)
- 1 kombucha SCOBY (see Note)

METHOD

Bring the water to the boil in a large pot and add the sugar, stirring to make sure it is dissolved.

Add the black tea and steep for about 10 minutes.

Strain the tea, transferring to your 2 litre (68 fl oz/ 8 cup) glass jar to cool.

Once cool, gently add your SCOBY and the kombucha from your previous batch, and cover tightly with a piece of muslin (cheesecloth), securing it with an elastic band.

At a typical room temperature, the fermentation will take about 2 weeks. The warmer your home, the quicker it will ferment.

Check it using a straw, sliding down the side of the jar, past the SCOBY, to test the liquid. Take your sample from as deep in the container as the length of the straw will allow. The longer it ferments, the less sugary and more vinegary it will get. Too sweet, and it needs more time.

To bottle the kombucha, gently lift the SCOBY out of the jar and place it on a plate. It will either need to be stored in the fridge, covered with kombucha to keep it happy, or used to make your next batch of kombucha.

Keep 125 ml (4 fl oz/½ cup) finished kombucha to add into your next batch.

Pour the rest of the finished kombucha into glass bottles with tight-fitting lids and seal. Leave it on the bench for about another 4 days to fizz up (this is the second ferment).

With each batch, the SCOBY will grow a 'baby'. This is what you can use to get a second jar of kombucha brewing, or simply leave it with the mother. The bigger the SCOBY gets, the faster your kombucha will ferment.

You can add flavour to your kombucha during the second-fermentation process. Once you have bottled your brew, experiment by adding fresh fruit juice, whole or pulped berries, or spices, such as ginger. Tighten the lid and leave it out at room temperature for 4+ days. This is also a way to add more effervescence.

Note

Buying a kombucha SCOBY: your first port of call should be contacting your local food co-op or online community forum – you will more than likely find someone locally with SCOBY to share. Alternatively, SCOBYs can be bought online and are usually sent vacuum-sealed with a little fermented tea; use this to start your first batch.

Chapter Thirteen

Drink Me

Drink Me

I am famously bad at labelling things, particularly jars and bottles of food. There's a tomato-y looking jar in the fridge that might be relish, or maybe it's pizza sauce, or could it actually be very old baby food? Maybe don't eat it. There's a bottle that looks like milk, might be kefir, could be yoghurt. I acknowledge it is not an ideal system. At the back of the fridge, though, there's a promising bottle with a label that clearly reads: lemon barley cordial. It's a family favourite. A safe bet. As safe a bet as the ice cube tray being empty right now, which is a shame because this cordial is best served iced. Life is fickle.

Hot Chocolate Mix

This is a lovely and useful thing to have in your pantry. Obviously, it's used to make up hot chocolate at a moment's notice when cold school kids tumble in the door or when someone thoughtfully lights the firepit in the backyard. You can also use it to sieve over cakes or desserts that are improved by a soft layer of chocolate powder.

MAKES 1 × 150 G (5½ OZ) JAR

60 g (2 oz/½ cup) unsweetened cocoa powder
115 g (4 oz/½ cup) caster (superfine) sugar
¼ teaspoon salt

METHOD

Mix all the ingredients together and keep in an airtight jar in the pantry.

To make hot chocolate, add approximately 1 tablespoon hot chocolate mix per 250 ml (8½ fl oz/ 1 cup) full-cream (whole) milk to a saucepan and heat, whisking until the mixture is a uniform colour.

Add more mix if you like it more chocolatey. Use Vanilla Sugar (page 36) if you like it vanilla-y.

Pop it in a blender at the end to froth it if you like, but please be careful with hot liquid in a blender!

Coconut Milk

Making your own coconut milk is a great trick if you're a fan of chia puddings, as I find the tinned organic coconut milk is lumpy and hard to emulsify with the chia. It's also very straightforward and useful to know if you run out of coconut milk.

MAKES 1 LITRE (34 FL OZ/4 CUPS)

120 g (4½ oz/2 cups) shredded coconut
1 litre (34 fl oz/4 cups) hot water

METHOD

Put the coconut into a blender and pour the water over it. Leave to soak for 10 minutes, then blitz on high speed for about a minute.

Pour into a nut-milk bag, if you have one, and squeeze the solids until all the milk has been drained. Alternatively, pour into a muslin (cheesecloth)-lined colander, pick up the muslin and squeeze as much milk from the solids as you can.

You can dry or dehydrate the coconut for use as coconut flour, or discard in your compost.

Fresh homemade coconut milk will last in your fridge for 4 days, or you can freeze it for up to 3 months.

The milk will separate in the fridge, just shake it to recombine.

Almond Milk (Or Any Nut Milk)

My talented friend Karina Shepherd taught me how to make this. Karina worked with us for a few years in the beginning, many years ago now, and made something like ONE TONNE of sauerkraut by hand on a big wooden mandoline in the time she was here, and got our commercial kitchen humming before she began her own very successful wholefoods catering company, Dandelion and Mallow. I never make almond milk without thinking about Karina.

MAKES 1 LITRE (34 FL OZ/4 CUPS)

155 g (5½ oz/1 cup) almonds, soaked overnight and drained (or you could try cashew nuts, walnuts, macadamia nuts or hazelnuts)
1.2 litres (41 fl oz) water

METHOD

Place the nuts in a blender with the water and blend for 2 minutes. Line a bowl with a nut-milk bag or piece of muslin (cheesecloth) and pour the blended nuts and water into the bowl. Pick up the bag or muslin and squeeze the milk through, leaving the pulp inside. Pour the nut milk into a jar or bottle and place in the fridge. The nut milk will last for 3–4 days and will need a shake before use as it may separate.

Chai

My relationship with chai began when I was eighteen years old. I'd just moved to Sydney to university, and my college was between the uni and Glebe Point Road. There was a cafe called Badde Manors just along Glebe Point Road – it's still there – that sold the best chai, way before the insanity of chai lattes: just proper chai tea brewed in a pot with hot milk and honey and fresh ginger. I can still smell it, and see the filtered light on the red booth seats and feel the bubbling of anticipation and euphoria at being able to study medieval history all day, with a nine-floor uni library and the best chai tea imaginable across the road from each other.

This recipe is the product of many years of trying to recreate the Badde Manors chai.

MAKES 140 G (5 OZ)

5 cm (2 in) piece fresh ginger (see Note)
40 g (1½ oz/½ cup) loose-leaf black tea
17 g (½ oz/¼ cup) whole green cardamom pods
17 g (½ oz/¼ cup) whole cloves
30 g (1 oz/¼ cup) whole peppercorns
2 cinnamon sticks, broken up
1 star anise (optional)
honey, to serve

METHOD

First, finely chop or grate the ginger and place on a tray or plate and leave to dry out overnight. (This step isn't totally necessary, except if you live somewhere with high humidity.)

Put all the ingredients into a blender or high-powered food processor and pulse briefly until the spices are broken up.

Store in an airtight jar in your pantry for about 6 months.

To make the chai, put a cup of your favourite milk (I love soy chai) into a saucepan on the stove, and add 1 heaped teaspoon of the chai spice and stir well. Heat over a moderate flame – do not boil! – and when it starts to bubble around the edge, take off the heat and let it steep for 5 minutes. Strain into a cup. Sweeten to taste with a small spoon of honey.

Note

I use fresh ginger for this and store it, and it's always been fine. If you are in a warm climate, be careful it doesn't go mouldy, or substitute powdered ginger to be safe. Alternatively, you could make up the chai and add fresh ginger as you use it.

Lemon Barley Cordial

I first made lemon barley cordial when we moved to the farm ten years ago and I inherited the most productive lemon tree in the world. The tree is almost as old as I am, and most years it produces massive amounts of juicy fruit. Every house needs a lemon tree – put one in a pot if you have no space and move it with you until you can put it in the ground. Lemons stay ripe on the tree for ages, so it's not like you have to harvest the whole lot in one go. You'll be picking lemons to accompany fish, or to make a slice, or clean your barbecue, or to make someone with a sore throat hot lemon and honey. When you find yourself with leftover lemons, make a batch of this and stash it in the pantry. Made up cold with ice on a hot day, it's delightful.

MAKES 1.25 LITRES (42 FL OZ/5 CUPS)

250 g (9 oz) pearled barley
1.5 litres (51 fl oz/6 cups) water
4 lemons
495 g (1 lb 1 oz/2¼ cups) white sugar
2 teaspoons citric acid

METHOD

Put the barley into a large saucepan with the water. Add the lemon zest, thinly peeled with a potato peeler. Juice the lemons (you want approximately 200 ml/7 fl oz of juice) and set aside.

Bring to the boil and simmer with the lid on for 40 minutes.

Pour the barley water through a sieve, keeping both the water and the barley (use the barley in a salad, or in bread-baking, or you can toast it in the oven and eat it for breakfast with berries). Discard the zest.

Put the barley water back into the saucepan and add the lemon juice, sugar and citric acid. Heat and stir until the sugar dissolves.

Ladle the cordial into hot sterilised bottles (see Note on page 86) and close the lids tightly.

Serve to taste with still or sparkling water, approximately 1 part cordial to 4 parts water. Once opened, keep in the fridge.

Chapter Fourteen

In
for a
Quick
Dip

In For a Quick Dip

I had two new year's resolutions. They were:

1. Being able to walk through my house without bits of stuff sticking to my feet
2. Make all the dips

So far I'm not doing brilliantly with either.

My house really isn't that dirty, but there's a lot of outside tracked inside by children, farm crew, and the occasional farm dog. It's a pretty busy kitchen, and if the farmhouse floor is not vacuumed or swept pretty regularly, it really shows. Adam does the vast majority of the cleaning here, he is excellent at it, but he uses up an enormous amount of his domestic work allocation cleaning up the kitchen. I cook, and I make a LOT of dishes. And making dips makes more dishes, as I know you know. Far out, I know people who don't compost because it's messy and time consuming. I suspect they're not making pesto. Which is a shame because fresh homemade pesto is the bomb.

So if it's a clean floor or homemade olive dip – what's it going to be? Can I have both?

While I contemplated whether a clean floor really was that important, I soaked too many chickpeas, so now we've got hummus for days and a food processor to wash up and a floor to sweep. But still: fresh homemade hummus that is smooth, creamy and garlicy. Mmmmmm.

Basil Pesto

Never underestimate basil pesto. With a jar in the fridge, you've got a fast-food dinner almost made, to stir through pasta (see page 34). It's also delicious on toast under fresh tomato, dobbed onto pizza with mozzarella and sun-dried tomatoes, you can make a salad dressing out of it, toss hot steamed veggies through it, stir it through couscous, bake it into bread and add a spoonful to everything from mashed potato to soups and stews for a flavour hit. I try to never be without it, and in the depths of winter if I don't have any basil, I'll substitute spinach, kale or rocket (arugula).

MAKES 1 × 300 G (10½ OZ) JAR

60 g (2 oz) parmesan cheese
bunch of fresh basil or 100 g (3½ oz/2 cups)
    basil leaves
2 garlic cloves, minced
40 g (1½ oz/¼ cup) pine nuts, lightly toasted
2 tablespoons fresh lemon juice
125 ml (4 fl oz/½ cup) olive oil
½ teaspoon salt

METHOD

Place the cheese into a food processor and blitz until fine.

Add the basil, garlic and pine nuts and lemon juice and blitz.

Add the oil and blitz again.

Taste and season with salt.

If it's too thick you can add 1 tablespoon water at a time until it's the consistency you like.

To store, scrape the pesto into a clean jar and pour a thin layer of oil over the top before refrigerating. It will keep for 2 weeks in the fridge.

Baba Ghanoush

We grow too many eggplants (aubergines) every year. Not just a few too many, but way too many. It's like a mind blank every spring when I put in the eggplant seedlings. Why don't I just plant one? Maybe because in my heart of hearts I know that all those eggplants will yield jarfuls of beautiful smoky baba ghanoush? So, in go all the plants, and for a few months we're awash in this delicious eggplant dip, scooped up with crackers, spread across dinner plates underneath warm roast veggies, on every cheese plate and afternoon tea table from December until March, when I finally pull out the failing plants and promise myself to plant fewer next spring.

MAKES 1 × 500 G (1 LB 2 OZ) JAR

3 large eggplants (aubergines)
2 garlic cloves, peeled
1 tablespoon apple-cider vinegar
2 tablespoons tahini
1 teaspoon salt
½ teaspoon ground cumin
1 teaspoon smoky paprika

METHOD

First, put your eggplants into a hot (180–190°C/350–375°F) oven on a baking tray – no oil, don't cover – and let them cook for about an hour until the skin is dark and thin and crisp. Take out of the oven and cover with aluminium foil for at least half an hour until the eggplants cool down and the skin separates easily. Peel the skin off and cut off the stalk end, then sit the eggplants in a colander over a bowl to drain for another half an hour.

In a food processor, finely grind the garlic first. Add the eggplant flesh and the vinegar and pulse until combined. Add in all the other ingredients and pulse until combined.

Keeps well in a sealed jar in the fridge for up to 10 days.

Chicken Liver Pâté

Our chicken liver pâté recipe was originally given to me by our friend Jodie Petrov, who got it from her Uncle Vic. Jodie and Uncle Vic, I think, used Grand Marnier, but we prefer Cointreau. We made this in big batches in Thermomixes for a number of years in the commercial kitchen for sale at the farmers' markets until we decided to just sell the chicken livers instead.

This pâté is pretty fantastic, and if you turn up somewhere with this in a little pot with a layer of butter set on top and some homemade crackers, no one is going to forget it.

MAKES 1 × 300 G (10½ OZ) JAR

1 bacon rasher (slice), finely chopped
1 garlic clove, finely chopped
60–80 g (2–2¾ oz/about ¼) onion, finely chopped
125 g (4½ oz/½ cup) butter, plus 80 g (2¾ oz) extra
250 g (9 oz) chicken livers, washed, sinews removed
½ teaspoon ground or freshly grated nutmeg
½ teaspoon cracked black pepper
handful of fresh basil, or 2 teaspoons dried basil
2 tablespoons Cointreau
1 tablespoon cream

METHOD

Sauté the bacon, garlic and onion in a saucepan or frying pan with 125 g (4½ oz/½ cup) butter over a low heat until cooked, about 5 minutes.

Add the remaining ingredients except the extra butter to the saucepan, stir all together and cook over a low heat until the livers are thoroughly cooked, about another 5 minutes.

Transfer to a food processor and blitz very thoroughly until smooth, or puree with a hand-held blender.

Melt the remaining butter in a small saucepan over a low heat.

Put the pâté in a jar or pot and cover with the melted butter.

This keeps in the fridge for about 1 week if you've used very fresh livers.

To make this in a Thermomix, blitz the bacon, garlic and onion for 5 seconds on speed 7 (MC on).

Add the butter and sauté for 4 minutes at 100°C (210°F), speed 1 (MC off).

Add the remaining ingredients and cook for 5 minutes at 100°C (210°F), speed 4 (MC on).

When thoroughly cooked, blitz for 1 minute on speed 9–10 until super smooth.

Transfer the pâté to a jar. Melt the remaining butter and pour it over the top of the pâté to seal.

Hummus

We eat a lot of hummus in this house. We eat it smeared on flatbread and sprinkled with paprika, smoothed onto dinner plates and covered with savoury mince and pine nuts and crispy kale, on lunchbox wraps and toast and crackers and pita chips, and to dip veg sticks in on the way to gymnastics/netball/soccer training.

MAKES 1 × 500 G (1 LB 2 OZ) JAR

1 × 400 g (14 oz) tin chickpeas, drained (see Note)
135 g (5 oz/½ cup) tahini
juice of 1 lemon
3 garlic cloves, finely chopped
3 tablespoons olive oil
1 teaspoon ground cumin
½ teaspoon salt
3 tablespoons water

METHOD

Put all the ingredients, except the water, into the food processor and whiz until smooth. Slowly add the water, testing the consistency until you have the smoothness you like. (I use about 3 tablespoons water because I love hummus smooth and creamy – use less if you like it chunkier and thicker.)

Keeps in the fridge for about 2 weeks.

Pumpkin Hummus

Pumpkin hummus is like hummus on steroids. There's something about adding the warmth of pumpkin to the chickpea dip that makes it just about twice as good.

MAKES APPROX. 440 G (15½ OZ/2 CUPS)

250 g (9 oz/1 cup) cooked pumpkin (squash)
3 garlic cloves, very finely chopped
1 × 400 g (14 oz) tin chickpeas, drained (see Note on left)
1½ tablespoons lemon juice
3 tablespoons tahini
1 tablespoon water
1 tablespoon olive oil
1 teaspoon ground cumin
½ teaspoon smoky paprika
1 teaspoon salt

METHOD

Place all the ingredients into a food processor and whiz until very smooth. Adjust the water for a thicker or thinner consistency.

Store in the fridge for 2 weeks.

Note

This is even better if you can use dried chickpeas. Cook 200 g (7 oz) dried chickpeas in lots of water with 1 teaspoon bicarbonate of soda (baking soda) for 30–40 minutes, or until tender, then drain and use.

Salsa

I wrote this 'recipe' down at my first proper cooking gig at Rose Blues Cafe on Glebe Point Road in Sydney. I still have it – it's on the back of an order docket and it's a list of ingredients only. No measurements or any instructions – my nineteen-year-old self obviously assumed I would know how much of everything to use.

Here's a more helpful version:

MAKES APPROX. 750 G (1 LB 11 OZ)

4 ripe tomatoes, finely chopped
2 celery stalks, finely chopped
1 red capsicum (bell pepper), finely chopped
125 ml (4 fl oz/½ cup) olive oil
2 tablespoons lemon juice, or lime juice
1 teaspoon dried chilli flakes
½ teaspoon salt

METHOD

Put the tomato, celery and capsicum into a bowl and mix together with the olive oil, lemon juice, chilli and salt and season with freshly ground black pepper.

Use immediately or preferably leave, covered, in the fridge for a day before use to allow the flavours to blend. This keeps, refrigerated, for about 1 week.

At Rose Blues we served this with deep-fried potato skins and sour cream and grated cheese. Still a great combination of delicious things, and a family favourite here.

Olive Dip

This was the last recipe added to this book, because as we were testing and re-testing everything, at one lunch table there was my middle teenage daughter surrounded by delicious from-scratch things with a sneaky tub of her favourite olive dip from the supermarket, nibbling it off warm homemade Breadsticks (page 47).

Olive dip is really just mayonnaise with chopped olives through it. You can totally make it, and your version will not have any of the massive long list of chemicals and other weird stuff added to it. Can we get our teenagers to eat it? You can if it tastes the same. And if you put it in an aesthetic jar. And then when it runs out and you're busy and they want olive dip – you need to show them how to make it.

MAKES APPROX. 375 G (13 OZ/1½ CUPS)

250 g (9 oz/1 cup) Whole Egg Mayonnaise (page 84)
125 g (4½ oz/1 cup) black olives, pitted and finely chopped or processed

METHOD

First, make your mayonnaise. I swear it will only take you a few minutes. Scrape it into a bowl and set aside.

Wash your food processor then put the olives into it and chop them finely.

Scrape your mayo back into the food processor with the olives and blitz briefly together until well combined.

Great for #cottagecore picnics, better than a bought jar.

We can do this.

Doug's Avocado Dip

My grown-up and wonderful nephew Doug Beckinsale, now at university, had dinner at my house one night when he was six and earnestly recited a recipe from memory that he had seen being made (on *PlaySchool*) and that he thought I might like.

More than anything I *loved* the fact he gave me a recipe, one that he thought very hard about and carefully remembered, and I never forgot it.

Doug: Auntie Fi, I have a recipe for you. I think you should make it.

Me: Fantastic, Dougo! What is it?

Doug: Avocado dip. Here's how you make it. Mash one avocado up. Chuck in some cream cheese.

Me: *(interrupting)* Cream cheese, are you sure? Not sour cream?

Doug: *(thoughtful for a good minute)* No Auntie Fi. It's cream cheese. Then chop a tomato up really small, and chuck that in. Yep, that's it. Avocado. Cream cheese. Tomato.

Me: Dougo, you're excellent.

Doug: *(shy smile)*

He's the best.

So here's Doug's avocado dip.

(Now to be strictly honest, I added a couple of things. I really didn't think he'd mind, and if you were making it just for kids I'd stick with Doug's. But I wanted to make something marginally closer to guacamole. Sometimes, when no one is really hungry for dinner, we'll toast corn chips with cheese under the griller/broiler and eat them with this.)

MAKES APPROX. 500 G (1 LB 2 OZ)

1 large ripe avocado
2 tablespoons cream cheese, softened
1 ripe tomato, de-seeded and finely chopped
juice of ½ lemon
¼ red onion, very finely chopped

METHOD

Mix all the ingredients together – use a food processor if you have one handy. Season to taste with salt and pepper.

This keeps in the fridge for a week, is delicious on flatbread, or to pimp lunchtime wraps, or on sourdough toast for breakfast.

Thanks Doug. You're excellent.

Index

Thank You

This book was effectively years in the making and there are many people responsible for it coming together in the end. Thank you firstly to my beloved *Inner Pickle* readers from all those years ago – you encouraged me to cook, and to write about it.

Thank you to the team at Hardie Grant, particularly Anna Collett, Andrea O'Connor and Andy Warren. I was thrilled when Alan Benson, whom I've admired for years, agreed to photograph this book, and we all had so much fun working with him that we wished he would move in. Thank, Alan, for being a legend. Thanks to Jane Willson for picking this book up in the first place and asking Alan to work on it. Thank you to Jane Hann for her gorgeous styling.

Thank you to Laura Dalrymple for her timely and ongoing encouragement. Thanks to Matthew Evans for reminding me it's OK to make mistakes and renewing my confidence. Thanks to Karina Shepherd who worked with us for years in the kitchen at Buena Vista and who taught me so much. I'm super grateful to you.

Thanks to my totally fabulous Buena Vista kitchen crew – Sarah Worboys, Stephanie Debeck, Caroline Minnear, Ellie Burke – you're the best team ever, thanks for the hours and hours of food chats, your detailed recipe testing and your very good company.

Thank you to my wonderful recipe testers Naomi Weir, Rose Lyden, Suzie Beckinsale, Alex Crossing, Jodi Mullen, Rachel Walmsley, Stella Morrison, Jo Cunningham, Rosemary Russell, Bev Jordan, Vanessa Brecht, Sebastian Brecht, Ashley Brecht, Leah Horstmann, Linda Evans, Emmy King, Sarah Young and Penny Rushby-Smith; your thorough feedback made this book what it is, thanks so much for your time and effort. (Any mistakes or omissions are mine!)

Thanks to my girl gang, Lyndall Coulthardt, Linda Evans, Heather Philpott, Sarah Young and Lana Hall. Just knowing you're on a group speed dial makes my life better. Thanks for believing in me from the very beginning, you are the best cheerleaders ever.

Thanks to my dear friend Kirsten Bradley for the years of stringing bows and shooting arrows together, you have encouraged me so much.

Thanks to Vanessa Brecht for never letting go, always showing up and holding my hand forever, mostly dragging me along but making wherever we are going endlessly interesting.

Thanks to my parents for their constant encouragement and support, I don't take it for granted. You're the best.

Finally, thanks to Adam who makes my heart race and stacks the dishwasher and is never not grateful for whatever food is on the table, and to our beloved three – Henry, Matilda and Ivy – I hope this book is useful, I adore you, please eat proper meals.

Published in 2022 by Hardie Grant Books,
an imprint of Hardie Grant Publishing

Hardie Grant Books (Melbourne)
Wurundjeri Country
Building 1, 658 Church Street
Richmond, Victoria 3121

Hardie Grant Books (London)
5th & 6th Floors
52–54 Southwark Street
London SE1 1UN

hardiegrantbooks.com

Hardie Grant acknowledges the Traditional Owners of the country on which we work, the Wurundjeri people of
the Kulin nation and the Gadigal people of the Eora nation, and recognises their continuing connection to the land,
waters and culture. We pay our respects to their Elders past and present.

 A catalogue record for this
book is available from the
National Library of Australia

From Scratch
ISBN 9781 74379 807 2

10 9 8 7 6 5 4 3 2 1

Publishing Director: Jane Willson
Project Editor: Anna Collett
Editor: Andrea O'Connor
Design Manager: Kristin Thomas
Designer: Andy Warren
Photographer: Alan Benson
Stylist: Jane Major
Production Manager: Todd Rechner
Production Coordinator: Jessica Harvie

Colour reproduction by Splitting Image Colour Studio
Printed in China by Leo Paper Products LTD.

 The paper this book is printed on is from FSC® -certified forests and other sources.
FSC® promotes environmentally responsible, socially beneficial and economically viable
management of the world's forests.